THE JOLLY ROGER SOCIAL CLUB

THE JOLLY ROGER SOCIAL CLUB

A TRUE STORY OF A KILLER IN PARADISE

NICK FOSTER

Duckworth Overlook

This edition published in 2016 by
Duckworth Overlook

LONDON
30 Calvin Street, London E1 6NW
T: 020 7490 7300
E: info@duckworth-publishers.co.uk
www.ducknet.co.uk

For bulk and special sales, please contact
sales@duckworth-publishers.co.uk or write to us at the address above

This paperback edition published in 2016 by Duckworth Overlook

ISBN: 978-0-7156-5135-3

Designed by Meryl Sussman Levavi

A catalogue record for this book is available from the British Library

Printed and bound in the UK

For my parents

Thou shalt not kill.

—EXODUS 20:13

Be not afeard; the isle is full of noises,
Sounds, and sweet airs, that give delight and hurt not.
Sometimes a thousand twangling instruments
Will hum about mine ears; and sometime voices
That, if I then had waked after long sleep,
Will make me sleep again: and then, in dreaming,
The clouds methought would open, and show riches
Ready to drop upon me that, when I waked,
I cried to dream again.

—WILLIAM SHAKESPEARE, *The Tempest*

Contents

A Note from the Author

This is a true story. Although some names have been changed, no scenes have been invented. Items of text appearing in direct quotes come from interviews given to me or, in a couple of instances, interviews recorded for television. Otherwise, they are taken from documents drawn up by, or for, Panama's state or district prosecutors. All translations from the original Spanish into English are my own. Some passages quoted from blogs, e-mails, police notes, letters, and flyers have, occasionally, been corrected for spelling and grammar.

Where witnesses to events gave me conflicting versions, I chose the most credible source or the version I thought most likely. Any errors, of course, are my own.

Caribbean Sea

Isla Colón/
Columbus Island

Bluff Beach

Punch Beach

Big Creek

Isla
Carenero

Wizard Beach
Red Frog Beach

Bo Icelar's house

Bocas airport

Bocas Town

Casa del Sapo

Isla Solarte

Isla
Bastimentos

Almirante

Bocas Lagoon

Isla
Cristóbal

Dolphin
Bay

Darklands

Isla
Popa

the Brown house/Hacienda Cortez

Cher's island

The Jolly Roger Social Club

Split Hill

PANAMA

Chiriquí Lagoon

0 Miles   5

0 Kilometers   5

Chiriquí Grande

© 2016 Jeffrey L. Ward

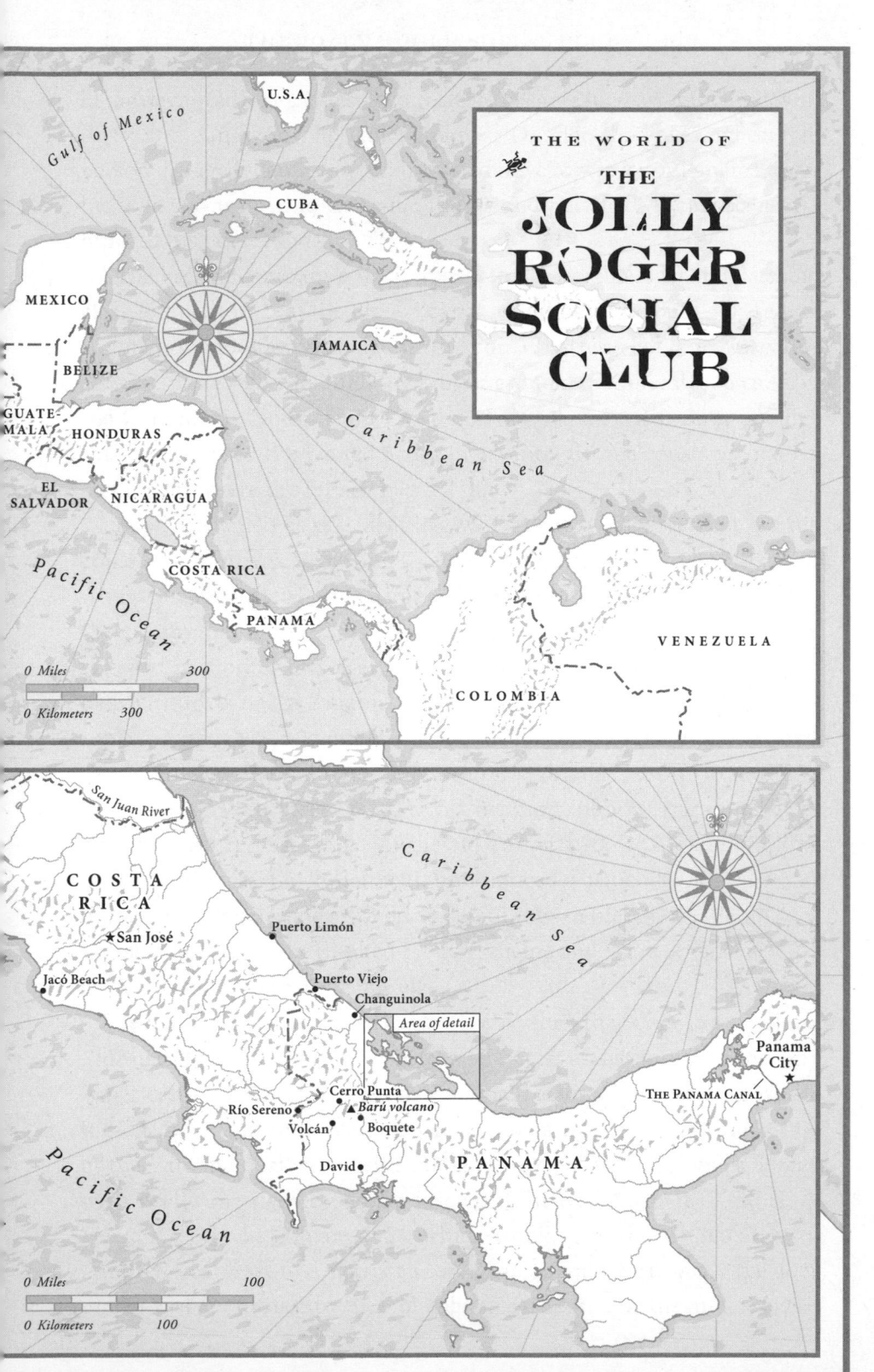

THE WORLD OF

THE
JOLLY
ROGER
SOCIAL
CLUB

U.S.A.

Gulf of Mexico

CUBA

MEXICO

JAMAICA

BELIZE

GUATE-
MALA HONDURAS

Caribbean Sea

EL
SALVADOR NICARAGUA

Pacific Ocean

COSTA RICA

PANAMA

VENEZUELA

0 Miles 300

COLOMBIA

0 Kilometers 300

San Juan River

Caribbean Sea

COSTA
RICA

Puerto Limón

★San José

Jacó Beach

Puerto Viejo

Changuinola

Panama
City

Area of detail

Cerro Punta

THE PANAMA CANAL

Río Sereno ▲ Barú volcano

Volcán Boquete

Pacific Ocean

David

PANAMA

0 Miles 100

0 Kilometers 100

THE
JOLLY
ROGER
SOCIAL
CLUB

Introduction

In 2011, my editor at the *Financial Times* asked me to write a feature on the real estate boom in Panama. I had just spent a few days in the country and had found it surprisingly modern and bustling. Panama occupies the narrow isthmus separating the Caribbean Sea from the Pacific Ocean. Its canal, completed in 1914—a remarkable piece of engineering in any age, and a considerable source of revenue—immediately set the country apart from its neighbors.

In Panama City, scores of high-rises poked at the sky on the waterfront, in a Latin copy of Dubai or Singapore. One of them was a dramatic, sail-shaped seventy-story tower called the Trump Ocean Club Panama, and it had just opened for business. Meanwhile, plans were afoot to turn a 3,460-acre former US Air Force base near the canal into a new urban environment with sleek business parks, malls, and thousands of new homes. It was part of the general ambition to transform this small, ideally located nation into a hub of the Americas, the perfect place for blue-chip corporations to locate their Latin American operations. I asked the communications director of the project to develop the old air force base if

Panama, long considered a developing country, was now about to join the ranks of the first world. "Yes," he replied, "absolutely!"

While I was writing my newspaper feature, I came across the story of an American expat known as William "Wild Bill" Cortez—a fearsome-looking young man in the photos—accused of killing five of his compatriots in Bocas del Toro, a remote archipelago off Panama's Caribbean coast, near the border with Costa Rica. Cortez had been apprehended on the run in Nicaragua, and promptly flown back to Panama to face the music. Under interrogation, he soon admitted to killing a total of six people: five American citizens and a Thai woman, married to one of the Americans. Cortez's victims had all been shot in the head, execution-style. His wife and presumed accomplice, Jane Cortez, was a tight-lipped young woman who, like Wild Bill, had been born and raised in North Carolina. At their home in Bocas del Toro, police found a stash of gold dental fillings and crowns, ammunition for an AK-47 assault rifle, and a number of credit cards and checkbooks that were not theirs. Bill had been described by a fellow expat as "the world's first capitalist serial killer."

In 2011, there were an estimated two thousand expats living more or less permanently on the tropical islands of Bocas del Toro, around two-thirds of them Americans. No one knew the true figure, but the number was certainly growing every year. Many homes were only accessible by boat. I wondered what kind of expat community Bocas del Toro was. Bloggers made arch comments about the kind of newcomer who washed up there. It turned out that Bocas del Toro—literally "Mouths of the Bull," or Bocas for short—is a place of sun-kissed beaches and pristine jungle. But scratch the surface and the islands of Bocas appear a whole lot more sinister: for thirty years or more they have been a key transit point for drug shipments from Colombia to North America. They were also known for their property scams. Among other things, unscrupulous realtors went as far as hawking tracts of land to people who already owned them, and trying to sell sandbars, only visible at low tide, hoping the gullible buyer wouldn't come back when the tide was high and the sandbar was underwater.

Most of all, the islands of Bocas del Toro had become a hangout for the type of expat who appreciates anonymity and who might want to disappear—from ex-spouses, tax authorities, the police. Many of these people adopt a false name, and few others seem to care. "The principle of live and let live has been taken to the extreme in Bocas," another expat told me. "Everyone here," he said, "came because back home they were either 'Wanted,' or unwanted." Some of them had precious few friends and family.

After 9/11, Bocas saw a huge new influx of expats. Even if it was the middle of nowhere, it was far away from likely terrorist targets. It was a place whose isolation forced an almost total self-reliance. It attracted the kind of person, often in their forties or fifties, the tail end of the baby boomers, who had given up on the idea that any government was going to take care of them.

From around 2002 onward, Bocas Town—the only large settlement in the chain of islands, with bars and restaurants right on the water—became a place to party. You could buy land or a house and, in a year or two, sell up and double your money. This was an accentuated version of what was happening in the United States: in the period preceding the housing crash of 2007, many American states saw years of double-digit house-price growth. A lot of folks thought there was no reason why house prices could not go up forever.

The disturbing Cortez story also connected with that global property boom and bust. Soon after he arrived in Panama in 2006, Wild Bill portrayed himself as a real estate developer with plenty of cash to spend, advertising *HASSLE FREE AND FAST CLOSINGS* in a local English-language newspaper. In Bocas it was known that Cortez was solvent and on the lookout for houses to buy. Piecing together accounts from locals and Panamanian and US news reports, I began to suspect that Cortez's numerous murders—if, indeed, he was the perpetrator—had property fraud at their heart.

Besides his real estate business and a Harley-Davidson repair shop, Cortez also ran a bare-bones drinking den called the Jolly Roger Social Club. The bar, open weekends only, was located four hundred yards from Bill and Jane's own home. The raucous parties at the Jolly Roger were the stuff of local legend. Some expats would not want to be seen within a mile of the bar, such was its reputation. But many others loved the place and its boisterous drinking games, and courted the company of Wild Bill himself. Cortez, with his beefed-up physique—it was widely assumed he took steroids—long blond hair, and Viking helmet, was defiantly larger than life. And so was his life story. His father was Mexican and had been an ambassador. He owned oil fields in Texas. He had a $10 million trust fund. Meanwhile, Jane said she was a veterinarian, but when shown a sick Jack Russell terrier she said she couldn't help as she only treated "big animals like cows," not dogs. The Jolly Roger Social Club flew a skull and crossbones and its motto was: *Over 90% of our members survive.* One oddity about the place was that, for a successful, even hard-nosed businessman, Cortez appeared to run his dive on what could only be described as altruistic lines. All the time he spent serving drinks behind the bar, and in the kitchen preparing greasy finger food, made a profit of little more than $20 a night. On top of that, the Cortezes had to pay for electricity and upkeep of the wooden structure, jutting out on stilts over the Caribbean.

But details of the Cortez case were sparse and sometimes contradictory. Panama's criminal justice system is flawed, and police have in the past used torture to extract confessions like Bill Cortez's. From the start I knew that I would have to navigate carefully through the leads that I was amassing, some of which would surely prove false. You have to keep your wits about you in Panama.

And yet, Bocas del Toro is seductive. It's easy to step off the plane and fall in love with the place and with its people; heaven knows, many have done so. The islands of the archipelago fringe a vast lagoon, where the sight of a native family setting off in their *kayukos*—canoes hollowed out from a single tree—gladdens the heart. Then there are the lobster cookouts with friends on the beach; the sound of the relentless, pounding rain on a corrugated iron roof; the multicolored bird-of-paradise flowers. In Bocas, many local families speak English with the lilting accent of the Caribbean, helping gringos settle in a bit more quickly. Here, witchcraft is taken seriously and shamans earn a decent living. All the locals, and indeed some expats, know which plants in the jungle to take for high blood pressure and rashes, and to soothe a hangover. In the 1980s, the English novelist Graham Greene wrote that Panama was "bizarre and beautiful." It still is.

Every paradise has its snake, of course, and often more than one. In 2011, soon after my first visit, former dictator Manuel Antonio Noriega arrived back in the country in handcuffs, after an absence of twenty-one years. In 1989, the United States had invaded Panama and removed General Noriega from power. He was detained as a prisoner of war, flown to Miami, Florida, and tried and convicted on eight counts of drug trafficking, racketeering, and money laundering. In the early 1990s, Panamanian courts had found the famously pockmarked Noriega guilty of murder in absentia, so Panama's hitherto most famous, if involuntary, expat was taken from the airport straight to jail. Meanwhile, his confiscated, once-opulent, hacienda-style mansion in Panama City was put up for auction twice. After Noriega's ouster, this was where a shrine to Adolf Hitler, voodoo materials, and ninety pounds of white powder were discovered. The white powder was initially reported as being cocaine but later found to be flour for making tamales. (The auctions, by the way, failed to attract a single bid.)

After I filed my story with the *Financial Times*, I followed the Bill and Jane Cortez case at a distance. I also got to know a group of courageous women, a close friend of one of the American victims, and three family members of another, who had banded together to see that justice was served. None of these women spoke Spanish and they all found Panama perplexing. But they were determined, resolute. They wanted to find out exactly what had happened at the Jolly Roger Social Club.

Meanwhile, the police investigation progressed at a snail's pace and Panama's wheels of justice turned very slowly. Then something changed: in the middle of 2013, a slimmed-down Cortez, speaking fluent, confident Spanish, started to acquire a public presence. He appeared on television and radio and became president of an outfit calling itself the Panamanian Prisoners' Association. He had achieved, however improbably, a kind of jail-bound notoriety, even a warped celebrity. How was this possible?

I had lived in Latin America for a decade and had been looking for a Latin American story that demanded telling. But far from everyone in Bocas del Toro wanted this story out in the open. Some thought it was bad for business, others that it brought shame.

"It's too raw," one expat guesthouse owner, a woman from Europe, told me. "This isn't the right time to tell it."

"When would be the right time?" I asked.

"In about a hundred years."

I don't agree. Many Americans—and other nationalities, too, of course—dream of a new life next to a white-sand beach and an azure sea—a place where you never need to switch on the heating or light a fire to keep warm, where it's pretty as a postcard and the living is easy. They want to start over in paradise. And in one such paradise, here was a strange American couple with an implausible and sometimes brutal backstory who were tolerated—even indulged—by so many of their compatriots. In the meantime, their neighbors went missing. Why were the expats in Bocas del Toro so slow to react? What—if anything—was it about Panama that made it the type of country where this sort of crime could happen?

1. The Tipping Point

he year was 1989, and the world was about to change. In June, the Chinese government took an iron fist to protesters by sending tanks into Tiananmen Square. By November, ecstatic East Germans had breached the Berlin Wall, signaling the beginning of the end of the Cold War. George H. W. Bush was in his first year of what would be a one-term presidency. In Beechwood Lakes, a middle-class subdivision in Hendersonville, North Carolina, family life went on, as it did everywhere. You could switch on your television and listen to national news anchors sent to a frosty Berlin to make sense of the hard, swift changes to the established global order, or you could look out your window and watch the squirrels scurrying over the moist carpet of leaves and the ducks floating on the still pond.

William Dathan Holbert, now ten years old, was an only child. His mother, Karen Moore, who was considered kind and pleasant by neighbors, had had him young. William Holbert, Dathan's father, worked in a farm machinery business and was seen around Beechwood Lakes a lot less frequently than Karen. The Holberts' two-story house—rec room, big garage, vast yard—occupied a corner plot on Mallard Trail. Outside,

Dathan had plenty of tracks to explore on his quad bike. The house is still there, although the Holberts are long gone from Beechwood Lakes. William and Karen divorced many years ago, too.

He was not gifted academically, but Holbert threw himself into sports when he started high school, and soon bulked up. His arm and chest muscles expanded, his neck grew thick. In particular, Holbert got serious about football. North Henderson High was a new facility back then, and the school wanted a big, successful football team to announce its arrival in the county. Holbert also got a girlfriend named Ryan Dunlap, a year above him, tall and slim with short dark hair.

William Dathan Holbert and Ryan Dunlap married on August 8, 1998. Holbert was eighteen and only turned nineteen the following month. A year after their wedding, the young couple became parents. Two more children followed in the space of four years.

With William and Karen Holbert divorced and gone their separate ways, the young married couple moved into William and Karen's old house on Mallard Trail. Holbert bought and took over an existing landscape gardening business. Ryan, meanwhile, stayed home and looked after their young children, later finding work as a bank teller in Hendersonville. One of Holbert's early landscaping jobs was in Beechwood Lakes. Often driving a large truck, he spent part of each day working in the subdivision he called home. His big truck also helped out with clearing people's driveways in the short but snowy North Carolina winters. There was money to be made pretty much year-round. Holbert was never short of the right landscaping tools and this prompted people to think that his business was flourishing. Some of the neighbors would look at the couple and think they were maybe a little too young for the responsibilities of parenthood. But, then, hadn't Karen had Dathan young, too?

One day, the Holberts' neighbor, Dianne Prohn, got an anxious phone call from Ryan about the Holberts' dog, a chow mix called Dax with a black tongue and lots of fur. "Ryan knew that I was fond of Dax," said Dianne Prohn. "She [Ryan] was worried that [Holbert] wanted to have the dog put down." The dog was healthy; there was no reason to put the animal to sleep. Looking back, she thinks maybe Ryan's call was a muted cry for help. Soon afterward, Dax disappeared and was never seen again.

Holbert apparently hadn't contacted a vet to have the family pet put down. It became a kind of open secret in the subdivision. "My understanding was that he [Holbert] shot Dax," said Ken Prohn, Dianne's husband. In fact, most people who wondered about the fate of the Holberts' chow mix were convinced that William Dathan Holbert had taken a firearm to the family pet. At around that time, his neighbors at Beechwood Lakes whispered about steroid abuse.

It was a perfect moment to get into the landscaping business in Hendersonville. Not only did Holbert have the advantage of family connections to procure vehicles and professional gardening machinery, Henderson County was buzzing with newcomers. The population of the county grew from around seventy thousand in 1990 to some ninety thousand a decade later. Some of these new arrivals were the so-called half-backs. These were retired folks from the Northeast or from the Midwest who had moved to Florida, found it too hot and humid, and so moved halfway—so to speak—back home. They discovered the picturesque valleys and plateaus of the southern Appalachians, with their long summers, falls bursting with red and gold, and relatively mild winters. Nature was bountiful here: the county's orchards sagged under the weight of fresh fruit, crates of vegetables crammed tables at farmers' markets, forest trails reeked of sap. Golf courses opened; lifestyle magazines advertised new gated communities. Bit by bit, Hendersonville—traditionally a genteel place—became more urban. The half-backs bought houses with yards that needed landscaping crews. The men of the Mexican community who traditionally picked the apples in the orchards were a reliable source of labor and stepped in willingly. For a young landscaping entrepreneur like Holbert, opportunities for lucrative contracts were all around.

But Holbert was "always looking for something easier," said one man operating another landscaping firm in Henderson County in the early 2000s. "He always wanted to make serious money. But he wasn't willing to make it work." Holbert's landscaping business, the man said, "kind of fell apart." Also, rumors started to spread about Holbert's behavior. A guy once owed him some money for a job. It was a recent debt in the low thousands of dollars, and Holbert, pumped up, weighing well over two hundred pounds at this point, went to the guy's house to see him about it. The guy opened the door not properly dressed, a shirt over his shoulders, underwear on. Holbert didn't get his money immediately because the guy told him that he'd only just gotten up. But when Holbert threatened to harm him, he soon handed over the cash.

With the debt settled, Holbert beat him up anyway. "You're lucky I didn't take all your money," he told the guy. Holbert—described by an acquaintance as the "ultimate jock"—started buying suits and ties. He wanted to try out other business ventures. In November 2001, he moved his family out of Beechwood Lakes and to a house in Saluda, twenty miles southeast of Hendersonville, where his father's family owned some land named Walnut Drive beyond the fire station. Saluda had a population of about seven hundred—it still does—and owed its very existence to the railroad. The railway up Saluda Mountain, close to the border between North and South Carolina, opened for business in 1878. But before the track up the Saluda Grade was constructed, people in the railroad community wondered how a grade as steep, in short stretches, as 5.1 percent could be tolerated by locomotives and wagons when any grade of over 2 percent is considered a challenge. Runaway trains became a regular occurrence, and the name Saluda would be forever associated with trains hurtling off their tracks.*

In Saluda, Holbert would spend time in the cafés on Main Street at breakfast time trying to strike up conversations with the local bigwigs. He had political aspirations, telling friends that he wanted to become mayor.

---

* In 1880, two years after the railroad opened, out-of-control trains accounted for the deaths of fourteen railwaymen. Nine more were killed by derailments in 1886; three died in 1890, and three more in 1893. Many more workers lost limbs, especially legs, or were injured from jumping off out-of-control locomotives. It was a near miracle that no passenger train derailed. The grim statistics continued until a system of safety tracks was put in and locomotive brakes were improved. Still, runaway trains hardly halted Saluda's growing prosperity: in the warmer months, every passenger train that passed through Saluda was met by vendors selling sandwiches and fried chicken. The "summer visitors," as the seasonal tourists were known, started to buy plots of land and build their own mansions. One general store opened in 1899, and it is still in business today. In some big or small way, everyone profited from the steam monsters puffing up and down the Saluda Grade.

Each time he pulled off Interstate 26 at the Saluda exit, there it was, as soon as he got off the ramp: a sign for Holbert Cove Road, named for his ancestors, an artery connecting downtown Saluda with the cabins and farms on the town's eastern flank.

But the atmosphere at the Holberts' house was often tense. One winter Holbert had an accident while sledding and hurt his leg. He blamed Ryan immediately. Friends invited for dinner saw Ryan cringe in embarrassment when he took to calling a pet cat "Nigger." Another dog the family owned met the same fate as Dax, the chow mix the Holberts had owned back in Beechwood Lakes. Depending on the source, the dog fell out of favor because it barked too loudly every time the postman came by or it growled at Holbert the wrong way, earning its master's displeasure. Whatever the reason, the second dog disappeared, too.

Holbert opened a pool hall in a small town in Polk County, downhill of Saluda. As a gesture of his ambition for the new business, he got some buddies to drop by the pool hall and paid to have a TV ad filmed. Everyone had fun racking up the balls and fooling around with the cue sticks, the cameras rolling. Holbert was a larger-than-life host with a commercial ready to air, so there was every reason to be optimistic. But the business fizzled out after a few months.

It was in 2003, at around the same time as the ill-fated pool hall venture, that William Dathan Holbert entered the lives of Marie and Kevin Hoover.

The couple first met Holbert when he took out a membership at their Body Shop fitness center in nearby Hendersonville. Marie Hoover still has the application form that Holbert filled out, kept in a drawer in her office in the Arden, North Carolina, branch of what is now a chain of Body Shop gyms. On the gym application form, Holbert wrote *Me* under "Employer," and *Lazy Ass* where it said "Occupation." Holbert stood out in that he was loud and brash, but it was a relative thing. Marie met a lot of people who filled the room and appeared superconfident at all times, the life and soul of any party that might kick off. At the gym, it kind of came with the territory.

Holbert and Kevin Hoover both liked working out and pumping iron and soon became buddies, hanging out together in the Body Shop in

Hendersonville. Marie, a trim, soft-spoken woman who wears her blond hair tied back, said there was no surprise about that, since they were both "Alpha males." Holbert might have described himself as a "Lazy Ass," but in the weeks after signing up for membership in the Body Shop he talked big about his landscaping business, which then was barely scraping by. In the end, he discarded the yard work altogether. Kevin and Marie Hoover met the Holberts for occasional dinners. Everyone was struck by how likeable and decent Ryan was.

Kevin Hoover was already a successful businessman, and there was every indication that Holbert, a younger man, was headed in the same direction, even if one of his many planned business ventures—opening an escort service—raised a few eyebrows. One other time, Holbert rented a building in Asheville to accommodate another in a long line of business ideas. But Holbert didn't pay the rent on the building and one day a man came to the Hendersonville gym looking for his money. Holbert stepped out of the gym into the parking lot to talk to the man. With the door closed, Marie couldn't hear what words were exchanged, but she saw the man swiftly turn around and leave the parking lot. "The guy looked pretty shaken up," said Marie Hoover.

The Hoovers' relationship with Holbert intensified when Kevin expanded and bought another gym in a strip mall off Hendersonville Road on the south side of Asheville early in 2004. This time, it was a gym that was already open, but its owner wanted to sell up. It appeared to be the chance that Holbert was looking for: the opportunity to learn the ropes of running a business from a man with a proven track record who knew exactly what to do. Kevin Hoover agreed that Holbert could help out managing the new Asheville branch, the third in his Body Shop chain. It was a loose arrangement, and the understanding was that Holbert might eventually operate the Asheville gym in partnership or as a kind of franchise, provided he could secure the required financing. In the meantime, Holbert was not going to be paid a salary for the time he spent running the new Body Shop in Asheville.

Acquiring the gym meant making a number of quick decisions, notably the question of whom to hire. Kevin and Marie were tempted to start afresh and take on some new staff at their new Asheville branch. For instance, they briefly wondered what to do with a young woman with long, dyed-blond hair from Greensboro, North Carolina, named Laura Michelle Reese. She was tasked with cleaning up at the gym and doing light administrative work. Her colleagues knew little about her, other than that she had been adopted as a child. It looked like Laura Michelle, who was twenty at the time, might be let go. On the other hand, she was quiet and unremarkable and had, in truth, all but passed under the Hoovers' radar. But Holbert insisted that hiring matters were within his remit as branch manager.

"[Holbert] said, 'She's good, she's fine,'" recalled Marie Hoover. And so Laura Michelle Reese stayed.

The Body Shop in Asheville was a forty-minute drive from Saluda. Holbert rented a small apartment nearby to save commuting up and down I-26 from his family home in Saluda every day. Meanwhile, when Marie Hoover drove up the highway to Asheville to check out how the new operation was going, she sensed that Holbert and Laura Michelle had become very close. Holbert didn't yet own a single exercise bike or dumbbell at the Body Shop in Asheville and Laura Michelle was a low-level employee, yet Marie said, "It was like the gym actually belonged to them, like it was their gym." Marie told her husband that something was up. There was another development, too: without any prompting, Holbert started to send Marie brief, handwritten notes. This was unusual in itself, but it was the content of the notes that was really unwelcome. The notes informed Marie of something to the effect that she should be proud of her race, proud of being a white woman. Marie stashed the notes at the back of a drawer in her office and later threw them out. "He was getting weirder," recalled Marie. Holbert had been given—or had grabbed for himself—a position of authority and control, "and it just went to his head."

Still, the Hoovers and the Holberts found some time to laugh and share a joke together. *The Sopranos* was a hit TV show at the time and at the water cooler Marie and Holbert would casually discuss the latest episode, with its story lines of glamorized violence and Mafia killings. "He said that he was going to become a Tony Soprano," said Marie Hoover, referring to the principal character in the show, an Italian American mobster. "At the time I took it to be a respect thing, that he wanted money and power."

One day Kevin Hoover was riding in a car with Holbert at the wheel and they got pulled over by a traffic cop. Holbert had to show the cop his driver's license. Kevin spotted the date and told Marie about it. "He had always claimed he was three years older than me," said Marie. "But he'd been lying." Holbert, it turned out, was really a year younger than Marie. On the application form where Dathan had given his occupation as "Lazy Ass," he had also written his birthdate as September 12, 1975—adding precisely four years to his age. Although this was undoubtedly odd, you could laugh about it, too. But much worse was to come: Kevin got a call from his banker in Hendersonville alerting him to some unusual spending patterns at the Asheville branch of the Body Shop. Gym managers routinely buy such things as vitamin supplements wholesale that are offered retail to members. But here was Holbert writing checks for a mattress, a television, and a bunch of other things. Taken together, the value of the checks that Holbert had written amounted to around $20,000. Kevin Hoover confronted Holbert about it.

At this time, things were coming to a head between Holbert and his wife, Ryan. The mattress and the television had been bought for the apartment on Turtle Creek Drive in Asheville where Holbert was supposed to crash during the week to avoid the long drive back to Saluda. But Holbert wasn't living there alone. He had set up a parallel home in the apartment with Laura Michelle Reese, spending weeknights with her. In the spring of 2004, Ryan found out the truth about her husband's setup with Reese. It came about when Holbert called a cable TV company to get a connection and—coincidentally—the technician sent by the cable company was one of Ryan Holbert's relatives. The news was passed on to Ryan, who was understandably distraught to find out that her husband had been living a double life. Dathan and Ryan Holbert officially separated on May 21, 2004.

Holbert and Reese decided it was time to move on from Asheville. They left behind a city that was in the throes of change. John Boyle, a reporter for Asheville's *Citizen-Times*, originally from Virginia, moved to western North Carolina in 1995. "There wasn't much here," said Boyle of Asheville in the mid-1990s, "just three or four nice restaurants for lunch."

The Grove Arcade, the city center's landmark shopping mall that had first opened its doors in 1929, was bricked up. Asheville's fortunes started to change at about the turn of the millennium, when the Grove Arcade was restored to its period glory. The years that followed, said Boyle, were "explosive." Asheville started to attract cool, fashionable young folk from all over America. There were new eateries advertising farm-to-fork meals; brew pubs were set up; art galleries appeared. Here and there in the downtown you would catch the smell of incense sticks. It was all hippy-chic, self-consciously progressive.

Later, the Hoovers discovered that not only was Holbert writing Body Shop checks for personal use, some of them bad, he had also contacted a broker a few short weeks after he started running the Asheville gym. He had claimed to the broker that he owned the business. Holbert had wanted the broker's help to sell the Asheville Body Shop—the gym that Kevin Hoover owned.

On March 17, 2005, at the age of twenty-five, Holbert paid a fee of $155 to file for Chapter 7 bankruptcy. Under a Chapter 7 bankruptcy, a debtor who gets into financial difficulty and cannot pay his debts requests that a trustee take possession of all his assets. The trustee then liquidates the assets and uses the proceeds to pay creditors.

Holbert declared real estate worth $560,000, split fifty-fifty between the Holbert family home in Saluda and another house on Indian Woods Trail in Laurel Park, Henderson County, North Carolina. The bankruptcy documents showed the full extent of Holbert's overreaching: unpaid credit-card bills of $11,500; auto loans worth $28,765; a string of unpaid hospital invoices; unpaid phone and utility bills. The pretty, clapboard house on a corner plot in Laurel Park, a middle-class neighborhood much like Beechwood Lakes, was a buy-to-let investment. But it had gone badly wrong: Holbert's tenant had gone away and he did not find anyone else to move in to pay the rent that covered his mortgage payments. According to bankruptcy records, Holbert had monthly mortgage payments of $1,750 for the family home in Saluda and $1,720 for another property. The math didn't add up, whichever way you looked at it. In his Chapter 7 application, Holbert described himself as a self-employed landscaper with a total monthly income, after payroll deductions, of $1,667. But his expenditures were recorded as $3,765. It was proof he was living well beyond his means. At the time of the Chapter 7, Ryan Holbert was working as a bank teller and earning $8.50 an hour. Holbert previously appears to have insisted to Ryan that he be the family's sole provider, so for a long period not even the wage from the bank was coming in. According to records of the Holbert's divorce proceedings, *The Man* [Holbert] *has requested that the Woman* [Ryan] *not work and stay at home with the Offspring.*

Unsurprisingly, Chapter 7 debtors don't have the easiest access to credit after a court has discharged them. But otherwise, it can be seen as a new beginning. Indeed, according to a sign posted in the Federal Bankruptcy Court in downtown Asheville, it should be seen as one: *The Mission of the U.S. Bankruptcy Court for the Western District of North Carolina is to maintain order on society by providing a fresh start for the economically devastated debtor and the maximum and timely distribution of assets for creditors.*

In Holbert's case the fresh start was setting up home with Laura Michelle Reese in a rental property in the town of Casar, one hour and fifteen minutes east of Hendersonville. Casar was a third the size of Saluda. But Casar was just where the couple slept; their real business was elsewhere. In April 2005, mere weeks after filing bankruptcy, Holbert resurfaced in nearby Forest City, North Carolina, with a new venture: a white supremacist bookstore.

The store, at 136 West Main Street, was called Southern National Patriots. Captain Chris Lovelace of the Forest City Police Department recalled that it sold "stickers, bandanas and swastikas." The police department put the store under what Lovelace termed "pretty intense" surveillance soon after it opened for business. Concerned local voices prompted them to act. There was an e-mail from the superintendent of Rutherford County schools saying that some students from a local middle school had walked into the store and Holbert had told them that "blacks are not allowed." Other calls came from established business owners on

Main Street, particularly at the end where Southern National Patriots was trading, saying that the presence of Holbert's store was driving away customers from their stretch of Main. There were other complaints from local residents who thought that Holbert was trying to indoctrinate the town's more impressionable youngsters. Specifically, the problem was that Holbert went out onto the sidewalk with a megaphone to encourage townsfolk to attend meetings. In parallel, Holbert rented space at an out-of-town clubhouse—the kind of venue habitually attracting wedding receptions and big birthday parties—to drum up interest in his venture.

By now Holbert weighed around 240 pounds and kept his head shaved. His high school buddies would hardly have recognized him. He had a swastika tattooed on his upper back, a warthog across his right shoulder, and a cross on his left arm with ARYAN PRIDE written above it.

Megaphone in hand, Dathan handed out flyers to passersby on Main. They were titled, *Southerners, a Call to Action!*

Are you tired of being a second class citizen in the country your father build [sic] for you? Are you sick of the ethnic and cultural cleansing of our White Southern Children by MTV and Rap Music? . . . Do you wonder why everything popular promotes everything you find disgusting and revolting? Are you angry at losing your jobs to hoards [sic] of cheap labor overseas? Are you horrified at the onslaught of illegal aliens pouring in and ravaging our job markets and culture? Does "tolerance" make your stomach churn? In this new American Empire you are a criminal to want the same rights afforded to the growing hoard of minorities.

Are you proud you are Southern, and not ashamed of your rich heritage? Being so your honor calls you to take part in the fellowship, and plan for the saving of our future. [. . .]* Everyone must do their part or we will vanish from this Earth. Now is the time, and the stage is set. The future is ours by birthright. The end of the oppression of the Southerner is at hand!

The flyers announced that the first general meeting at Southern National Patriots would take place at seven p.m. on Thursday, April 28, 2005. At the foot of the flyer, in bold type, underlined, the store's address

---

*Ellipses in brackets—[. . .]—are used to indicate my omissions; ellipses without brackets are as in the original source.

in Forest City was spelled "Forrest City."* No matter: between thirty and forty people showed up that April evening.

Plainclothes members of the police department were in a crowd of mainly folk from out of town to hear Holbert, his finger poking the air, rant against the people who were "breeding us out." There seemed to be an economic message, too, for the people of Forest City. This was a community that had been hit hard by the closure of Florence Mill, a hulk of a textile mill a block from Main Street that had shut down in 2001. Cotton, wool, and flax had been spun at Florence Mill since the 1890s. Textiles were to Forest City what the railway had been to Saluda. Much later, in 2010, Facebook would invest a reported $450 million in a massive new data center near the town, providing much-needed jobs. But that moment was still a long way off. Few people could, surely, have predicted this in 2005. On Main Street, there were some storefronts boarded up, which made the place look down-at-heel, but you could get a haircut in four different places and pawn your jewelry. Some people still threw nickels into a shallow fountain on Main for good luck. In a trick of the light, the nickels at the bottom of the fountain looked as big as quarters. All in all, to more than a few textile operatives who were out of work, the future of Forest City must have seemed rather bleak.

"They're taxing us to death," said Holbert at the meeting. "They're removing our jobs!"

Holbert did all the talking, but Laura Michelle Reese was a constant presence, her eyes rarely straying from her companion. And, although the general meeting at the store looked like it was Holbert's gig, the business license for Southern National Patriots had been taken out by Laura Michelle. In what had the feel of a prepared statement, Holbert told a news reporter from a local TV channel: "Our culture, we feel, is the pinnacle of achievement in Western society and has been destroyed for the past hundred years or so after the Civil War."

Holbert also spoke with the police after the meeting. "Their plan

---

* During the Civil War, there was a Nathan Bedford Forrest who was a lieutenant general in the Confederate army. In April 1864, Forrest led his forces in an attack on, and capture of, Fort Pillow in Henning, Tennessee, a battle in which many African American Union soldiers were killed. Forrest was also an early member of the Ku Klux Klan.

was to hold regular meetings [at the store]," said Lovelace. "But it didn't take off."

One night, Holbert and Reese packed up their stuff and left town. They also left their rental in Casar without warning. The owner of the rental found some empty pizza boxes and a stack of correspondence that appeared racist. Holbert had always been polite in his dealings with police officers in Forest City and never said anything negative about law enforcement, Lovelace recalled. It was also true that Holbert and Laura Michelle Reese had not committed any offenses in town. With Holbert and Reese gone, the folk of Forest City got on with their lives, and most of them forgot all about the man who had brandished a megaphone for a couple of months at the west end of Main.

A few days after the couple's departure, Captain Lovelace received a greeting card in the mail sealed with a sticker depicting the Confederate flag. The card was a thank-you note from Holbert. The message inside read: *KEEP UP THE GOOD WORK. SAVE THE SOUTH!*

After fleeing Forest City, Holbert and Reese drove to the town of Oak Island on the North Carolina shore. According to the local police, they spent two or three months there and in nearby Wilmington, North Carolina. Oak Island is popular with retired folk and vacationers who want a quiet stroll around the marina or along the beach. For the most part, it's solidly middle-class.

A plan was hatched. Holbert forged the deeds to a pleasant detached house at 1004 West Dolphin Drive, posing as a medical doctor named Luke Gregory Kuhn who said he owned the place. He deliberately chose a property that had been empty for long periods, and he forged deeds and an earlier bill of sale. The town was quiet, it was post–vacation season. Holbert called a number on a flyer put out by a developer looking for houses to buy. The developer was searching for homes to renovate and then flip. Holbert, in the guise of Dr. Kuhn, told the buyer that he was selling it quickly because he wanted to help his elderly godmother who needed the money. That's why he was prepared to let it go for considerably less than its market value. The deal was done in a couple of weeks, and the developer didn't carry out a title search. In early October 2005, the man handed over $200,000 to Holbert as partial payment for the house.

The real owner was a retired woman who lived in a small town outside Charlotte, North Carolina. Weeks later, she drove to Oak Island to find her vacation home gutted. There was a man inside making renovations who adamantly claimed that he had bought it, and he showed the owner the papers he said proved it. But it didn't take long for him to realize he'd been tricked. Holbert and Reese, meanwhile, cashed the $200,000 and left in a hurry, decamping to Ireland before the police could pounce. After several weeks they returned from Ireland and embarked on a road trip across America, stealing vehicles to get from place to place. Now Holbert started using a new alias—Donald Lee Bruckart—and obtained a false Kentucky driver's license. Reese began using the alias Laura Bruckart.

The US Department of Justice put out a "Wanted" alert for Holbert. The charge was real estate fraud. Things were getting even more serious: by the time of the alert, Holbert had also assaulted a Kentucky state trooper. *Use Caution*, warned the notice. *HOLBERT is known to be a white supremacist. HOLBERT has a tattoo of a Nazi Swastika/Confederate flag on his chest.* The notice informed law enforcement agencies that *HOLBERT may be traveling with his girlfriend, Laura Michelle Reese.*

In his office in Forest City, Captain Lovelace said that Laura Michelle Reese was a "silent voice" at Holbert's side. At first sight, this appears a contradiction. But what Lovelace meant is that Reese was able, at the very least, to give wordless support to her partner. She may also have even incited him to do certain things. "He always looked to her for confirmation," said Lovelace, recalling his experience of the couple's operations at Southern National Patriots. Captain Lovelace was one of the first to wonder about the precise role and influence of the inscrutable young woman. He wouldn't be the last.

Still only twenty-six, Holbert was sought nationwide. Reese, by this time, was twenty-two. Holbert appeared on the television crime program *America's Most Wanted*, to the mortification of his parents. Ryan and Holbert's divorce had since come through, but Ryan's high school friends could only imagine her anguish, with three young children to provide for.

Holbert and Reese were by this time driving across America, never spending much time in any one place. They traveled to Wyoming, where they were stopped by highway patrolmen in Sheridan County one freezing day early in February 2006. It was a routine check, but the officers became suspicious that the vehicle was stolen—which it was. When they ran the alias through the system, they saw that Donald Lee Bruckart was wanted in North Carolina. Luckily for Holbert, the vehicle he had grabbed was a Jeep Cherokee, an SUV with a high clearance. Fearing arrest, Holbert chose to speed away. He hit the gas pedal, and a car chase ensued. The officers have a video of Holbert and passenger Reese veering off a country road in a blizzard, determined to reach freedom. But it was an unequal contest. The patrolmen had no way of catching Holbert, as the officers' vehicle was a sedan with an undercarriage close to the ground.

That day, Holbert and Reese escaped—but there was no longer any safe hiding place for them in America.

Holbert and Reese were now fugitives, about to embark on a long run from the law. Holbert later said in jail, with a wink, that a combination of "planes, trains and automobiles" took him and Reese to their new life in Central America, but the truth is more prosaic: the pair went on a cruise.

First they made it the twenty-three-hundred-plus miles to Fort Lauderdale in Florida without raising suspicion. From there they very likely sailed on a cruise liner either to Nassau in the Bahamas or to Grand Cayman, and onward to Puerto Limón on Costa Rica's Caribbean coast, a place described in a cruise company's advertising material as a "zesty little slice of heaven." In Puerto Limón, Holbert and Reese skipped the shore excursions offered to the cruisers—the canopy zip-line tour that took you "close enough to touch tiny orchids," the sloth sanctuary visit, and the banana field railroad ride—and simply jumped ship. When the cruise ship sailed away from Costa Rica, Holbert and Reese weren't on board.

The pair did not linger in Puerto Limón; instead they made for Puerto Viejo, thirty-five miles southeast, a seaside community hovering in the uneasy space between funky beach town and drug den, the kind of place where hotel staff warn their guests against wearing jewelry or nice wristwatches on the streets at night. Holbert rented a beach house for himself and Reese, and things were not too expensive, but none of the nice things they wanted came free, either.

Holbert and Reese arrived in Puerto Viejo at around the same time as another American, Jeffrey Arlan Kline, a lawyer from Rockford, Illinois. Kline had racked up a string of misdemeanors for driving under the influence of alcohol and driving an automobile recklessly. Kline had, in fact, a long history of alcohol dependency. Like Holbert and Reese, Kline had exited the United States under what charitably might be described as a cloud. After failing to pay child support to his former wife, he left Illinois with the former couple's nest egg by wiring money to a bank account held in his name in Costa Rica. In Puerto Viejo he rented a ground-floor bedroom in a modest beach house.

Eventually the case against Kline came before the hearing board of the state of Illinois. But the hearing board had, of course, no way of knowing—and, more important, neither did his daughters or his former wife back home in the States—that the body of Jeffrey Arlan Kline, a victim of murder at age forty-three, had been decomposing under a rough slab of poured concrete in Puerto Viejo for many months. And yet, almost certainly after Kline's death, an automobile purchase was registered in the former Rockford lawyer's name. If he wasn't driving that car, who was?

In Puerto Viejo, one American couple recalls a strongly built man, calling himself "Big Bill," and his partner, "Michelle," leaving town in a hurry, citing a family emergency back in America. Holbert and Reese remained in Costa Rica but switched the Caribbean Sea for the Pacific Ocean, ending up at Jacó Beach, a surfers' hangout on the country's west-facing coast, where the tall waves now fell on sand the color of ash.

Around this time, Holbert started to grow his hair long so people wouldn't recognize the shaven-headed mug shot they ran on American TV in news segments. He now became Wild Bill, a name that would stick; Reese, meanwhile, introduced herself as Jane rather than Laura or Michelle. Still carrying tens of thousands of dollars in banknotes from the Oak Island fraud back in North Carolina, and from other scams, Holbert splurged. Any vacationing couple might do the same, still hazy about the exchange rate and the sudden blast of tropical heat going to their heads. The place they rented in Jacó Beach was a detached house at the end of a winding pebble drive, palms in the garden bent in the wind. It was a nice property, beyond the reach of most of the surfers. It was also much more secure than the town's simple beach shacks. Inevitably, though, the time would come to move on.

Precise details of the couple's stay in Costa Rica are difficult to ascertain, and Holbert—it goes almost without saying—is an unreliable witness to his own movements. This was a period when Holbert and Reese tended to keep to themselves, at least in comparison to their subsequent time in Panama. The authorities recorded them staying in a beach house named Fiesta when they were in Puerto Viejo, but had few other details. In any event, Holbert and Reese were both trying out new assumed names and backstories, settling into them, fine-tuning twists and turns of lives that never were, tossing aside the parts that didn't fit. Lots of gringos (North Americans and northern Europeans touring or living in Latin America, *gringa* when referring to a woman) did the same thing. Here, everyone grew a bit in stature, sometimes a lot. There was a fear of humble, spindly realities, of lives half-lived, half-realized. Fact and fiction blurred for many folks, but most maintained some sort of equilibrium. However, in Holbert and Reese's case no balance was possible: fiction overwhelmed the few thin strands of fact.

Local people were hardly on the lookout for American fugitives. They had their own lives to live, and simply making ends meet is considered success enough for most in Central America. But Holbert and Reese knew it was wise to avoid drawing unnecessary attention, so the couple laid low. Among other gringos in Central America there was—and still is—an unspoken rule that you don't pry into other people's business. Introductions are usually on a first-name basis, and everyone wears the gringo uniform of shorts, T-shirt, and flip-flops. Outside the yachting crowd, which is seasonal anyway, a preppy label here and there or well-kept teeth are some of the few markers of wealth. Folks aren't unfriendly, but it's not a gringo thing in Central America to bake a pie to welcome the couple who has just moved into the next cabin. Long-term expats will usually raise their eyebrows gently when a newbie arrives and enthuses, wide-eyed, about his new environment. Such comments are usually indulged with good humor. After all, most long-term expats once went through the gringo honeymoon period. But all honeymoons end, and the rhythm of life flattens out. Comments on the vagaries of the weather, anecdotes about keeping boats afloat and cars on the road, and gripes about mild overcharging are discussion staples among the expats. It takes a long while, if ever, to gain a person's trust to progress to more substantial topics. And, generally, people draw a line at discussing previous lives in North America and Europe. Gazing at the crashing surf at sundown puts a bad marriage or a failed business—or much worse situations—into uncomplicated perspective.

Years later, when a law enforcement officer in Panama asked Holbert about his marital status, he said that it was in Costa Rica that he and Reese had made their vows. He could not recall precisely where. His marriage certificate was, it seemed, one of many documents that he had left behind in the rush to leave Bocas del Toro, the remote Panamanian archipelago where he and Reese eventually put down roots. The marriage certificate would never be found, but many other documents would be—a big pile of printed, signed, stamped sheets of paper that told the story of Holbert's assets.

The Pan-American Highway snakes southeast from Jacó Beach all the way to David—with 140,000 residents, Panama's third-biggest city. You can do the journey in a day's drive, if the customs officers don't give you too much grief at the border. David is an airless place on a hot plain, cattle country all around, its squat buildings pressed flat to the ground. The Super 99, a big new hulking box of a supermarket part-owned by a past president of Panama and offering 24/7 shopping, was an instant local landmark when it was built, towering over its neighborhood. You know you're getting close to the city when the push buttons appear. These are pay-by-the-hour motels, surrounded by walls on top of which ersatz turrets perch, medieval-style. People get in by pushing a button, hence the name. Panama is a small world, and many who came into contact with Holbert—his friends and neighbors, the local reporters—are still there. By no means is everyone prepared to talk about why he finally felt at home in Bocas del Toro, their brushes with him in David and in the expat mountain towns of western Panama, or why no one stopped him sooner.

When I arrived in David in March 2014, the city was getting back to work after Carnival weekend. I left my hotel early on my first morning in town to look for a cup of coffee and something to eat. The air-conditioning in the coffee bar was too fierce for my liking, so I went out into the street to find a shaded spot to have my breakfast. A crowd had gathered on the main square, named Cervantes Park, and I walked up to see what was going on. They were watching a municipal worker as he cut the grass with an electric trimmer.

David is full of casinos, which operate around the clock and attract day-trippers from Costa Rica. They are like casinos anywhere in this hemisphere: rows of slot machine players in a trance; overweight men loading stacks of low-value chips onto numbers at the roulette table; girls on stools flicking the ice around the soda in their tumblers, staring at the fat male gamblers. But the city has some attractive refuges, too, including a nice coffeehouse with inviting sofas and smiley baristas three blocks from Cervantes Park. Here, a little glass cabinet on the wall contains a wide selection of Spanish-language self-help and get-rich-quick books: *The Legend of the Leader*; *How to Start a Conversation and Make a Friend*; *My Mentor Is a Millionaire*.

When Holbert and Reese arrived in David in early 2007, they maintained the low profile they had adopted in Costa Rica, at least at first. Holbert rented a modest single-story house in a decent but hardly prosperous neighborhood. According to his own notes, the pair spent four months in David. The couple also had days out at a small community on the Pacific shore ten miles from the city. This was Playa Barqueta, much visited on weekends for its proximity to David but practically deserted much of the rest of the time.

Within ten blocks of Holbert's David rental there are six or seven churches. There are the Mormons and evangelical setups, some in former retail spaces, one in what used to be a car repair shop. A large sign advertises a chicken restaurant, a cartoon bird shrugging its shoulders, grinning. On Holbert's former street, fermenting mangoes litter the ground, their smell like vinegar. A tangled spaghetti of power and phone cables crosses out the sky; pairs of grimy tennis shoes dangle from some of these, marking out the territory of drug dealers. At night, all you can hear is the din of crickets.

Years later, Holbert would call a man named Mike Smith his "best friend," although when Holbert and Reese came to David for the first time their paths did not cross. Mike Smith and Fran Tilbury, an American couple in their late fifties, moved to Panama in 2003. Smith, originally from Oregon, is a tall man, broad-shouldered, with big, weathered hands. He runs a solar panel business from his home in one of the nicest suburbs of David, which he built himself, overseeing the construction, the way you need to in Panama. The demands of running a small company mean that he spends most of his time in David. Tilbury, meanwhile, likes to hang out at their other home, a house next to the ocean in Bocas del Toro, the archipelago off the Caribbean coast on the other side of the isthmus—"over the mountain," in the parlance of the expats. When they coincide in David, the couple spend a lot of time under a shady patio next to their pool, chasing lime-green cane toads away from their two Jack Russell terriers, whom Smith calls "the girls." When Scott McAda, another expat, also in his fifties, joins them for a drink next to the pool, he keeps a lookout for the toads, too. If the dogs bite them, expecting sustenance, the toads' venom can kill. McAda, a cosmopolitan man, worked for Acer, a computer manufacturer, in China for fifteen years and had a stint working in Helsinki, Finland, too.

Western Panama is the country's Expat Central.* Few North Americans or Europeans choose to settle in David. Sometimes it attracts couples of mixed nationality, invariably the man a gringo, the woman a Panamanian. It may be a place of sparse entertainment, but the city at least has the

---

*Eastern Panama, meanwhile, is one of the wildest places in the Americas and attracts very few expats. The Pan-American Highway peters out some 175 miles east of Panama City in the mountainous jungle of the country's Darién Province. It's the only stretch of the Americas between Alaska and Tierra del Fuego that has no road running through it. It was on the inhospitable Caribbean coast of Darién in the 1690s that Scotland hatched a plan to become a global trading nation by setting up a colony of around twenty-five hundred people. In an atmosphere of near hysteria, Scots committed as much as half of the country's wealth to the Darién scheme. But a combination of disease, poor planning, and dwindling supplies of food finished off Caledonia, as the colony was known. Almost two thousand colonists lost their lives in the ill-fated venture, which bankrupted Scotland and was an important factor in weakening Scottish resistance to union with England. Predictably, the jungle wasted no time in reclaiming the settlement: almost nothing remains of Caledonia now except a name on the map, Puerto Escocés (Scottish Port).

advantage of a couple of hospitals. Smith and Tilbury say they are there for the warm climate and the generally good private health care that those hospitals offer. "I'm a smoker," says Smith. "Smokers' insurance only costs me a hundred bucks in Panama." Smith has a comfortable home and a solid business, and you sense he doesn't need to economize, but maybe he likes a bargain.

The area has a mountainous spine and the country's coolest climate is found in a clutch of upland towns close to David, a few miles short of the Continental Divide, originally colonized in the late nineteenth century by Swiss Germans and other Europeans. A visitor in the mid-twentieth century would have heard German and English spoken on the country lanes here. This was a period when war and poverty brought still more European settlers. In the temperate climate they grew strawberries, watermelons, salad leaves, and, above all, coffee. A first-generation Croat owns one of the main market-garden operations, up in Cerro Punta, Panama's most elevated town, and sends his produce across the country. Cerro Punta is no more than a rambling village, in fact, a place where vacationing Panamanians buy tubs of strawberries and cream, and put on windbreakers and scarves to guard against the sudden cool whenever a cloud crosses the face of the sun. Lower down, Volcán is another mountain town, bigger than Cerro Punta, these days even a bit sprawling. The place was named after an extinct volcano, Barú, that looms nearby. That a section of Volcán is called Nueva California says a lot about the optimism of the early arrivals, who included a Swede whose descendants went on to corner the local coffee market. On the other side of the volcano is Boquete, a mountain community considered a more worldly, even quite ritzy, alternative to Volcán. Boquete was Holbert and Reese's next stop after David. He says the couple spent three months there in a rented house.

If the swirling mists, verdant hillsides, and freshly ground coffee were not reason enough, Panama has put together "the most appealing program of special benefits for retirees you'll find anywhere in the world today." This is according to *International Living*, a magazine that has given people overseas retirement tips and advice since it was set up as a modest newsletter over thirty years ago. Retirees with a pension of $1,000, or slightly more in the case of a couple, qualify for residency and automatic discounts on energy bills, half-price movie tickets, and reductions in health care. You are allowed to import your household possessions duty free; and the Panamanian government offers a particularly sweet tax-free deal on buying new vehicles. If you invest in property above a certain threshold, you don't even need to prove a monthly income.

Volcán and Boquete have attracted many such pension program applicants, boosting the local economy, although perhaps not by as much as the Panamanian government had hoped. Some were awarded their pensioner's residency status a decade ago when the threshold was set at a pension of just $750 a month. Had they been living in America, some folks in the program might have been close to the breadline, but in Panama much of what you needed to eat grew on trees in the yard and fell into the dirt when ripe, or was sold on the street for the equivalent of spare change. This is a climatic sweet spot, too, where you needed neither heating nor air-conditioning. But Panama is the developing world, after all. Traffic police are a low-level irritant on the roads. Cops want $20 not to write a speeding ticket; failing to pay up means a visit to the police station and a long, dull wait as punishment. To the working-class, or working-poor, locals, the impoverished gringo pensioners must inevitably be wealthy. Panamanians toil in fields and coffee plantations, work in stores, or build and fix things for scant reward. So, the gringos—who have the luxury of being able to leave their own country to go to another one without having to work there—must, necessarily, have a good amount of money. It is difficult for Panamanians to see it any differently, unless they are familiar with life in North America or the prosperous economies of Europe, and most aren't. When many locals are living on very much less, the expat pensioner with an income that wouldn't stretch far in North America can, here in Central America, look around and feel just a bit richer. They can usually afford to employ someone to clean their homes; perhaps cook their meals as well. Wealth is always a relative thing, after all.

After Boquete and Volcán, the third magnet for expats in western Panama is the lush islands and headlands of Bocas del Toro, on the Caribbean coast. Real estate is touted to foreign buyers in all three locations, and crooks will surely always be part of the deal, but it is only in Bocas del Toro that the property market became full-on frothy, attracting an even less scrupulous class of real estate operator than in the mountain towns— true bottom-of-the-barrel types.

"People would get in touch with certain real estate agents in Panama from North America and Europe. These guys would offer them a tour of Panama to get an overview of the housing market," said Okke Ornstein, a Dutch radio journalist based in Panama City. But these were real estate agents whose main business was plugging properties in Boquete; they had nothing else to sell at all. The realtors came up with a simple trick that involved no gimmicks; no one needed to be buttered up for a sale: "They drove them through the hottest parts of Panama and then, finally, up they went to cool Boquete," said Ornstein. There was relief all around. Everyone could breathe properly again in the fresh mountain air. It was here that the tourists bought their retirement homes.

The roads above Boquete's diminutive town center twist and turn as they rise; everywhere are blue jacaranda flowers and white lilies. Comfortable houses sit behind fences. On one bluff overlooking the valley there is a small chapel painted white at the far end of a long lawn. A sign outside reads: THIS PROPERTY IS NOT FOR SALE. People come to Boquete from all over the world, attracted by the delightful countryside and a climate that is never too hot or too cold, an *eternal spring* in the blurb of the publicity material of the gated communities.

Around April 2007, Holbert rented a room above a supermarket on Boquete's main square, directly opposite the place where the decommissioned American school buses, widely used as public transport in rural Panama, arrive from David with a screech of their brakes. The best guess is that there are now about seven hundred people from North America and Europe in Boquete, versus around four hundred in Volcán, but it is difficult to know precisely how many there are as not all expats become residents by joining, for instance, the pensioners' program. There are some gringos living in Boquete as tourists who have to exit the country every six months to renew their tourist status—the "visa run," it's called locally. Newcomers and locals lead mainly separate lives; one expat said that the Boquete gringos wanted "a slightly segregated lifestyle" in a place that is "rigidly organized."

In his room above the market, Holbert set up a fake psychiatry office, calling himself Dr. William Reese. "In no time I had twenty clients," he said later. "They were all old women who just wanted to talk." He charged $80 a session but said he didn't like the town. "I want to live with Panamanians!" said Holbert. "Americans bitch about everything." The main square where Wild Bill dispensed advice as Dr. William Reese is also where Boquete's town hall is located. The townsfolk help out with chores in the expats' homes, but they have concerns all their own, too. (Fast-forward to 2014, and take a look at the wall on the main square across from the town hall. Someone has glued an enlarged photocopy of the identity card of a young man and written the word THIEF below it.) Meanwhile, Holbert arrived at his own view of the expats. He said that "out of a hundred, ninety-seven will be damaged and three will be normal." Holbert and Reese were still generally keeping their heads down in Boquete, although this would soon change. They became customers of an English bookstore in the village of Dolega next to the highway between Boquete and David. There was plenty of stock: libraries in the former Canal Zone had lots of books to dispose of, and many hundreds of these turned up in the English bookstore in Dolega. Here, Holbert bought books on historical figures like Napoleon Bonaparte and Adolf Hitler; Reese liked true crime stories.

One day Holbert called an American expat in Boquete who had put her comfortable house up for sale, arranging to meet the woman and her husband at their house to inspect the property with them. But when Holbert phoned to confirm the visit and the woman told him to come along but that her husband had been called away on business, Holbert cut the call short and never contacted the woman again.

Although the two towns are less than ten miles apart as the crow flies, it takes over an hour to drive from Boquete to Volcán, because there is no direct road: the volcano and a deep, wild ravine are in the way, so you have to skirt them. In about August 2007, Holbert and Reese moved to Volcán and actively sought out the company of their fellow expats. Holbert seemed odd, loud, larger than life, determined to be the center of attention. He set up a Harley-Davidson repair shop in the town and called it Vikingo Motor Sports. Holbert's motorbike business was next to a workshop, cluttered and dark inside, where several men made leather goods for horses. Vikingo Motor Sports is long gone but the men are still there, driving studs into their saddles. Holbert's business card had a black Viking helmet and read "William Adolfo Cortez."

Holbert was six feet tall and looked like he took steroids. He introduced himself as a serial entrepreneur. Reese, often frumpy and sullen, said she was a veterinarian. At social events Holbert wore a Viking-style helmet with long, curled horns like the one on his business card. His boisterousness and his firm desire to be the focus of attention in a crowd were noticed by just about everyone. His reputation preceded him most places he went in Volcán; someone less self-confident might have attracted more comments about the feasibility of his chosen line of business. After he left Volcán, one expat woman said: "What was he thinking of? A Harley-Davidson shop here? You hardly see regular motorbikes here, let alone Harleys. People get around in pickups or on horses. This is a farming community!" But perhaps the expats thought it didn't matter so much anyway. Holbert was hardly short of money to fund his hobby bike shop: he told pretty much everyone he met in Volcán that he had inherited a large sum of money from his parents, people heard the sum of $30 million mentioned, and that he had gold in a bank vault in the Cayman Islands, and beachfront property in Cozumel, Mexico. Sometimes the tales were richly extravagant: in the Caymans, Bill and Jane entertained gold buyers with parties, they said. They invited lords and ladies and rich people. Naturally, they had to provide the cocaine and Bill also did a bit of cocaine to fit in with his guests.

Many of the long-term expats have a precise memory of meeting Holbert for the first time because he threw a big party to announce his arrival in Volcán. David Dell, a Welshman who came to Panama with his Dutch wife, Lydia, by way of Vancouver, Canada, remembers that it was held in a now-defunct restaurant called Daly's, a diner run by an American.

Holbert booked the whole place and put up the money for everyone's food and drink. "It was a smorgasbord-style buffet," recalls Dell. A country-and-western band hovered at the edge of the party, ready to plug in their guitars, as they did most weekends, to play a few covers. Holbert strode over to them. "No, not tonight, no music." As one of the guests observed later, "He didn't want anything or anyone to take the spotlight away from him."

Around two weeks after the party, Dell and his wife met Holbert and Reese at the house of a mutual friend. The Dells' home was away from the center of Volcán but nonetheless stood close to the busy main road that bisects the town. The Dells spent days at a time at another house, this one on the coast. They were considering making their seaside house their main home, with the idea of moving out of the mountains. Their Volcán house was not formally up for sale, but that didn't mean that the Dells weren't open to offers, and so the couple were happy to talk about the property if they detected interest. Dell recalls the meeting well: "Jane said to us, 'I really like your house, but it's not secluded enough.'" By the expression on his face, it seemed that Holbert wasn't really attracted to the house. But then, a little over a month later, something odd happened. The Dells got back from their place on the coast and found that someone had broken into their Volcán house. "The thief hadn't bothered to take the TV. All the food was still there. But whoever had got in had used a crowbar to force open a filing cabinet. They didn't need to force it, actually, as the cabinet wasn't locked. It seems they ran off when the house alarm started to ring," said Dell. "What did that say to us? That the thief was looking for our papers and documents. That he was looking for the deeds to the property."

After the break-in, Dell—who, before retiring, used to produce a television program on crime prevention in British Columbia called *Mugshots*—gathered a number of items that the burglar had moved. He put them in a plastic bag and took it to the police, thinking that they might have the burglar's fingerprints on record, or at least would want to record the prints Dell had recovered. "But the attitude of the police was, nothing was really stolen, so why bother with any of this?" Dell kept that plastic bag for two years, and the police never did take an interest in it.

Most of the time gringos—small-level shakedowns on the highway notwithstanding—are ignored by the Panamanian police. The police force is one of the few institutions in the country where there is some degree of social mobility. It attracts people who want to make a steady living and get job security. The consensus is that only a minority of policemen in Panama are ready to risk going into the line of fire.

I take a room at a wooden guesthouse on a road branching off the highway close to the premises of Holbert's erstwhile Vikingo Motor Sports. Back in the day, the guesthouse was the home of Volcán's school principal. Built in the 1950s, wood was at that time the only viable building material in the highlands. Trees grew all around Volcán and bringing concrete up the road from David, in those days unpaved, was prohibitively expensive. Jorge, the owner, said that there was no key to the door of my room, so I would have to leave it unlocked. "Someone left with the key," he said. "But don't worry, no one ever steals anything here." I can hear a sharp, barking chorus of a dozen guard dogs on Jorge's lane through the torrential rain falling outside his establishment. Volcán is an ugly town in a pretty place, but after a hot soup and a glass of red wine, the dining room of Jorge's creaky wooden lodge begins to ooze a bit of charm, gives a feeling of well-being. The guesthouse has a community notice board in the lobby. People have pinned advertisements for farms for sale, bull semen, used household items. Someone is hoping to sell a 2003 Saturn that is *wrecked, driveable*. There is a flyer for a real estate outfit calling itself "Paradise Found."

After you have left behind the center of Volcán, marked by a bus stop and a couple of Chinese-run supermarkets, the road to Río Sereno—a small town next to the border with Costa Rica—is smooth and runs straight as an arrow for about three miles. If anyone felt like going out for a ride on a Harley in this part of Panama, the itinerary would likely include this stretch of the Río Sereno road. A ninety-degree turnoff ten minutes out of town brings you to a group of holiday cottages around a trout pond. On a lawn shaded by mature oaks there are half a dozen stalls. This is Volcán's weekly farmers' market.

The market is a fixture on Volcán's gringo social calendar. Next to the trout pond a café does a swift trade in eggs and pancakes and coffee. Regular customers sit back in their chairs, legs crossed, relaxed. There is much talk of hiking routes. Several newcomers hover less confidently at the edge of small groups. Some of the older men tip their hats when they greet a woman. Most of the expats live on tracts of land and semi-suburban streets populated with Panamanians. Gated communities designed for North Americans and Europeans never took off in Volcán, not for want of people trying, but because this is fundamentally a much more individualistic destination than Boquete—not so well-dressed, living on thinner pensions, but in its own way a kind of ballsy place nonetheless.

I begin chatting with a youngish American man dressed in a black shirt and black skinny jeans who tells me, apropos of nothing at all, that he has trouble understanding people who don't believe in UFOs. But we negotiate ourselves around this potential conversation-killer and, after exchanging a few pleasantries, I find out that the man and his mother live in the house that Holbert and Reese had occupied when they were in Volcán. They invite me to come over that same day.

When we get there, I am surprised. This modest property was hardly the place you would expect the rich kid with the gold stored away and the fat-cat inheritance to hole up in. Holbert and Reese lived on what is basically a residential street lined with houses of varying build quality, each house set back from the road behind large yards. The earth road is deeply pitted, with large stones poking out of the surface here and there. Some plots are empty and have been used to dump garbage. One is being used as a dentist's office; it advertises the services on offer on a board fixed to a gate with the various dental interventions hand-painted in sloping, irregular script. The young man, who is called Richard, and his mother, June,* show me around. It turns out that Richard is staying in Panama while some family trouble in the United States is getting sorted out. It was June who took over the property after Holbert and Reese moved on from Volcán. "This part was just weeds when we got here," says June, pointing

---

* Not their real names.

at the edges of the yard where she has planted bougainvillea and irises. The concrete house has bars on its lower windows and contains two rooms and a bathroom. The paint of the interior walls is smudged and peeling in places. In the first room, someone built a mezzanine sleeping space under the eaves to create an extra bedroom, which makes the kitchen below it a bit cramped, but the arrangement suits June when Richard comes to stay.

Before the day is over, I tag along with Richard and June to a weekend market on the grounds of a school. Here there are many more Panamanians than at the farmers' market. Everyone is searching through crates of clothes that seem to have been sent here from thrift shops. There is a batch of shirts with different names of chefs and their restaurants sown into the pockets, a heap of men's chinos are marked "imperfect," and there is another pile, this one of dark-blue parkas with furry hoods, which I assume have been dispatched to the wrong place—even on the coolest night in Volcán, you wouldn't need to wear one of those. In another room there are piles of pretzels, small packets of oatmeal, and unmarked tins—everyone is asking the vendor what is in them. Before I take my leave of Richard and June, I ask June about Holbert and Reese. What did the folks in the street have to say about them? "I just thought Bill was a big fat slob," said June. "And then his fly-by-night business, the bike thing . . ." June trails off; her shopping done, she is ready to go back home. Then she recalls something else: "They say Bill used to get Jane to shower naked outside in the yard. That was something people thought was really weird."

One day in late 2006 Lydia Dell remembers talking casually with an American man in late middle age, and his wife, perhaps a decade younger than he was, who appeared to be from the Far East. They had come to stay in Volcán for a few days to check the place out. Lydia doesn't recall that they were actively looking to move to the town, but expat home prospectors come and go in Volcán. Some stay; many move on. That's the way things are. But what stuck in Lydia's mind is that when she asked the woman if she was from Thailand, the woman replied that no, she wasn't from Thailand but, rather, from Indonesia. "And Indonesia was a former Dutch colony. We learned about it at school back in Holland. That's why I remember talking to the lady."

The woman's name was Manchittha Nankratoke Brown, and she called herself Nan for short. She might have lived for a time in Indonesia, or felt that it was convenient to cover up the fact that she was originally from Thailand. There exists a document drawn up by the Panamanian authorities in 2005 certifying her husband, Michael Watson Brown, as a small-scale agricultural producer on twelve acres of cleared land in the Darklands Peninsula of Bocas del Toro. The document shows that, like Holbert and Reese, the Brown couple used Dutch passports as their main form of identification. Michael Brown's real name was Michael Francis Salem. The couple were homeschooling a son, Watson, who was in his mid-teens and loved to skateboard, like many boys his age. Little is known about Manchittha other than that she liked to cook.

In Panama, people intent on controlling their contact with the authorities by going off grid in a remote place are often successful. Darklands is a densely forested peninsula shaped like a hammerhead jutting out of the mainland. There are no roads and the only way to get around is by boat. It's a perfect place to be anonymous, maybe even to feel safe. A year after passing through Volcán, the lives of Brown, Manchittha, and Watson were about to collide with William Dathan Holbert.

For the couple from North Carolina on the run, change, inevitably, had to come. Vikingo Motor Sports had customers, but not enough of them. Holbert was cooped up with Reese in a dump of a two-room house in a town that approximated the middle of nowhere. Holbert found Michael Brown on Craigslist, the pared-down website offering classified ads for everything from used clothing to friendships. Brown had a property for sale in Bocas del Toro. Around Thanksgiving 2007, Holbert called Brown to find out more about the home he had advertised. They arranged to meet.

One day, before Holbert and Reese moved out of their house in the shadow of the volcano, the pair found themselves in a casual discussion of the stock market with a few other expats. Holbert said: "If this system goes down, I won't starve. I'll go to a rich person's house and kill them all." Apparently, his threat went unchallenged. And Reese, who kept her mouth shut for a lot of the time, suddenly broke her silence: "Folks aren't going to believe what we've been doing here when we're gone," she said.

2. Bocas del Toro

hen Graham Greene arrived in the town of Bocas* on Columbus Island (Isla Colón in Spanish) in 1979 as Omar Torrijos's guest,† he had a sense of impending doom—"a feeling that I would never get away." The wet weather had not helped; "the island seemed to be sinking back into the sea under the weight of the storm." After a visit to a dull agricultural fair, a terrible dinner, and a night of fitful sleep in a hotel room with neither air-conditioning nor a mosquito net, Greene was looking forward to catching his flight. The next morning, as the airplane lifted off into a clear sky, he saw dozens of islands scattered in the bay

---

*A note on nomenclature: The province of Bocas del Toro, consisting of a large slab of mainland containing the provincial capital Changuinola, is always called by its full name. But Bocas del Toro can also refer to the archipelago and the promontory of Darklands. Where a reference is to the province, I indicate it as such. The only town in the archipelago is also, formally speaking, called Bocas del Toro, but newcomers and locals alike invariably abbreviate this to "Bocas" or "Bocas Town." Expats also often call the archipelago "Bocas," but the context usually makes clear whether the reference is to the archipelago or the town.

† In 1979, General Omar Torrijos was the unelected de facto ruler of Panama.

of Bocas del Toro below him. Next to Columbus Island was the cigar-shaped Carenero Island, and farther off the islands of Popa, Bastimentos, and Cristóbal, with the Darklands Peninsula thrust alongside them. In his airplane, Greene realized that it was possible to see "how each piece had once fitted into another."

Greene might have liked the town a bit more had he visited at the turn of the twentieth century. Flush with profits from the banana trade, Bocas had a theater, a cinema, consulates, and even a cricket pitch. French, German, Italian, and English were spoken on its streets. Ladies' fashions arrived in longed-for boxes from Paris and London. It was mainly immigrants from Jamaica and Barbados, among other places, who did the backbreaking work on the plantations. Some arrived after working on the Panama railroad and, later, the first attempt at a Panama canal. But disease ravaged the banana crops on the island and a disastrous fire in 1904 hastened the town's demise. The golden age of Bocas ended definitively in 1909 when the United Fruit Company, the dominant local banana producer, decamped to the mainland and set up its head office there.

Greene's overriding impression of stagnation in Bocas would remain accurate until the 1980s, when speedboats started to use the calm bay as a stop-off for cocaine runs from Colombia, bringing money to the local economy and arguably changing Bocas permanently. Later, a new type of foreign resident came to settle, first in a trickle, then a wave, encouraged by overseas relocation publications touting Panama as "the world's best retirement destination" and—in the specific case of Bocas del Toro—"the undiscovered Caribbean." Panama attracted a more intrepid type of foreign newcomer than Mexico, then the most popular gringo retirement haven: it was farther away from the United States and Canada and, for most people, was something of an unknown quantity. And Bocas del Toro was the back of beyond: Panamanian newspapers published in Panama City still routinely call it *la alejada provincia de Bocas del Toro*—the faraway province of Bocas del Toro.

When Malcolm Henderson first arrived in Bocas del Toro in 1997 with his wife, Pat Buckley Moss, an American artist, there were around twenty or thirty expats—mainly North American—living there. "We were a bag of oddballs, but we were united," said Henderson, an Englishman who

had been a soldier in the British Army and later ran a gallery in the suburbs of Washington, D.C. "We knew everything about each other, how
many ex-wives we had, and how many children. It was just like one big
family. We felt very lucky." It was chance that brought Malcolm and Pat
to Bocas. The couple had found an unexpected gap in their schedules and
decided to fly down to Costa Rica to visit a Native American community
they had read about, with the plan to learn from them how best to
slow down their pace of life. But nature intervened: torrential rain and a
washed-out road forced a change in plans. "We had the chance to fly to
Bocas, and we took it," said Henderson.

The next day, on impulse, Henderson put down a deposit on a house
on Carenero Island—directly across a three-hundred-yard passage of
water from Bocas Town—and also some land, farther away from Bocas
Town on the Darklands Peninsula, now the location of a farm where
Henderson lives. He freely admits that there was no due diligence. "I
knew that if I delayed taking the plunge, my children would persuade me
to be sensible and not risk my health in an isolated tropical community.
It was a question of, do it then or never." This was a pattern that would
repeat itself many times over, as more and more expats came to Bocas del
Toro and bought—often very quickly—pieces of real estate they thought
conformed to their tropical island dream. After Henderson's snap decision, the couple spent several months setting up their main residence in
the house on Carenero Island.

When Malcolm and Pat arrived in Bocas del Toro, access other than
by plane was difficult, and services were often delayed and sometimes
canceled altogether when the weather was bad. The only paved road out of
Almirante—the mainland port serving Bocas—ran northwest to the border with Costa Rica rather than southeast toward the rest of Panama
(a highway connecting Almirante with David and Panama City was
finally completed in 2000). A former Baltic Sea ferry ship, repurposed in
Panama, sailed to Bocas from the mainland every Wednesday with supplies for the town's few food markets; expats would often plan their week
around that day.

The Hendersons' gringo watering hole was the Buena Vista, a bar and
restaurant of wooden construction built out on poles over the water, fish

swimming below. The expats held regular parties there, often costume events. They met to celebrate Halloween, Valentine's Day, Mother's Day, and Father's Day, as well as birthdays and the occasional marriage. The men sometimes put on grass skirts, with coconut husks chopped in two and strapped over their chests; the women either came as pirates or dressed up in a retro, 1960s flower-girl look, a choice—conscious or unconscious—of the decade when most of them were young and coming of age.

The Buena Vista is still there—"In those days, if you wanted to eat something other than chicken, beans, and rice in a restaurant there was really nowhere else to go," says Henderson—but it is no longer the only expat bar. The seafront is now lined with them, their daily specials, cocktails, and happy hour deals advertised out front. Young men and women, the sort who arrive in a place for a week and six months later are still there, tout bilingual menus to passersby, smiling broadly. Out back, wooden decks over the water catch the breeze. From time to time divers still pick old medicine and cologne bottles from the first years of the twentieth century out of the silt under the decks where the vacationers sit sipping their mojitos and caipirinhas.

A year or two after the Hendersons' arrival, *International Living* magazine ran a story touting Bocas del Toro as an expat retirement haven. A couple of features in American big-city newspapers followed. "The floodgates opened," recalls Henderson. "Things started to go wrong. There was a real hunger for land. People sold land they didn't own. The same plot of land would sometimes get sold twice. You could be offered the same piece of land three times in a week by three different people claiming to be the owner."

As it happened, one day Henderson was offered a piece of land for sale that he knew very well. "I had been back to England for a while and was having a drink at the Buena Vista. Possibly I looked a bit pale, as if I had just arrived in Bocas for the first time. Soon, a friendly North American man started a conversation with me. He said he had a few choice properties to sell. I let him carry on with his pitch. After a few minutes he unfolded a map and offered me a piece of land that was mine. I told him so. But the man just smiled at me and asked, 'Then is it up for sale?'"

Journalists and writers had shone a light on Bocas del Toro and the publicity attracted some of the worst real estate scammers. They had the perfect means at their disposal: a land registry office known to take bribes, a system of banking secrecy, and ultra-discreet corporation law. All this, in a country where the US dollar is legal tender. Real estate sharks could keep several steps ahead of the understaffed and pliable police by flitting from one Central American republic to the next. For crooks, it was no less a paradise than for the expats who liked boating, surfing, or just swinging on their hammocks in the dead of the afternoon. Some of these new gringo arrivals had already cut their teeth in nearby Costa Rica. They made the relatively short journey from the beach communities around Puerto Limón, which in the 1990s—on the back of the country's relatively sound infrastructure and well-advertised ecotourism credentials—had attracted a wave of newcomers from North America.

But at the turn of the millennium there was a perception that Costa Rica was becoming unsafe. Gangs of thieves moved quickly from one place to another, robbing houses and stealing vehicles. Some drove from coast to coast to steal, operating in places where they wouldn't be recognized. People thought Bocas del Toro had to be quieter and more secure than Puerto Limón because there was no road access. Any crime that happened there would be limited for the most part to kids stealing food from your kitchen or running off with your stereo system. This, at least, was the theory.

The classic racket in booming Bocas was for a promoter to offer land with an impeccable title recently delivered by the local land registry office. The sale price would be a bargain, practically too good to be true. The North American buyer would build his dream home and, with construction complete, finally move in. Only then, a letter would arrive from a firm of local lawyers, advising that its client—one of Bocas' most estimable families, often with useful political connections—already owned the plot of land, with a title dating back several generations. The embarrassed lawyer would propose that they reach an amicable agreement with the local family to buy their long-standing title. Though it might seem amazing that the land registry office could have overlooked an old but perfectly valid title, it was stranger still that the estimable local family waited until the last piece of furniture was carried through the front door before contacting their lawyers.

"Around 2003 or 2004," recalls Okke Ornstein, the Dutch radio journalist based in Panama City, "people were buying, often sight unseen, into land that was to be given over to projects like teak plantations and noni fruit farms.* Not only did the promoters sometimes not own the land they were selling, teak was a wood unfit for commercial plantation in Bocas, and the market for noni fruit was minuscule and would soon be swamped if even a tenth of the produce they promised was ever harvested."

Another dubious project marketed in Bocas in that period was a luxury tree-house development in a jungle setting. Ornstein rang the promoter when he heard about it. "I told him that I was handicapped, so could they fit the tree house out with an elevator? The promoter said 'yes, no problem.'" Needless to say, today's visitor to Bocas will not find any trace of a luxury tree house, with or without an elevator. Another realtor tried to sell a sandbar close to Bocas Town that, lying uncovered, would sometimes attract local youngsters wanting to play an informal game of soccer. The sandbar was all that was left of an island destroyed in a powerful earthquake that hit Bocas del Toro in 1991. But the realtor had to time his inspection visits carefully, as the sandbar was flooded by water at high tide.

Despite the smoke and mirrors, the hilly, green islands of Bocas del Toro, with their white-sand beaches, really are an ideal refuge for those fleeing colder climates, creditors, bad marriages, failed businesses, taxes, or the rat race. It can get stormy, as Greene discovered, but Bocas del Toro lies outside the hurricane zone. A habitable island in the bay with a secure title can cost as little as $25,000—a fraction of the price of something similar in the Bahamas or the Virgin Islands. There is a virtually endless supply of timber to build a home. Bocas has idyllic beaches for surfing and swimming, fresh fish, and cheap rum. Dolphins frolic in the lagoon.

---

* The pungent-smelling fruit of the noni shrub—commonly used in Polynesia as a folk medicine—has been promoted as a cure for various diseases, including cancer, although there is no evidence to support such claims. When sold commercially, noni juice is often mixed with grape juice to make it more palatable.

A dozen coral reefs offer divers and snorkelers a glimpse of beauty below the surface of the water. None of these is going away anytime soon.

As the years went by, Henderson started to notice a phenomenon. The expats would often build their houses in isolated locations. Their over-riding objective would be to have the best possible view and not be overlooked. "But houses that are hidden from view are at a higher risk of robbery," says Henderson. In addition, there was another problem with the preferred siting of the typical gringo dream home. Consider the indigenous people of Bocas del Toro. They built houses either well away from the water, where there was less risk of flooding, or on stilts right on the water at the end of a short jetty to guard against termites. But the half-on-land, half-in-the-sea building style favored by many expats achieved neither; it was picturesque but not well suited to this corner of the tropics.

Malcolm and Pat Henderson's marriage didn't survive their time in Bocas. Pat moved back to the States and Malcolm stayed in Panama at his beloved farm on Darklands, called Finca Tranquila for its peace and quiet. In truth, away from Bocas Town every corner of the archipelago is quiet, except for when a storm rages. The farm is virtually self-sufficient: he keeps chickens, some twenty sheep, and three horses, but no cows. "If you kill a cow, you have too much meat," says Henderson. "What are you going to do with it? There's nowhere to keep such a large amount of flesh frozen. But a sheep is the perfect size. You slaughter it and there is just enough for you for a week or so, plus meat to give your neighbors."

It was around Thanksgiving in 2007—and while Bill and Jane, as Holbert and Reese were known, were living in Volcán—that Holbert found Michael Brown's small ad on Craigslist. Brown had put his house up for sale on the south-facing side of the Darklands Peninsula, a place at the very edge of the archipelago. It was a large property—three bedrooms with high ceilings on the first floor, and a big reception room that faced a sloping lawn bisected by a stone path leading down to the floating dock. The roofed second floor had no windows or dividing walls and was open to the elements. This upper floor was empty, except for a skateboard ramp made of plywood that Michael Brown had constructed for his son, Watson. (Brown had two other children, a girl and a boy named Leanne and Marco, with his first wife, who was Jamaican, but neither of these older children lived in Bocas del Toro at that point.) The roof had a row of solar panels. The Browns had lived in their house on Darklands for about four years, and during this time they had planted crops on their land, making them practically self-sufficient. Their land was mainly virgin tropical forest, forty-five acres of it, but the bush that had been cleared was sown with pineapples, oranges, passion fruit, and plantains. The Browns also kept chickens, meaning they rarely left even for groceries. When there were errands to run, Michael Brown preferred to send a couple of local men he employed rather than go himself. On the occasions he ventured off his property, he would avoid going to Bocas Town—full as it was with gringos passing through or in for the long haul—and instead went to stores in the more distant mainland towns of Almirante and Changuinola.

The Browns' house was in a particularly out-of-the-way part of Bocas del Toro and wasn't the kind of location people would visit on a whim. To get there from Bocas Town took around forty-five minutes by motorboat in calm seas, but when the wind blew and the water was agitated a skillful skipper would need to zigzag through huge waves and cut his speed. On those days the journey would take as much as twice as long. The route crossed the Bocas del Toro Lagoon, passing Dolphin Bay on the starboard side, through a channel of about two hundred yards hacked through a stand of mangroves, and then it rounded the northern and eastern shore of Darklands, making a sharp right turn at Split Hill (Loma Partida in Spanish). This is Darklands' most distinctive feature: Split Hill, actually a separate island, is a piece of land that looks like the end of a finger that has been hacked off its hand. The passage of water between the hand of Darklands and the finger of Split Hill is the location of a store selling boat fuel, detergent, cooking oil, beer, and potato chips. There are Native American houses, thatched and built of wood, protruding from the shore on narrow stilts.

After Loma Partida you're about ten minutes from the Browns' house by motorboat. Although the Browns kept to themselves, Mike Smith and

Fran Tilbury got to know them a bit when they were staying at their own house on Loma Partida. Smith recalled a tasty Thai meal that Nan prepared for Fran and him one day, and Nan's enthusiasm when she was cooking it. If Smith found out little about Michael Brown when they were eating together, that was pretty much par for the course for gringos in Central America. (Brown said he had run some sort of import-export business in the Far East, but the details were vague.) Watson Brown, his teenage son, made a firm impression on Mike Smith, however: "He was a great kid. He was smart. They were homeschooling him and he was looking forward to going to college." Smith recalled going up to see Watson's second-floor skateboard ramp: "It was a huge, U-shaped thing." On that isolated farm on the shore of Darklands, aside from the skateboard ramp, Watson had few of the material comforts that many other boys with American fathers might take for granted. There was no mall to wander around, no cinema, no evident group of friends to bond with. Watson was seventeen years old that Thanksgiving in 2007. He would never make it to college.

Unlike Malcolm Henderson, the Browns led a sustainable lifestyle more out of necessity than choice. In fact, Brown was a man who needed to keep a low profile. He had grown up in south Florida and had been in and out of jail since his teens—the police picked him up for the first time at age thirteen for breaking into a car. Like Holbert, he used a plethora of assumed names: Michael Csafka, James Hall, Bob Zell, Michael Zildgen, and, more fancifully, Captain Johan Tortugas. Michael Brown was born in 1948. He had been a career criminal thought to have been running drugs in the Far East after doing much the same in Florida in the 1970s. This was a time when many of the narcotics entering the United States came through the Caribbean islands. Brown was wanted by the Broward County Sheriff's Office for kidnapping a law enforcement officer; he had escaped from an American prison in 1980 and had been a fugitive from justice in the state of Florida ever since. After a period living in the Far East, he chose Panama as a place to lay low. With his sixtieth birthday approaching, it appears that Michael Brown—for all intents and purposes—was retired from a life of crime. His principal nest egg was kept in an HSBC bank account in Hong Kong, which he could gradually withdraw from at local ATMs.

Brown's house was remote from the noisy entertainment of Bocas Town—an attraction for some people but a deal breaker for others—but it had a number of features prized by gringos where homes in the archipelago are concerned. It had plenty of land and wasn't in a place a casual visitor would stumble across; it had a nice view; and anyone checking how solid the structure was by inexpertly tapping the walls would probably have convinced himself that the house would resist the worst storms of the rainy season. Holbert made the road trip to Bocas del Toro alone and left Reese in their rented house down the dirt track in the shadow of a volcano. To get there, Holbert had to backtrack almost as far as David and then drive his station wagon up through another valley and across the Continental Divide. Fronds and ferns encroach on each side of the concrete road, claiming it back to nature. Three hours out of Volcán, the view opens up, and on a clear day you can see the Caribbean and the outline of Darklands. But when clouds race in, Darklands is quickly obscured and the sea turns from azure to blue-black. Michael Brown went by boat to fetch Holbert on the jetty at Chiriquí Grande, a convenient access point for the southern shore of Darklands.

Holbert stayed with the Browns for three days just before Christmas, gaining their confidence. Brown confided to Holbert that he had peddled drugs in Thailand and had been offered a place in an American witness protection program in exchange for his testimony (this is most likely false). Brown also explained to Holbert that back in 2002 he had set up a Panamanian shell company, Latitude 9.10, Inc., with bearer share certificates. This was the legal vehicle he used to buy his house. So there was no need for a notary or an attorney to be present for Holbert to buy the property from him: the person physically holding the paper was the owner. This is how the system worked in Panama at the time: a lawyer would set up a Panamanian company and issue a corporation charter. The corporation would have its complement of directors who could hold meetings in any way they wished—around a table in a boardroom, by e-mail, by phone, by fax, or whatever, and in any location they wanted, anywhere in the world. In parallel, bearer share certificates would be issued.

What gave the setup its peculiar turnkey character had to do with the proxy directors appointed by the lawyer setting up the deal. These would be people trusted by the lawyer, but they would know little of—and care even less about—the arrangements of the corporation they were supposedly agreeing to direct. You would typically find law firm receptionists, staffers, or quite simply someone renting out his or her signature for a small fee acting as a director for this type of shell corporation, particularly where expats were concerned. But it hardly mattered that the directors were an unknown quantity for the potential buyer of a shell corporation. As soon as these people became directors, they, in effect, ceased to hold the title: each of them would immediately sign an undated resignation letter. This bundle of resignation letters completed the vendor's package. It is almost certain that in December 2007 Michael Brown explained the whole procedure to Holbert as he laid out the documents in front of him. To make a deal happen, all you needed to provide as the seller were the corporation charter, the bearer share certificates, and the signed, undated resignation letters provided by the proxy directors.

Across Latin America, and also in Spain, corporations are known as *sociedades anónimas*, literally anonymous societies, and the Panamanian bearer-share and proxy-director version of it was perfectly and unimprovably discreet.* From the buyer's perspective, all that needed to be done, formally speaking, was to set up a new board of directors. At the time in Panama this was an operation that cost about $500 in legal fees. And, of course, the old directors did not need to be present when the new directors were put in place in the lawyer's office, since these old directors had already resigned.

After three days with the Browns, their house-hunting guest returned to Volcán with the bearer shares. According to Holbert, Michael Brown had sold him the house in Darklands and the Browns had moved on.

---

* It probably was not a matter uppermost in Holbert's mind, but the system was attractively tax efficient, too, as no transfer duty or tax was levied on the transfer of bearer shares from one owner to the next, even where the shell corporation had been set up with the express intent of being a vehicle for real estate ownership.

Holbert subsequently spoke little about his purchase. Holbert told the few people who inquired that Michael Brown had left no forwarding address. Watson stopped sending e-mails to his half sister and half brother, Michael Brown's Jamaican children, and they became worried. Michael Brown, meanwhile, had a sort of financial manager—an old buddy from the old business—who saw that money was being drained from the HSBC account by daily withdrawals at an ATM in Bocas Town. Brown appeared to have disappeared into thin air. But nobody filed a missing persons complaint.

One person who didn't inquire about Michael Brown/Salem was Steve, his younger brother by four years. Steve Salem and Scott McAda—Mike Smith's friend living over the mountain in Boquete—today find the coincidence barely believable, but sometime in 2008, Scott McAda called a man in Miami he didn't know who earned his main living as a sea captain taking vacationers to the Bahamas and, sometimes, Cuba. For a couple of decades Steve Salem had sailed his vessel out of Bayside en route to the Bahamas. Each time the routine was to load the boat with donated goods intended for churches in the Bahamas to distribute to needy children. The holidaymakers were naturally happy to be associated with an act of charity. When he got to the docks in the islands Steve would give the kids Kool-Aid while he unloaded his cargo of school desks and bicycles. But Steve Salem had an occasional sideline as a repo man, and it was in this capacity that Scott McAda got in contact with him. Following McAda's call, Salem came down to Bocas del Toro for the first time in his life. He sailed right past the house where, until a few months previously, his brother Michael had resided. Steve had no idea that Michael was living there, he said. He had no idea his brother was in Panama, for that matter. He could have been anywhere in the world as far as he was concerned. The two brothers had lost contact; Steve Salem had also not met either of Michael's wives and none of his children. The brothers had not been in touch for over two decades because Steve said Michael had become "a very brutal man."

Steve Salem recalls two incidents from the brothers' early adulthood in Florida. One time, the pair were out fishing and Steve badly lacerated one of his fingers. "He wouldn't help me at all. That was a kind of red flag as far as I was concerned." Another time, Steve and Michael were in a car looking for a parking place outside a convenience store. Michael found a spot that he thought was his, but apparently just as he was about to slot in his car, another man he hadn't seen drove into the same parking place. The man smiled at Michael in a friendly way and gestured as if to say, I'll be in and out real quick. "But Mike got out of the car and beat up the guy for it. He pounded him. It was brutal. My brother appeared gentle, at least until someone pissed him off.

"He learned a lot from our father, who was a snake-oil salesman, the kind who would sell miracle cures for this and that, vitamins with exotic labels. He worked the fairs up the East Coast from where we lived in Florida as far north as Pennsylvania. He'd be pitching his wares from the back of a truck wearing a full Indian headdress."

It was a hardscrabble existence in the Florida of the 1960s: the arrangement was that Steve's father would give his wife $60 a week to pay for household expenses. There were five siblings in all. "She didn't always get the money," says Steve, "but I didn't feel deprived. What I know is that my brother learned a lot from our father and from his colorful, deceptive lies." By Steve's reckoning, Michael spent most of his life in prison. "He would never be out of jail for more than a few months at a time."

Holbert picked up Reese from Volcán and they swiftly moved into the Browns' former residence. Holbert and Reese had played Bonnie and Clyde on the run in Wyoming, and now they wanted to play Wild Bill Hickok and Calamity Jane, introducing themselves to neighbors as Bill and Jane Cortez. He renamed the Brown house "Hacienda Cortez," announced to anyone passing by on a large sign embellished with a skull motif. Much as she tried to be unassuming, Reese could not help but stand out. She was a quiet, mousy woman, noticeably overweight in a place where young women tended to look after their figures. She didn't seem to be an obvious match for Holbert, and people wondered what the mutual attraction was.

Although the Browns' house was a forty-five-minute speedboat ride from Bocas Town, Holbert and Reese wasted no time in setting up a bar.

The Browns' property had several hundred yards of shore on either side of the house where the bush ended abruptly at the water. Close to land, the seabed was topped with silt streaked with sand. Holbert and Reese converted an old wooden boathouse on the Browns' land into a drinking den. The jungle is so dense here that the only way in and out of the boathouse is over the water. Even the Browns' old home, which was four hundred yards away from the boathouse at most, could not easily be reached on foot. The structure had a big open deck just above the water and a curved bar with a tiled top at dead center. There were a couple of bathrooms behind the bar to the left. To the right of the bathrooms was a kitchen, a cramped space with a range and a pair of cupboards. Upstairs, Holbert kept a couple of rooms where his guests could crash after a party until first light came.

Holbert named his bare-bones bar the Jolly Roger Social Club and it became a kind of minor druggy focal point of Bocas expat life. His new friends and acquaintances liked the name Wild Bill. People guessed he must be full of steroids because of his size, and he wore a horned Viking helmet so often that it became his trademark, just as it had been in Volcán. In a photograph from this period, we have Holbert, his chest protruding, his bearded chin pushed out, mouth forming a sneer, red-blond hair worn long, swept back, and tied up with a band. Beside him, Reese's lips make a half smile, quizzical, her face a moon, tan upper arms almost as heavy as her husband's. Behind them, a clutter of Harley-Davidson memorabilia, metal glinting, is pinned in approximate rows to a wall.

The Jolly Roger Social Club offered "24-Hour Security" and "All Services." Holbert had a flyer printed that said: *Pull up yer boat and play!* Another one said: *When yer having so much fun you don't want to leave!* The location of the bar was given as Cutthroat Cove, a name that doesn't appear on any map. Wild Bill was the self-declared Minister of the First Church of the Inebriation. Holbert drew a cartoon picture of himself for the flyer with an ink pen. His strands of hair are standing on end as if connected to a Van de Graaff generator. Most disturbing is the way he drew his eyes: two dizzyingly dense spirals of ink with no pupils or whites.

The Jolly Roger Social Club was an undiluted piece of Americana, tables and chairs on the souped-up front porch of the revamped old boat-house, with the cash bar out of reach of the rain. It was far from the only expat dive in the archipelago, but Holbert knew how to throw a party when he wanted to. In his customers Holbert saw money, the Panama-nian police said later, but not the couple of dollars they might pay for a bottle of beer or a hot dog.

The motto of the Jolly Roger Social Club was a cheeky yet now ominous "Over 90% of our members survive."

The opening bash at the Jolly Roger Social Club in early 2008 was Holbert's own meet-and-greet on the islands, his way of getting to know the community efficiently and quickly, just as he had done in Volcán. Douglas Ruscher, an American guesthouse owner in Bocas Town, origi-nally from just outside Cincinnati, Ohio, sailed out with around fifty or sixty other people to party with Wild Bill and Jane on that first night.

When I arrive in Bocas, at the end of March 2014, I go to meet him. It is around eleven in the morning, and the tourists are already out on their day trips. We sit on his porch and drink coffee. Ruscher is a pleasant man in his late fifties. He wears shorts and a polo shirt, the standard expat attire here. I can see my reflection, tiny and distorted, in his mirrored sunglasses.

In ten years in Bocas del Toro, Ruscher has built up a collection of Latin American crafts: pots and naive paintings; squares of cloth with images of parrots; pieces of wood carved to resemble monkeys that serve as placemats. They cover one of the walls of the porch. Among them is a mask from the collection of Bo Icelar, a reclusive antique dealer who used to live in Bocas. The mask is elongated with a prominent nose, Easter Island–like, inscrutable. It is one of many that Bo brought over from the gallery of Native American art he owned in Santa Fe, New Mexico. The rooms in his mansion were full of them. Ruscher was on friendly terms with Bo Icelar.

I ask him about the Jolly Roger's opening party. "I can usually take my drink," says Douglas Ruscher, "but that night I had four, five mojitos and collapsed. I remember nothing of the party after the first few cocktails. My friends told me later I fell to the floor and had to be dragged to the boat for the ride back to Bocas." In the last few years a number of unfortunate tourists have left their drinks unattended late at night in a noisy bar and woken up in the street, many hours later, with the mother of all headaches and minus their wallet or purse. Ruscher says with a rueful shake of his head that spiking tourists' drinks has lately become a "sport" in Bocas. But the Jolly Roger was aimed fair and square at seasoned gringo residents. It was too far from town to function as anything else, as you needed your own boat to get there. That meant a person should have been able to enjoy a drink without a worry in the back of his mind.

"Was Wild Bill grooming me by spiking my drinks? Yes, I'm pretty sure he was."

His low, gentle voice is almost lost among the whooping of gulls. I ask Ruscher about how he has adapted to life in Bocas. "A place like this makes you crazy," he says. "Let's take breakfast, for instance. Why have cereal and eggs in the mornings? If I want to I start with ice cream, steak, or a piece of fish. In Bocas you just do what you like." Back in the day, Ruscher had his own bottling business in Ohio. He would take off for a couple of months each year to travel the world. His wanderlust brought him to Bocas del Toro, and he stayed. "I feel lucky here," says Ruscher, spreading out in his rocking chair, hands folded behind his head. "You don't need so many material things."

After the first night of the Jolly Roger Social Club, the venue started to become a drinking den principally for the people who lived in the vicinity, meaning the Darklands crowd and the occasional yachtsman who put down anchor nearby. Holbert ran his flyer as an advertisement in the *Bocas Breeze*, a monthly newspaper published in English and Spanish, paid for by advertising, lying in piles in shops and hotels for visitors to pick up. The excitement of Wild Bill's opening night died down after a few weeks; people came to the Jolly Roger Social Club mostly to chat or play poker. A routine was established. The bar opened on Fridays and Saturdays in the middle of the afternoon. People climbed back into their boats and went home just before nightfall. Few people enjoyed being out on the sea in the dark, as the mangrove stands posed a constant threat. That meant that the last guests would be leaving at around seven p.m., depending on the month of the year. Otherwise you were reliant on GPS and a flashlight to dodge the mangroves, which wasn't easy.

Although dozens of people would show up for big parties, there was a hard-core group of about seven or eight regular guests. These included Cher Hughes, a businesswoman from St. Louis, Missouri, who had come to Bocas del Toro via Florida to enjoy the good life in the sun. Cher and Keith Werle, her husband, had built their own home on the bluff of a small island off the southern shore of Darklands, a mile and a half from the Jolly Roger Social Club and visible from it. The couple had met in a bar in Florida that Werle was running. Among the expats it was known that, as a young man, Werle had ambitions to make it as an actor in Hollywood, and he worked as a carpenter on film sets for a while and did some modeling jobs. Later, Werle set up as a contractor in Florida, and the home was a custom build for a couple with an active social life and plenty of visitors. Werle was a confident, good-looking man and people remarked that he was clearly a few years younger than Hughes.

Three or four other couples were regulars at Wild Bill's bar, including Mike Smith and Fran Tilbury. The vibe at the Jolly Roger Social Club could get a bit druggy, too, depending on the precise mix of guests, and particularly if there were younger folk there. Cocaine was almost as easy to get hold of in Darklands as in Bocas Town. If a couple of people went off quietly to the bathroom together, everyone knew not to disturb them.

Guests got used to the sight of Wild Bill in the kitchen, cooking up fries, hot dogs, cheeseburgers, and nachos. It was "real greasy food," Fran Tilbury said. Jane served beer and spirits at the bar. She had a reputation for being a bit moody and had a tendency to stare into space when no one was asking her for drinks. "Sometimes," said Tilbury, "it was like she didn't want to be there." Mike Smith said he would be surprised if Bill and Jane made even $50 profit in a good weekend—it was usually less. And that's not factoring in the fixed costs: they had to light the place, keep the booze cold, and clean up afterward. His cooking done, Holbert enjoyed spinning his tales with his hand clasped around a glass of Panamanian white rum, which he liked to think of as his trademark, along with his horned Viking hat. He sometimes quizzed people about how they owned their homes, if they had dummy corporations with bearer shares. There was never any discussion of politics; only occasionally did people talk about religion. The Smiths said Bill boasted of owning a town in Mexico "just outside Cancún." He had inherited a fortune from his father. There was also talk of owning oil fields in Texas, gold kept in vaults in banks in the Cayman Islands. The stories were variations on what Holbert and Reese had told the expats in Volcán. Douglas Ruscher, who was only ever an occasional visitor to Holbert's bar, remembers that Wild Bill claimed to have a "ten-million-dollar trust fund" and that his father had been "an ambassador." Meanwhile, Jane claimed to be a veterinarian. "But she said that she only treated big animals like cows, not smaller ones like dogs," recalls Ruscher. Reese said the same thing to a German lady living near Malcolm Henderson's farm. "I love animals and I know about them," said the German expat, "and I can tell you that Jane was no vet."

Around this time, Holbert was thirty years old. At the time Mike Smith said he thought Wild Bill was "about forty." Most people thought he was in his late thirties at least. Holbert's size and his bearing led his guests at the bar to assume he was about ten years older than he really was, and he did nothing to correct that impression. And if any of the regular drinkers at the Jolly Roger Social Club wondered what a man who claimed to be so wealthy was doing running a dive that brought in a relative pittance each weekend, then they kept it to themselves. At the same time, some of Holbert's younger guests no doubt enjoyed the prestige of being close to a multimillionaire, the reflected aura of such a glamorous character. A couple of Darklands expats said these people were just short on money and were looking for a cheap night out. They would "kiss Bill's ass" to get one.

Several of Holbert's fellow expats in Bocas tell the same story: on dark nights, Holbert would enjoy riding the Browns' old motorboat with its powerful engine going flat out, skimming over the flat water with the lights off. Only the local *kayuko* dugout canoes, or maybe a late-night swimmer, would be out in the dark with no lights. It was a kind of Russian roulette in reverse, the figurative gun pointing away from the holder, the risk loaded on everyone else.

3. Welcome to Panama

I got obsessed by that damned thing. I quit my job and spent two years researching," said Ovidio Díaz Espino, the Panamanian author of *How Wall Street Created a Nation*. "I wanted to give Panama its own history, only to find it didn't want one."

It was 1997 and Díaz Espino was employed as a junior attorney at J. P. Morgan in New York City. At a chance meeting at a Christmas party, an American film producer told Díaz Espino that Panama had been created in part as the result of a deal hatched in New York's Waldorf-Astoria hotel. Intrigued by the conversation, Díaz Espino spent the next few days at the main reading room of the New York Public Library, checking the basic facts. Back home in Panama for the Christmas holidays, he told his family about his plans to delve into the history of his country's independence movement, to find out who did what, and why. Who, ultimately, was responsible for Panama's coming into being as a sovereign nation? But his family's reaction to the news was lukewarm at best.

The subject matter was not entirely new. Earl Harding, a reporter on the *World*, a now-defunct newspaper owned by Joseph Pulitzer, unearthed documents in Panama in the early years of the twentieth century that formed the backbone of his 1959 book, *The Untold Story of Panama*. Harding showed that a number of mainly American investors not only profited handsomely from Panamanian independence, but they needed Panama to wrest full control over its own affairs from Colombia to make their gains. For his part, Díaz Espino's focus on the money trail in Panama, and naming names in a country unaccustomed to this type of personal scrutiny, was a novelty. "The book created a debate about our history," said Díaz Espino. "There were so many holes, so many gaps, incomprehensible things. When Panama seceded from Colombia in 1903 there was almost no bloodshed. Why was that? There was so much that just didn't make sense." Back in New York City, Díaz Espino found out that a film production company in Hollywood had been looking into making a movie about the emergence of Panama as an independent country, and the subsequent building of the canal, but had dropped the idea. The problem with the Panama story was that "there were no good guys," said Díaz Espino. "For it to have worked, the good guys would have been the locals who got screwed by the Americans. Bottom line, they dropped the story."

Panama lies on the world's greatest crossroads, straddling North and South America, the Atlantic and Pacific Oceans. Like much of the rest of Spain's colonies in Latin America, Panama's independence movement found its feet in the first part of the nineteenth century. On November 28, 1821, a group of Panama's most powerful landowners and merchants—white, locally born men who were descendants of the colonizers—decided to annex their province to Greater Colombia, which was governed from Bogotá. Attempting to go it alone would make Panama an easy target for the Spanish, who would surely wreak revenge on its people, so fully fledged independence was not considered a viable option. However, the alliance with Bogotá caused problems, too: administrators and the business elite in Colombia wanted an increasingly large share of the revenue from the trade that flowed across the isthmus. As for the large black and mixed-race population of Panama City, Colombia's rule that only members of the landowning class would be allowed to vote—meaning,

Panamanians who owned property, and who were white—was a simmering injustice. A biracial man named José Domingo Espinar, a surgeon who had been Simón Bolívar's* personal secretary, started a separatist movement among Panama City's urban poor. For a few brief months in 1830 Espinar's group took control of the bustling port town. The following year, Panama's white elite called in Colombian soldiers to quash the uprising, fearful of a repeat of the slave rebellion in Haiti that had led to independence from France almost three decades earlier.

By the 1840s the narrow crossing point of the isthmus between the city of Colón on the Atlantic coast and Panama City on the Pacific coast was the favored transit point for Americans from the East Coast seeking their fortunes, or simply a better life, in California. The California gold rush boosted the economic argument for investment in a speedy, safe crossing of the isthmus that reduced the risk of contracting tropical diseases such as malaria and yellow fever, which were rife. As things stood, prospectors would sail to the Atlantic side of the isthmus, disembark, and trek with mules through dense jungle to the Pacific side, where they would wait for a ship bound for San Francisco. Work started on the Panama Railroad in 1850, linking Colón and Panama City. When it opened in 1855,† travelers willing to pay $25—some $700 at today's value—could shorten the trip from the northeast of the United States to San Francisco to a little over two weeks. (Even before the line was finished, a third of its investment had been recouped as the railroad management could charge a hefty fee for the ride on an incomplete track, since any way of shortening the journey time was a blessing.)

The forty-niners triggered a boom in Panama. Rental prices spiked as demand soared, causing a housing frenzy. It was Panama's first real estate bubble. There was a huge demand for housing, bars and restaurants, warehouses (and whorehouses). One historian noted that drinks at the Silver

---

* Simón Bolívar was born in Caracas in 1783. He led Venezuela, Colombia (including Panama at the time), Ecuador, Peru (together with José de San Martín), and Bolivia to independence from the Spanish Empire. Greater Colombia's successor states were Colombia, Venezuela, and Ecuador.

† It was only in 1869 that railroads finally linked the eastern United States and California. During the American Civil War (1861–65) the Panama route was used to move gold, munitions, and soldiers from coast to coast.

Dollar Saloon in the now-abandoned Atlantic coast port of Chagres cost seven times what you would pay in New York City.* As the gold rush became a stampede, prospectors had to wait their turn in Panama City for onward passage to California as ships' crews were often depleted when sailors decided to join the massed ranks of gold prospectors. Every extra day that the gold prospectors had to wait to leave meant more money in the tills of local businessmen.

But as the stories of fortunes made by gold-seekers began to dry up, so did the waves of prospectors passing through Panama. The railroad was still profitable for its US and British financial backers in spite of diminishing returns since it offered the only reliable crossing of the isthmus. But for many Panamanian entrepreneurs it was a different story. They had invested heavily in accommodation and related businesses to service the needs of a dwindling number of gold prospectors. These local entrepreneurs had rightly identified the forty-niners as a cash cow, but many were caught with their pants down when the cash cow simply wandered away. Some of the Chinese workers brought in to build the railroad stayed in Panama and set up their own stores, ramping up competition. Meanwhile, the Colombian government only returned to Panama a tenth of the taxes it charged the railroad, causing resentment among the Panamanian authorities who felt they deserved more cash in their coffers.

Panama's post–gold rush stagnation was only temporary. The railroad showed that, despite the threat of disease and torrential downpours, complicated works of engineering were possible in the tropics. As the United States grew in confidence, politically and economically, a Central American canal began to be touted as a necessity. In 1869, President Ulysses S. Grant evoked a canal in his first address to Congress, later establishing an Interoceanic Canal Commission. The commission was hesitant about the prospect of routing the canal through Panama: the experience of building a railroad was generally positive but construction had been blighted by landslides. Meanwhile, there was an easily identifiable route through Nicaragua that was closer to the United States; this featured upward of a hundred miles of navigable lakes and rivers, and offered the

---

* Matthew Parker in *Panama Fever: The Epic Story of the Building of the Panama Canal.*

lowest pass through the Continental Divide. On top of that, Nicaragua was offering the land for free. A majority of commission members came down on the side of the Nicaragua option when it filed its findings in 1876, and US policy would favor Nicaragua over Panama for the next quarter century.

But a French—rather than American—team was the first to attempt to dig a canal—and they chose to build it in Panama. Rather than route the canal through a system of man-made lakes and locks close to the site of the railroad—eventually, the American-built canal would follow this broad plan—the French decided to build a sea-level canal, devoid of locks. Work began on the mother of all big ditches in 1881. Three decades after the forty-niners had brought boom, and then bust, to Panama, the local merchant and business class bristled with confidence once again. The family names of the Panamanian elite were, in great part, the same names found today. These elite Panamanians were known as the *rabiblancos*, named for a delicate bird with a long white tail. Some of these families would come to shun Ovidio Díaz Espino for daring to expose what he considered to be the truth about their ancestors.

The French project was the dawn of a brand-new boom in Panama. Thousands of workers from France and other countries needed a roof over their heads and food in their stomachs. Around fifty thousand mainly English-speaking newcomers from the islands of the West Indies came to work on the canal. The French management, meanwhile, arrived in Panama with much fanfare; high society was having a ball. The chief engineer, a respected and experienced Frenchman named Jules Dingler, engaged the locals with his charming and attractive family and his collection of thoroughbred horses that he rode around the isthmus. Meanwhile, hundreds of millions of francs, many risked by small, individual subscribers in the French provinces as part of a vast public offering, had been invested in the most expensive construction project ever. But the venture ultimately collapsed in 1889; the French discovered how difficult it was to move mountains in Panama. As many as three-quarters of the French engineers hired for the project died from malaria or yellow fever, or in accidents. When the money ran out, the excavation equipment was left in the jungle where it stood. Wooden tools were soon on their way to being devoured by termites. Panama City became increasingly run-down, dirty, and dangerous. For chief engineer Dingler, there was unbearable personal tragedy: both his children died of yellow fever in Panama, then his wife succumbed to the same illness and perished. Inconsolable, he ordered his horses shot.

The French company's stock was virtually worthless when it became clear to investors that the French canal would never be built—there was simply not enough money left in the pot. What was left, and was valuable, were the rights to build the project granted by Colombia, owned by the Compagnie Nouvelle du Canal de Panama, a French company. But this presupposed the United States intervening in the construction and picking up where the French had left off.

Newly installed as president in 1901, Theodore Roosevelt applied his considerable energy to getting a canal built, believing it to be critical to American security. He also came to favor a route through Panama over the Nicaragua option. This was in spite of the fact that Colombia was engaged in a bitter civil war that was likely to complicate negotiations over a future canal in Panama, which was part of Colombia (in comparison, Nicaragua was relatively stable, politically speaking). But the Panama cause had two indefatigable supporters: William Nelson Cromwell, a high-rolling Wall Street lawyer, Washington lobbyist par excellence, and the legal representative of the old Panama Railroad; and Philippe Bunau-Varilla, a Frenchman with pronounced aristocratic airs who had become wealthy despite his modest beginnings in life. Bunau-Varilla had invested heavily in the ill-fated French scheme and was a relentless, ferocious promoter to rival Cromwell.

Teddy Roosevelt appeared to get his way when the Spooner Act of June 1902 mandated, after heated debate in Congress and a close vote, that any American-built canal be sited in Panama. Negotiations between Washington, D.C., and the Colombian government in Bogotá over the terms of the Panama deal were never going to be easy, with Colombia at war with itself. The two respective foreign ministers put pen to the Hay-Herrán Treaty in January 1903, which would give the United States a hundred-year lease to construct a canal and operate it. However, the document was not ratified by the Colombian legislature. By the middle of the same year, President Roosevelt's frustrations with the turn of events in Bogotá were tempered by a new development. A Panamanian separatist movement, or at least the beginnings of one, was making advances to the American government in the person of Manuel Amador, the former chief physician of the Panama Railroad. Amador, a man who had worked under Cromwell, the silver-haired lawyer and political fixer known as "the Fox," was pushing for the Americans to finish the job that the French had started. In September 1903, Amador paid a visit to Bunau-Varilla, identified as the go-to man, in his suite at the Waldorf-Astoria in New York. Amador calculated that the Colombian troops stationed in Panama could be paid off with relative ease since their salaries were already in arrears. Money would also be needed to bolster the country against Colombian reprisals. Bunau-Varilla was in on the plan. He promised Amador to make efforts to get money for the Panamanian rebels.

Díaz Espino, the Panamanian writer, and Harding, the American reporter, have made a convincing case that a consortium of Wall Street financiers, in a deal brokered by Cromwell, bought up the stock of the Compagnie Nouvelle, the French canal company, for cents on the dollar, gambling that one day they would be able to sell them at a huge profit. The syndicate subscribed $5 million, more than enough funds to buy all of the French stock. If the punt was a success, the deal would reap many times more, since before the Hay-Herrán negotiations opened, the management of the French canal company had touted its assets to the US government for $40 million. The plan worked to perfection. On November 2, 1903, US warships blocked sea-lanes to prevent Colombian troops from reaching a rebellion that broke out on the isthmus. Panama declared independence the next day after paying off the Colombian soldiers according to rank, using funds that originated in the United States (from $50 in gold for the lowest ranks to a whopping $80,000, it is said, for General Esteban Huertas, who was in charge of Colombian forces in Panama). The United States was the first country to recognize the new nation. Three days later, the two countries signed a treaty granting rights to the United States to build a canal and indefinitely administer a canal zone.

At the signing ceremony, not a single Panamanian was present or even invited. Philippe Bunau-Varilla had schemed to get a mandate from the Panamanian separatists to negotiate on Panama's behalf. The result was that a ten-mile-wide strip around the route of the canal, excluding Panama City and Colón at either end of it, would be given to the United States in perpetuity (the draft agreement that had spooked Colombian lawmakers two years earlier had only laid down a hundred-year lease). The American government finally agreed to pay $40 million for the assets of the Compagnie Nouvelle and $10 million directly to the Panamanian government. Soon afterward, the records of ownership of the Compagnie Nouvelle were, effectively, lost. What happened was this: the shares of the Compagnie Nouvelle were originally recorded in a register alongside the names of their owners. But, subsequently, the stock was converted into bearer share certificates, meaning that whoever had the certificates in their possession owned them and could do with them as they wished. These owners of bearer share certificates thus became perfectly anonymous, and there was no formal record of anyone who received the proceeds of the $40 million sale. But this did not mean there was no paper or money trail elsewhere. Rumors about who was behind the massive purchase of Compagnie Nouvelle stock persisted. On March 22, 1906, the *New York Times*—a resolutely Democratic newspaper and no friend of Teddy Roosevelt—opined that the history of the Panama Canal was "one long track and trail of scandal."

Meanwhile, the law firm of William Nelson Cromwell invoiced the Compagnie Nouvelle for the eye-watering sum of $800,000 in legal fees—some $22 million today—in a long document that appeared to boast of involvement in helping the Panamanian separatists. On a trip to Panama, Earl Harding, the reporter for the *World*, dug around in the best traditions of investigative journalism and found his way into the personal records of Manuel Amador, the onetime Panama Railroad physician who became his country's first president. It turned out that the Panamanian separatists hugely inflated the cost of running the new army in the months after independence (weapons and munitions had simply been taken from the Colombians after the soldiers and their officers were paid off). American officials of the Panama Railroad company were not spared the revolution's largesse, either. But it was the leaders of the independence movement who benefited the most, with President Amador apparently the recipient of a check for $100,000. For his part, Díaz Espino, the lawyer-turned-historian, showed how Amador's government attempted to cover up the money trail by a law passed in Panama in 1904 with the express intention of concealing the bookkeeping of Panama's first months as an independent state. And when, four years later, a Panamanian minister of finance tried to re-create the bookkeeping of that early period, President Amador stopped him, according to Díaz Espino. The president told his well-meaning minister of finance that the first million dollars was, quite simply, unaccounted for.

In 1909, some of the fog lifted surrounding the investors who bought up the stock of the Compagnie Nouvelle on the cheap when a copy surfaced of what purported to be a memorandum of an agreement among the members of the mysterious syndicate. The document set out the price per share that would trigger a purchase and the minimum price needed to produce a sale. Among the members of the syndicate were J. P. Morgan, merchant bankers Isaac Seligman and J. Edward Simmons, lawyers Henry W. Taft and Chauncey M. Depew (a serving US senator), and—with a subscription of $1,333,333—William Nelson Cromwell.

None of the whiff of scandal got in the way of Roosevelt's exhortation to "let the dirt fly!" By the time the United States had finished building the canal and it opened for business in August 1914, the most conservative estimate of the death toll was twenty-five thousand—five hundred lives for every mile of construction. A goods train full of excavated material would have stretched four times around the globe. The new canal cut eight thousand nautical miles off the trip from the east coast of the United States to its mainland ports on the Pacific, consigning the perilous rounding of Cape Horn to the history books. On independence, Panama's currency became the US dollar and, with plentiful jobs available in the American Canal Zone, many Panamanians learned English. Over the years the Canal Zone sprouted schools, clapboard homes, churches, barracks, parking lots filled with shiny sedans, baseball diamonds, subsidized movie theaters, landing strips buzzing with aircraft, and stores (in fact, commissaries) selling exactly what you would find back home. Happy families lived out their lives in a cocoon of bold, tropical primary colors; the unhappy families disintegrated, slowly, as they do everywhere. The Stars and Stripes fluttered in the breeze as the world's ships moved from one ocean to the other.

By the mid-1960s, some thirty-six thousand US citizens lived in the 553-square-mile enclave. Those who were there for the long haul, rather than military personnel on temporary postings, were known as the "Zonians." Some spent half their adult lives in the Canal Zone without the need to learn any Spanish. Panamanians working in the Zone had to be out by nightfall if they were not employed as servants. Understandably, this provoked profound resentment against the United States among locals who were also often in awe of the gleaming modern world on display on the other side of the fence, literally close enough to touch. American music and fashions were a magnet to many young Panamanians in the 1950s and 1960s, as they were, of course, to young people in many other countries. But sheer proximity matters. The Panamanians were left merely gazing at it all, with no ticket for the ride. Many times, their attitude hardened into pure ambivalence. Think of it as a tough guy's pair of clenched, tattooed fists, one spelling out LOVE, the other HATE.

In 1964, *Time* magazine ran a story claiming in its title that the enclave was "More American Than America," a curious conclusion given the Canal Zone's lack of private enterprise. All Americans in the Zone were on the government's payroll through the US armed forces or the Panama Canal Company. American influence in Panama oozed out into the Panamanian backcountry, thanks to the presence of so many Americans in the Canal Zone and also—for a time—other US facilities away from the canal, such as Río Hato Army Air Base, which was used by the air force until 1948. American military personnel, families, and infrastructure provided employment to locals who adapted to the newcomers' language, learned how to cook the food they wanted to eat, and opened American-style drugstores. As the years went by, the strength of American influence tended to reinforce the idea that Panama was a quasi protectorate of the United States. This effect lingers, even in places as geographically remote as the islands and bays of Bocas del Toro.

R. M. Koster is an American writer who arrived in the country by means of a posting to the Zone in the late 1950s. Koster cowrote *In the*

Time of the Tyrants, the definitive account in English of the dictatorship that ruled over Panama from the late 1960s to the final days of 1989. His thick New York accent, however, belies almost a half century lived on the isthmus. "American retirees come down here and they think they are still in the States," said Koster. "That's a mistake."

Two of the canal's key protagonists had mixed fortunes after ships started to sail through the big ditch. Back in France, his country's failed canal venture over, Philippe Bunau-Varilla lived a life of elegance and refinement, in spite of losing a leg at the Verdun battlefield in World War I. He passed away at the age of eighty. Meanwhile, William Nelson Cromwell, the fixer who gambled big on the Panama Canal and won, died in 1948 with no heirs. He left $19 million in the bank.

In 1968, John and Susan Freivalds, a couple of young, recently married Peace Corps volunteers from Minnesota, arrived in Panama for what was supposed to be a two-year posting. Seven years earlier, the Peace Corps Act had been passed by Congress with the stated purpose of promoting "world peace and friendship." The men and women, for the most part college graduates in their twenties, were sent abroad to developing countries "in conditions of hardship if necessary." The highest number of Peace Corps volunteers serving overseas was reached in 1966 and, although the program still runs successfully today, in the public mind it is probably most associated with the mid-1960s to mid-1970s, when some volunteers hoped that by signing up they would avoid being drafted for service in the Vietnam War.

John Freivalds was tasked with setting up a farm cooperative in the settlement of Río Sereno in Chiriquí Province, close to Panama's border with Costa Rica. He and his wife, who subsequently divorced, were excited at the prospect of traveling to Panama; Río Sereno was at the time a remote place, but they at least both spoke Spanish. "The Peace Corps was a big deal to us," said Freivalds, who was then twenty-four. Rather than being motivated by idealism, "I was a practical sort of guy and I wanted to see how the world worked from the ground up. We wanted to go there and see what we could do to help out." Freivalds said that, later, employers would view the Peace Corps reference on his résumé favorably. "I think it showed them I was a survivor."

The farm co-op plan made perfect sense in theory since it was prudent for small producers to pool their resources to get produce to market quickly. Milk, for instance, would spoil in a short time in the heat if it was not rushed to buyers, and the dirt road leading out of Río Sereno became a river of mud in the rainy season. But the main players in Río Sereno were big cattle ranchers who had no interest in a farm co-op. Freivalds had his co-op teaching materials and all kinds of charts and data—even an electricity generator—but it was difficult to get the thing started, and initially "just a dog and an empty bag of potato chips" would be in the room when he opened his meetings. On top of that, the locals found it difficult to understand why the Freivaldses were there at all. Río Sereno was basically the middle of nowhere. "Why would people they perceived as being wealthy Americans come to such a place? Right after we got there, a young kid saw an airplane in the sky and said, 'Is it coming to get you?'"

Despite some cases of vote rigging, by the late 1960s Panama had evolved into a broadly democratic country—never a perfect democracy, but a democracy nonetheless. Following pressure from the United States, the army structure that Panama had essentially inherited from Colombia in 1903 was disbanded the following year. General Esteban Huertas, who had been in charge of Colombian forces in Panama—and had accepted an $80,000 bribe to change sides—started to get too big for his boots. A fresh financial incentive did the trick and Huertas sailed off to Europe with some like-minded friends, ostensibly to study the militaries of the countries of the Continent. With a view to making a clean start, the army was replaced by a police force called the National Guard. It provided employment to young men with few other options available if they came from lower-income families with no strings to pull. Nonetheless, the National Guard took on some of the airs of an army, slowly, as Panamanian students were offered places at military academies in other Latin American countries. One such military academy graduate was a short, ungainly young man who, while undergoing training, said little and hardly drew attention to himself: Manuel Antonio Noriega, the illegitimate son of an accountant whose mother died when he was still an infant.

In the early 1960s, Noriega attended the Chorrillos Military Academy in Lima, Peru. It was in Lima that Noriega was charged with raping and beating a prostitute so savagely that she almost died. But the US Defense Intelligence Agency helped to get the charges dropped, sensing that Noriega might be useful to them in the future. Noriega got lucky: the American spooks might not have taken the low moral ground had it not been for the fear that the recent Cuban revolution might spread communism to other countries in America's backyard. Now Noriega owed the United States a favor in return.

With the Cold War in full swing, Panama's National Guard became eligible for US aid. The mid-century National Guard was a proto-military force despite the fact that Panama was in the enviable position of having no enemies or territorial threats. But in the late 1960s the National Guard was the object of a threat, that is to say, the threat to the status and well-being of its senior officers. When Arnulfo Arias, a populist politician supported by swaths of poor voters in rural areas, was sworn in as president on October 1, 1968, he soon made it clear that he intended to make purges; he had a long-standing grudge against the National Guard because of, among other things, their repeated harassment of and attacks on his supporters. Arias was not a man who could be easily manipulated, and there was an unpredictable streak to his personality. By mid-October a group of senior National Guard officers led by Major Boris Martínez—and supported by Omar Torrijos, who outranked Martínez, but who controlled fewer men—pounced and took power. It was supposed to be a temporary measure, but military strongmen of increasing brutality were to rule Panama for the next twenty-one years. The *rabiblanco* elite still prospered, but it was now the soldiers—in the main mestizos (mixed Caucasian and Native American, such as Torrijos), blacks, and *zumbos* (mixed black and Native American, like Manuel Antonio Noriega)—who called the shots.

For Manuel Noriega, the coup was particularly good news. The young officer was tasked with stamping out an insurgency in Panama's western highlands, specifically in Chiriquí Province, where a small but determined band of armed Arias insurgents used the mountainous terrain and proximity to the porous border with Costa Rica to maximum advantage. Under Noriega, guerrillas who were caught were routinely tortured and killed, as were some peasants suspected of supporting the insurgents (the guerrillas sometimes responded by dealing National Guard members they captured the same fate). It was a job that suited Noriega perfectly. The military takeover also meant that another serious charge against Noriega was quietly dropped, even though the case had been prepared by the district attorney and was ready to go to court. It was alleged that Noriega had raped a teenage beauty queen in a field after a village festival and had given her younger brother a severe beating. The allegation of rape and beating were two of many crimes that Noriega would never have to respond to, let alone be prosecuted for.

At their Peace Corps posting in the sprawling village of Río Sereno, in Chiriquí Province, at the end of 1968, and with insurgents lurking in the surrounding countryside, John and Susan Freivalds were thus in the wrong place at very much the wrong time. A patrol from the National Guard commanded by Manuel Antonio Noriega came calling, suspecting that the two young Americans might be helping the guerrillas. John and Susan were carted off on a long trek to the city of David, the capital of Chiriquí Province, sixty miles away over atrocious, almost impassable roads. Freivalds said that Noriega was "a run-of-the-mill thug. He hadn't yet blossomed into what he became, although he did walk around with four hand grenades strapped to his chest." Noriega told Susan to ride a horse part of the way and made her put on a military cap and carry a rifle. "Noriega was always matter-of-fact," said John Freivalds. "He would ask, 'What have you been doing? There has to be an investigation.' As far as he was concerned, we had to be there for a nefarious purpose, what with having left a comfortable life [in the United States] to come here." After a couple of nights locked up in a jail in the backcountry, the Freivaldses arrived at David with the patrol. John was locked up again with some male political prisoners; Susan was in the cells with a bunch of prostitutes. Noriega passed by. Freivalds asked him, "Are we under arrest?" Noriega replied, "No, if you were under arrest it would be much worse."

"If anything happens to me," Freivalds had warned a Panamanian friend in Río Sereno, as the military launched their coup, "go to the co-op and call the US embassy from there." Risking his life, the friend did as he was asked. Thanks to his efforts, the alarm was raised and an American consular official secured the Freivaldses' release from jail. The next day, the couple were driven to Panama City. A security officer from the embassy debriefed them. "We told him about how Noriega put Susan on a horse looking like a soldier. We were saying, 'I wonder why they did that?'" The security officer explained that if there was an ambush, it would have been Susan who would have gotten the first bullet.

Before they were deported from Panama, cutting short their expected stay by about a year, John Freivalds caught a glimpse of the front page of a local newspaper. "The headline said, 'Peace Corps Conspired Against the Junta,'" recalls Freivalds. "It was surreal, but we were young then, and a bit naive, too." Far from the clutches of the National Guard, John Freivalds subsequently followed events in Panama on and off from wherever in the world he happened to be.

Manuel Antonio Noriega had already started his climb to the top of the greasy pole of the military machine that ran Panama. In February 1969, Boris Martínez, who had advocated a land reform program and had started to cut down on the graft practiced by the National Guard—in some ways, if not others, he was a principled man—was deposed by Omar Torrijos. (Shortly after he was ousted, a couple of Torrijos's associates offered Martínez ambassadorship of any embassy he wanted. It was a lucrative opportunity. This offer was curtly rejected by Martínez, who settled in the United States.) Noriega guessed right and sided with Torrijos when the countercoup came. Noriega was rewarded by Torrijos with the post of head of military intelligence and his new boss promoted him to the rank of lieutenant colonel.

Torrijos was an inveterate womanizer and was frequently drunk, and also he had a ruthless side to his character. Some opponents to military rule were murdered on Omar Torrijos's orders in the months after he took over as Panama's strongman. But Torrijos had a certain folksy charm, and this, coupled with an increasingly hostile attitude on the part of many Panamanians to US presence in perpetuity in the Canal Zone, propelled a number of intellectuals to Torrijos's door. These included the English writer Graham Greene, and the Colombian journalist-turned-novelist (and, later, Nobel Prize winner) Gabriel García Márquez. The intellectuals barely bothered befriending the puppet presidents whom Torrijos installed to give the country a false veneer of democracy. As de facto ruler of Panama, General Torrijos did his dirty work at arm's length, which is why he came to rely on "my gangster," as he called Noriega. By the late 1980s, references to Noriega in the American press were becoming increasingly common. "I was surprised when his name kept popping up," said Freivalds. Noriega also makes a brief, silent appearance toward the end of the book *Getting to Know the General*, Graham Greene's near love letter to Torrijos, who flew the English writer first-class on trips to Panama.

In late 1979, Torrijos entertained a controversial guest: the shah of Iran, Mohammad Reza Pahlavi, accompanied by his wife, Farah Diba, and an entourage that included his personal physician, his head of security, and several hundred pieces of luggage. The shah, long supported by the United States, had been ousted by Ayatollah Khomeini's Islamic revolution of January–February 1979. The couple fled to Mexico by way of Egypt, Morocco, and the Bahamas. In October of that year the shah traveled from Mexico to New York for medical treatment of lymphatic cancer. What happened next was President Jimmy Carter's worst nightmare. On November 4, 1979, a group of Iranian students supporting Khomeini's Islamic revolution took over the US embassy in Tehran. Following the release of thirteen women and African Americans, fifty-three American diplomats, soldiers, and citizens were held hostage with the pledge that they would be released in exchange for the shah. The former Iranian leader and his queen became the most uncomfortable of hot potatoes. Mexico refused to take the shah back, and any country taking in Mohammad Reza Pahlavi—hated by swaths of Iran's population for his autocratic rule, corruption, greed, and the activities of a cruel secret police under his command—would likely gain the ire of the unpredictable Ayatollah Khomeini, Iran's new ruler. Omar Torrijos was in Las Vegas, Nevada, to see a boxing match, when he heard of Mexico's decision to suspend its offer of refuge for the shah. That was the moment an idea occurred to the general that would place his small country center stage in the eyes of the world. In Las Vegas, Torrijos was preparing to gamble for high stakes.

In December 1979 President Carter sent Hamilton Jordan, his chief of staff, to Panama to see if Omar Torrijos would make good on his offer to take the shah off Washington's hands. From the US perspective, getting the shah out of America would be a wise move, with so many American hostages very much in harm's way. Jordan was also tasked with convincing the shah that by leaving the United States, President Carter's chances of freeing the hostages would improve. The shah's negotiating position could hardly have been weaker—if America now wanted him out, there was little he could do about it. (With no apparent irony, it pained him that Torrijos, his proposed host, was a dictator.) The decision to allow the shah to travel to the United States in the first place had been the subject of months of discussion in Washington. Torrijos, meanwhile, a glass of whiskey in one hand, a cigar in the other, agreed to Jordan's request in a matter of seconds; President Carter called to thank Torrijos personally in Spanish. The presence of a man whose fate was closely linked with that of the hostages in Tehran, and the resulting media attention, was surely a boost to the general's ego. Since the signing of the Panama Canal Treaties* with President Carter in September 1977—under which the canal would become Panamanian property on December 31, 1999—Torrijos had rather slipped off the radar of the world's media. Most of all, the shah was an extremely wealthy man: when the deal was done, Torrijos's guest deposited $12 million in a numbered Swiss bank account controlled by the general (according to Colonel Roberto Díaz Herrera, a high-ranking member of the National Guard).

Most of today's first-time overseas visitors to Panama arriving by air touch down at Tocumen International Airport to the east of the city. If they are on a modest budget, chances are they will have booked a room

---

*The first of two treaties, often referred to as the Neutrality Treaty, gave the United States the permanent right to defend the canal from any threat that might interfere with its service to ships of all nations. The second treaty, formally the Panama Canal Treaty, set the date on which Panama would assume full control and ownership of the canal.

in one of the towering hotels of the central Cangrejo section of town. By day, it is a banking and business district with, at street level, deeply fissured concrete sidewalks. At night, gloomy men wearing baseball caps wait their turn in twenty-four-hour pawnshops. The neon of casinos burns the air. Prostitutes in high heels totter at the side of the road, oblivious to the screeching traffic. It all makes for an inauspicious start to a vacation or business trip. But as a deposed monarch who might well be targeted for reprisals by the new Iranian regime, the shah's itinerary in Panama hardly fit the mold. On December 15, 1979, Mohammad Reza Pahlavi and Farah Diba flew into Howard Air Force Base in the Canal Zone and from there were transported by helicopter to the island of Contadora, a weekend getaway island in the Pacific Ocean twenty minutes' flying time from the capital. Contadora is known for its pretty beaches, its orchids, and the sharks lurking offshore. The shah and his wife were accommodated in the beachside home of a wealthy Panamanian businessman who had served as Panama's ambassador to the United States. Of course, for the practical organization of the shah's stay in Panama, Torrijos had one name in mind: Manuel Noriega, chief of military intelligence.

There was popular opposition to the shah's arrival, with protest marches and demonstrations in the capital. The leader of one protest march, a university professor, was badly beaten by the National Guard and was fortunate not to suffer permanent brain damage. It irked many people that Torrijos's puppet government, in a rare gesture of independence from its military masters, had declared that Panama would not provide a safe haven for the shah—before Torrijos decided that he had a substantial amount to gain personally from taking in the accidental VIP expat.

Contadora covers less than a square mile and you can walk around it in an hour. The island must have felt claustrophobic to the shah and underscored the reality of the situation: he was well and truly trapped. In his memoir, *America's Prisoner*, Noriega wrote that the security arrangements "followed the principle of conducting operations in a way that would never alarm the subject we were protecting."* The Iranian security

---

* *America's Prisoner: The Memoirs of Manuel Noriega*, by Manuel Noriega and Peter Eisner, was published in 1997.

personnel traveling with the shah were, in Noriega's telling, "confused and intrigued by our subtle, almost invisible method of operation." Soon, the Iranian security people started to see things Noriega's way; "they recognized that our measures were intricate and worked . . . and started calling us magicians among security operatives." The shah would spend long periods staring out to sea past a hut that Noriega had built for his guards, frogmen, and listening devices. Noriega's team lounged around in the sun in their time off, drinking beer with their clothes hung out in the breeze to dry. Several antiaircraft weapons were hauled into place. Hardly a day went by without someone or other with connections to the National Guard arriving to pitch an investment scheme to the shah, who was wily enough to deflect them all. He was even offered the chance of buying Contadora itself, which had a $10 million price tag. But the shah could do little about the stream of payment requests emanating from Noriega and his staff: $21,000 a month to feed the frogmen and the security detail; $68,000 to pay for a security system that kept track of the shah's own phone calls from the house; and so on. Mohammad Reza Pahlavi was even asked to pay to have a school built in a poor neighborhood. It was hardly a voluntary donation and looked every inch a Noriega shakedown. Noriega pointedly remarked that he never saw the shah touch any money with his own hands.

The shah's stay on Contadora brought great disruption to the tourist traffic that was, and still is, the mainstay of the island's economy. Hoteliers were none too amused, but what could they do? Not for the last time, Noriega's extended presence in a Panamanian vacation spot would turn out to be a Midas touch in reverse for local businesses. But some holiday-makers did make it to Contadora. Walking along the beach one day, the shah struck up a conversation with a North American lady seemingly taking a vacation on the island. There was some lustful interest from the shah that was, apparently, returned by the North American woman. On the pretext of viewing some real estate, the shah was whisked off the island for a night for a rendezvous with the woman in the presidential suite of the Panama Hilton in the capital. The shah's romantic fixer was, of course, Noriega, who revealed that during Mohammad Reza Pahlavi's stay on Contadora, plainclothes operatives were used who did not seem to be intelligence operatives but who "instead [were] tourists, gardeners or common workmen who blended into their surroundings." So, was the shah's one-night love interest really a plainclothes operative? And if she was, did Noriega mean to make sure he had incriminating images taken at the Panama Hilton in his possession with which he might one day blackmail the shah?

Farah Diba liked to play tennis and go waterskiing. She had caught Torrijos's eye and the general passed on messages to her saying that he could provide her with anything she wanted. When the shah's wife ignored his clumsy advances, Torrijos instructed Noriega to film her when she was out enjoying the water. The Panamanian security detail was happy to get as close as possible to the waterskiing queen. The security men "enjoyed the view," wrote Noriega. "She was a very attractive woman." The films of Farah Diba at play in her swimsuit were sent off to Torrijos along with Noriega's regular reports of the progress of the stay of the former royal couple. As ever, Noriega filed his reports to his boss on audiotape rather than on paper, in line with his boss's long-standing request, as reading bored him.

No one was surprised that the shah's grave medical condition precipitated his departure from Contadora, and from Panama for that matter. The shah needed an urgent operation on his spleen. The obvious option was to have the surgery in Panama, but the shah and Farah Diba apparently did not trust the Panamanians, fearing that a sufficiently large bribe from the Iranian revolutionaries might result in the shah being put to death on the operating table. But for reasons of national pride, the Panamanians were loath to allow the operation to take place in Gorgas Hospital, a US Army facility in the Canal Zone. When his state of health became so serious that the shah was admitted to a hospital in Panama City, his American doctors called off the intervention. Finally, in March 1980, the shah was offered permanent asylum in Egypt. He flew to Cairo and received medical attention there; within four months, however, he died from complications that arose after surgery. In Iran, the following year, the hostage crisis reached its endgame. Two rescue missions ordered by President Carter were aborted, damaging his presidency and weakening his campaign for reelection. Finally, on January 20, 1981,

minutes after Ronald Reagan was sworn in as president, the fifty-two*
remaining American hostages were released by Iran into US custody after
444 days in captivity.

Noriega wrote that, when they said good-bye at the airport, the shah—
his life's journey almost over—had "the saddest eyes I had ever seen."
And when the time came for Farah Diba to leave Contadora, Torrijos
demanded that her used bedsheets be packed up and sent to him.

There was, of course, a time before Panama became a murky international
banking hub straight out of Central Casting, and R. M. Koster remembers it: "When I arrived in 1957, there was the National City Bank and
Chase Manhattan Bank in the Canal Zone. These were needed to service
the business of the Canal, after all. These two then set up in Panama City
and a trickle of other banks followed." But by the late 1960s, American
banks needed a new offshore banking center and Panama had a couple
of key advantages: the dollar was the national currency and there was no
central bank to impose restrictions; on top of this, shell or "dummy" corporations issuing bearer share certificates were permitted (Panama's leg-
islation in this regard was based on that of the state of Delaware). It also
didn't hurt Panama's case that the country was in the same time zone
as New York.

So in 1970 Torrijos introduced a banking law that was a deliberate
attempt to capture hot money in the Americas that needed a home. The
Panamanian strongman, so affable in his dealings with overseas states-
men, offered a measure of stability in his own person; the new law then
ushered in tax-free interest, unrestricted money flows, numbered accounts,
and no restrictions on denominations of accounts. In April and May 1969,
at President Nixon's request, Nelson Rockefeller, then governor of the
state of New York, headed a fact-finding team that visited twenty countries in the American republics to discuss aspects of US policy in the
region and to determine the conditions of each country. The itinerary
included Rockefeller's first meeting with General Torrijos. In September

---

* One of the hostages became seriously ill and was released in July 1980.

of the same year Omar Torrijos made an unofficial trip to New York and
met Governor Rockefeller in his city office. Investment bankers Goldman
Sachs hosted an elegant dinner in Torrijos's honor; the trip concluded
with a formal meeting with Secretary of State William Rogers. Torrijos
signed off on his new banking law in a decree in July 1970. Panama was
now a tropical Switzerland.

The ultra-discreet system neatly coincided with the interests of Chase
Manhattan Bank, in which the Rockefeller family members were the
largest shareholders. Around 90 international banks operated in Panama
at the time the shah came to stay, and by the mid-1980s the number had
risen to over 130, including branches of many big main-street banks from
North America and Western Europe. There was also a large outpost of
the Bank of Credit and Commerce International, an institution set up in
Pakistan that was later found to have been involved in money laundering
worldwide to a vast and unprecedented degree. Meanwhile, banking
secrecy was assured because heavy fines and even jail sentences were on
the statute book for bank officials who failed to maintain full discretion.
Banks aggressively chased business in Colombia, the center of the narcotics trade in the Americas. Vast sums of money flowed into Panama; by
the 1980s, Colombia would be the biggest single source of funds by some
distance. In Panama, the phrase "Nobody can resist a gunshot of a million dollars" is widely attributed to Omar Torrijos. It was true in his time
in power and it didn't stop being true after his demise.

As the years went by, Panama had more and more access to credit
from international lenders. Torrijos took full advantage and borrowed
hugely overseas to expand the public sector. Many new jobs created were
in the gift of National Guard top brass and were handed out to the usual
suspects: mistresses, brothers-in-law, sons, daughters. Communities used
to the general's largesse did very well out of it; Torrijos would travel with
cases full of cash and hand out money where he perceived a need or where
he was moved emotionally. R. M. Koster was surely not the only person
in Panama to have a recurring dream about finding a box of cash that
had fallen off the back of a National Guard truck.

Coclesito, a Native American community deep in the jungle that
occupies the central spine of Panama, was one such place that Omar

Torrijos visited repeatedly, always by plane, as it was difficult to reach overland. He developed a sentimental attraction to this village of modest houses crammed in a clearing in the forest. Torrijos even had a house built there—a neat, compact wooden chalet that now serves as a museum. One such flying visit to Coclesito proved to be his last: on July 31, 1981, Torrijos boarded a de Havilland Twin Otter aircraft with his latest mistress, a young woman who was studying with one of his illegitimate daughters. The weather was atrocious, and the pilot knew it, but Torrijos insisted on making the trip. According to some witnesses, the Twin Otter appeared to explode in midair. The wreckage was found strewn across a large portion of mountainside. Colonel Roberto Díaz Herrera, Omar Torrijos's first cousin, who turned against Manuel Noriega in the 1980s, later claimed that the crash was no accident. He maintains that a bomb was placed on Torrijos's plane and that Noriega was behind the incident. With Torrijos out of the way, Noriega may have calculated that he would be able to seize power. The cause of the crash was never properly identified or explained.

With the passing of Omar Torrijos, into Panama's vacuum of power strode four high-ranking military men. Leading the military in Panama meant ruling by decree and was a sure route to great wealth. Noriega, Díaz Herrera, and two other officers came to what might charitably be termed a gentlemen's agreement on a line of succession. Noriega had to bide his time, but he had access to everyone's secrets and was ready to play a long game. In August 1983 the quiet, pockmarked boy from the wrong side of the tracks became de facto ruler of Panama, two years before he was due to take over. The days when his youthful tormentors called him "Pineapple Face" because of his deep acne scars were long gone. His National Guard colleagues who had subscribed to the agreement setting out an orderly line of succession were, quite simply, outmaneuvered. They had been fools to trust Manuel Antonio Noriega.

4. The Story of Bo Icelar

In spite of the poor profits at their cash bar, and Wild Bill's limited skills at the stove, Holbert and Reese's Jolly Roger Social Club remained in business for all of 2008, with Bill's skull and crossbones flag fluttering in the wind above it. That the bar was in operation at all was principally thanks to ads placed in the *Bocas Breeze* that brought in the curious; the continued patronage of middle-aged drinkers with homes near Darklands like Mike Smith and Fran Tilbury, and Cher Hughes and Keith Werle; and a bush telegraph brought up to date for the twenty-first century: the regular text messages that Holbert sent to a motley group of acquaintances in the archipelago reminding them that his bar was open and he was presiding over it. *You are summoned to the Temple of Inebriation*, he wrote. *The knight has called his people to the table. You my fellow lords will honor me.* And: *For you Facebook Nazis, leave your fuckin' cameras at home.* "It only made sense later," said one expat who received Holbert's group messages, "but he was afraid people would post photos on Facebook and someone would recognize him back in the States." Holbert and Reese never had family to visit—Wild Bill's story was that he was an orphan, so this was naturally a limiting factor—but neither did any friends come visit them from the States or anywhere else. Nobody seems to have found this unusual.

Holbert's text messages were sent to a group that included expats in their late twenties and early thirties—his own age group. One Canadian who left Bocas del Toro for Volcán during this period couldn't figure out why the younger people living full-time in Bocas were there, and how they supported themselves financially, particularly those who owned powerboats and lived in quite comfortable homes: "Everyone had a fake story, and we would go home afterwards and wonder, Really? Bocas filled up with schemers, dreamers, and fly-by-nights. If you were gregarious and bought drinks for everyone, you'd fit right in."

The more the owners and patrons at the Jolly Roger Social Club got to know one another, the more esoteric the conversation became, particularly when an older group of drinkers was present. His cooking done, Wild Bill would wonder out loud about the mysteries of pre-Colombian temples in Mexico, monuments like Chichen Itza in the Yucatán. And then there was Teotihuacan, just outside Mexico City, a huge pyramid that left you out of breath by the time you had climbed the steps to its flat top. Holbert introduced himself as William Adolfo Cortez and told everyone his deceased father was Mexican. This gave him a prerogative to speculate. "How could those little guys build such massive things?" asked Holbert. "They were only four feet tall!" Holbert dreamed of visiting Easter Island, that speck of land in the vastness of the Pacific Ocean famous for its monumental statues, called *moai*, created by the early Rapa Nui people. "He was passionate about all that stuff. It was his belief that aliens or beings from outer space had built those temples and statues, not the Aztecs or anyone else," said Fran Tilbury.

On one occasion, Mike Smith and Fran Tilbury had to attend to some legal paperwork. Tilbury had gone alone to a notary's office and for some reason the notary couldn't accept the signature that Smith had provided. That meant that Smith had to travel on short notice to see the notary. Wild Bill offered to help house-sit for Smith in David. "So I had Bill and Jane come take care of the girls," said Smith, referring to the couple's two dogs. "And look after my home, too. I gave him access to my computer. I mean, he had access to everything." How was Holbert able to win the couple's trust? Mike Smith said: "We were basically—well, I thought—we were friends. Once we met him, we used to have dinners together," said Smith. "They'd come over and we'd cook dinners, or we would go to their place [the Browns' former house]." It's fair to say that Mike Smith and William Holbert are both men's men, and there was a bond there, but there were disagreements, too: "When he used to get into his weird Satan shit, I'd say, Bill, see you later." Sometimes, Holbert put on his Viking horns for what have been described as Satanic parties at his bar. Fran Tilbury said: "That was usually when he was 'round a bunch of young people, when he had an audience." Another expat said that Jane, most of the time, "had nothing to say." She just stood behind the bar staring at the horizon and the view of the stiff clumps of mangroves in the bay.

In 2008, Smith and Tilbury sometimes spent weeks at a time apart. Fran Tilbury was at their Bocas home on the island of Loma Partida (the couple had a nearby rental property, too, and this needed looking after). Mike Smith, meanwhile, was in the city of David, finishing off the construction of their main home. One day Holbert asked Tilbury if she knew what to do if someone was bothering her. The implication was: if someone was bothering her when Mike Smith wasn't around to sort things out. Holbert said that the best way of dealing with that person was to shoot him or her, take the body out to sea, and dump it overboard. Tilbury let Holbert know that his method could be improved. "So I told him, first you cut their stomach open. That way they don't float." Mike Smith said later, helping his wife tell the anecdote, giving her kindly encouragement: "You gotta remember, Fran's a fisherwoman from Alaska. She knows about these things." Tilbury added: "We were just talking hypothetically, after all. He said you could also put weights on them to make them sink faster." Smith continued: "That's what [Wild Bill] said, 'You have a problem over here, Franny, you shoot the person with a shotgun if you have one. Then I'll come over there and we'll take care of the weights. Don't worry about it.'"

Even in remote Darklands, the Jolly Roger Social Club had stiff competition for the gringo dollar. Every Sunday at lunchtime there was a big expat get-together at the Rana Azul (the Blue Frog), an open-air restaurant on the north shore of the peninsula run by Josef, an expat Austrian.

Josef had owned the land since 2007 and he set his restaurant up at approximately the same time as Wild Bill opened the Jolly Roger Social Club on the Browns' former property. Like Holbert, he lived next to his business. You really did see blue frogs scurrying across the undergrowth and along branches, so the name was apt. At the Rana Azul, guests sat at big tables, each one accommodating a dozen or more people. Above the tables, awnings kept the sun and the rain away. Josef's setup obliged people to get to know their fellow diners. Draped from the beams holding up the awnings were the flags of twenty or so countries that gave splashes of color. They were all different sizes, suggesting they had been collected over time or had been donated by the patrons. The restaurant is still there, located in a clearing fifty yards from the water, squat palm trees all around. In the high season, boats crowd the jetty. Sparks fly out of Josef's pizza oven, but most customers opt for the traditional European food cooked up by Josef and the changing cast of itinerant European twenty-somethings who help him out in return for a place to stay. Josef's specialty is beef Stroganoff, served with buttery, soft, south German egg noodles called spaetzle. He built the brick pizza oven himself, arched in the style of the ovens he saw in Italy, where he once lived for a while. For the beef Stroganoff and spaetzle it was as simple as recalling his childhood. When the plates are cleared away, the ladies present—for the most part middle-aged—dance to Latin pop music in a circle next to the tables. There are frequent screams of laughter. These are the sort of tunes you hear all the time on Panamanian buses, the beat too fast to hum to. The European kids behind the bar and the occasional Panamanian guest look on, smiling. Later, some of the menfolk place their wide-brimmed hats on the scrubbed tabletops, stand up, and sway to the music.

For many, Sunday lunch at Rana Azul is the high point of the week's social calendar. On other days of the week the main point of contact with the rest of the gringo community is the shortwave radio broadcasts that announce the weather for the day, the odd joke, and bits of gossip. (Sample broadcast from a man identifying himself as Captain Bob: "When you feel old, just remember, all the cells in our bodies renew themselves every seven years. There's nobody around whose age is more than ten.") At other times, Josef caters for the excursion boats operating

out of Bocas Town. They pull up to his jetty full of tourists needing sustenance on their way back from baking on a glaring-white beach or after a
spot of snorkeling.

At the Sunday get-together at Rana Azul, like pretty much all other
gringo bars, pairs of expats sometimes leave the tables quietly and walk
up to the bathroom housed in a wooden shack set back from the restaurant along a deck walkway. There is nothing the host can do about
recreational drug use. We are in Bocas, after all. Here, marijuana and—
especially—cocaine go with the territory.

Holbert and Reese came to the Rana Azul for Sunday lunch from time
to time. A few people noticeably stiffened when they saw Wild Bill's hulking frame approaching along the long jetty. Plenty of folks did what they
could to avoid talking to him, but at Rana Azul that wasn't always easy,
since the arrangement was deliberately communal. Holbert was as boisterous here as he was everywhere else; when he wasn't talking, he stared
at the person speaking with his pale eyes, rarely blinking. Reese, as ever,
tended to keep her mouth shut as the conversation bubbled all around.

"It's not so easy to live here," said Josef, referring to Darklands. "You're
far from everything. You begin to ask yourself, What about emergencies?
Who will come running? What will happen when I get older? People
wake up from the dream one day when they are set up with their house.
Basically, they are just waiting for the time they can pour their first drink.
Every paradise has its snake, after all."

Holbert and Reese got around Darklands, and made forays to Bocas
Town, in a powerboat they bought from another expat soon after arriving. This was a slim, thirty-two-foot vessel with a pair of powerful Evin-
rude motors. This type of model is designed to be driven fast and is
often called a cigar boat. It is now roped to a mooring behind the police
station in Bocas, its black hull—uncommon in Panama—bobbing up
and down over the oily film that attaches itself to the surface of the
water here in the center of town. On the flying bridge of Holbert's old
boat, a couple of white leather chairs face the steering wheel and the
controls. Above the chairs is a stainless steel frame with fabric—now
frayed and worn—stretched over it, marking out a small, shallow cabin.
Next to Holbert's boat behind the police station is a longer, bulkier,

sport fisherman's boat. This one was impounded after a drug bust. Both vessels are just sitting there rotting away.

Holbert took great care of his cigar boat, said Johan,* an old friend of Bill's from his Bocas period. He kept the inside spotlessly clean. The white leather seats were buffed to shine to perfection. "For Bill, that boat was all about freedom," said Johan. Bill drove the boat fast across the glassy waters of the lagoon with heavy metal music blasting over the roar of the motors. He had zero interest in fishing. After a year in Darklands, Holbert's routine was "parties, drink, and women," said Johan. It is now September 2014; almost six months have passed since I first arrived in Bocas. I meet Johan at an address on the scruffy outskirts of Bocas Town almost immediately after I make a short phone call to introduce myself. Johan says, "Come right over." Almost no one in Bocas seems more damaged by the experience of knowing Holbert than this man. He is powerfully built, and when I ask questions he looks at me intently, concentrating on what I'm saying, not missing a word. He has this in common with Wild Bill.

"I remember one time Bill's boat got scratched on a dock because the indigenous [Native American] guy helping out had forgotten to attach the fender. Bill screamed at him, 'I'm going to kill you; your life isn't worth that scratch.'" When Holbert paid Johan a call in Bocas, the very first thing Holbert would do was slam a bottle of Seco Herrerano on the table. This was Wild Bill's favorite brand of white rum, distilled in Panama. "It might have been mid-morning," said Johan. "That didn't matter. Bill just wanted to share a drink. He started drinking really early in the day."

I'm about to conclude the interview and say good-bye to Johan and walk back to the center of Bocas Town when I notice a local man riding an old bicycle in circles in the road next to where we are talking. We carry on talking about Johan's life in Bocas. Things haven't gone well lately for Bill's old friend. He gets animated as he continues his story. It turns out that in Bocas some expats have pointed fingers at Johan, shut him out of their social circles. He is tarnished by the association with Wild Bill and is shunned by some of the gringos, but in a lethargic, indolent way, as if

---

* Not his real name.

the deep heat of the tropics saps the will of anyone with half an idea of confronting him. On top of that, there is a lingering regret: Holbert had big plans for a deal with Johan. The project was to work together on upgrading a weed-strewn airstrip near David and building a hotel and casino next to it. Johan thinks it would have been a success, had Holbert been around to get it started. He really seems to believe this. After all, there are plenty of small private planes buzzing in the skies above western Panama, bringing tourists, investors, and whatever to this part of the country.

Fifteen minutes later, the man on the bicycle is still there, making his circles in the road. Johan says, "Don't worry. He's just checking you out. He's selling coke." Finally, the man on the bicycle goes on his way. Usually gringos get offered drugs in a whisper every half hour on the streets of Bocas if they are strolling around. The selling style of the man on the bicycle is one I haven't seen before.

This is how William Dathan Holbert described his time in Darklands in the e-mail he sent to the Panamanian journalists from his prison cell in David: *I was a person with problems. I was ashamed. I couldn't sleep and I couldn't rest because of the shame. That is when I discovered liquor (and specifically Seco Herrerano). This was the best medicine for my conscience. I drank half a gallon of rum a day. I changed into a guy who loved to party and I lived a crazy life. I hooked up with other women and the friends I found were bad people. I started working for the cartel again as a hit-man, but this time I did it voluntarily. I was given the instruction to kill a partner of the boss of the cartel. In return, I would get his house and his position* [in the cartel] *as an art trafficker.* But things at home were taking a turn for the worse: *My wife was very unhappy and didn't understand what the matter with me was. There were times when I wasn't drinking and we would live peacefully. But there were also times when I just wanted to drink and to live my life in a crazy way.* In Holbert's account, his role in the cartel diversified. He was no longer just a gun for hire: *When I was working for the cartel I was a debt collector and an enforcer. Wherever I went, I took a pistol with me.*

I paid no attention to my wife. She left me time and time again. I always asked her to come back to me. When Holbert was living with his first wife and children in North Carolina, his recollection to the journalists in his e-mail was that *Everyone could look in and see someone doing very well with a happy family.* Now, everyone could look in and see a man who had accumulated all the accoutrements of a moneyed life in the sun: *I bought a Harley Davidson, a small airplane, a powerboat, a yacht. But I was miserable, too. How could I ever be happy? My wife wanted us to leave Panama and the crazy life we had. She never knew about my dirty jobs, she just thought I was an investor. That's what everyone in Bocas believed.*

By the early months of 2009, after a year of living in the Browns' old house, Darklands could no longer contain Holbert's ambitions. He needed to play on a bigger stage. Bocas Town was where most of the gringo big shots lived. Reese was getting moodier, clamming up in the Jolly Roger Social Club when she should have been cheerful for the customers. Reese was tiring of Darklands, that much was clear. The wilderness simply wasn't her thing. A period in Bocas Town would do her good. Holbert and Reese lived a mile and a half from Cher Hughes and Keith Werle—a couple who had a reputation for liking to party—but although Holbert and Werle were close, the vivacious, smiley, and worldly-wise Cher Hughes had next to nothing in common with plain Jane Cortez. Still, Holbert reckoned the bar hadn't outlived its usefulness, even if its takings were meager compared to the runaway success of Josef's Rana Azul. So the Jolly Roger Social Club would stay open. But Bocas Town beckoned, and Holbert was ready to move on to the next phase of his plan.

Bo Icelar was born Barry Lawrence Eisler in Maryland on September 17, 1951. As a young adult, he changed his name from the Germanic "Eisler" to the Anglicized "Icelar." Bo Icelar moved to Bocas del Toro in 2004, although at the beginning he was an on-off expat, traveling back and forth from Santa Fe, New Mexico, while his house in Bocas Town was being built. For a couple of decades he owned the East West Trading Company, an art and antiquities gallery in Santa Fe selling Native American artifacts, African art, and nice pieces of jewelry that made popular gifts. In Bocas, there was a new name change: he introduced himself as Bo Yancey.

Icelar had run into some trouble with the authorities in Santa Fe. Native Americans and collectors—and the intermediaries who supply the collectors, and the treasure hunters, or looters—have long been engaged in a keen dispute over the status of buried artifacts. After the adoption of the Native American Graves Protection and Repatriation Act (NAGPRA) in 1990, it became a criminal offense to traffic certain Native American cultural items. In New Mexico, there were concerted efforts to clamp down on the theft of sacred objects and artifacts dug up from public or tribal lands. Oftentimes, the looting took place at, or very close to, human burial sites. In 1994, following a raid masterminded jointly by the Federal Bureau of Investigation, the National Parks Service, and the Fish and Wildlife Service, federal agents confiscated eleven objects deemed sacred by the Mescalero Apache tribe from the premises of Bo Icelar's East West Trading Company.*

In the years that followed, Icelar came to tire of Santa Fe, according to Sharon McConnell, a longtime friend who also lived in the city. "Santa Fe lost its charm for Bo," said McConnell. "It became too precious. He wanted to make a big change in his life. He found out about Panama and decided to travel there. He wanted a quieter life and he wanted to be closer to nature." Icelar was a tall, broad-shouldered man with curly, reddish-brown hair. He had a lizard tattoo on each upper arm. He liked to keep fit and he had a passion for martial arts. On February 7, 2005—around six months after he had started building his Bocas home—Bo Icelar declared Chapter 7 bankruptcy, wiping out over $55,000 in personal debts. He took a significant amount of money overseas, together with a large collection of artifacts and jewelry.

---

* According to Phil Young, a retired National Park ranger familiar with the East West Trading Company raid, most art and antiquities store owners convicted under NAGPRA run businesses that are "90 to 95 percent legitimate." But the markups on illegal artifacts is often extremely high. Young says that it is greed that motivates looters, dealers, and collectors of illegal artifacts, but he has also noticed that "time and again, people who have had a run-in with the authorities [for selling items outlawed by NAGPRA] have paid a penalty that goes beyond the judicial system." In New Mexico, Young has seen divorces, bankruptcies, even a suicide. "It's another level of indebtedness."

Bo Icelar built his house on a three-acre plot in Big Creek, three miles outside Bocas Town. Here the land is low-lying, fertile. In 2005, Big Creek was the most expensive place in Bocas to own a house, and it still is. There are a couple of hotels there with pretensions of being resorts, but for the most part this is a wealthy residential community of comfortable, recently built mansions with big yards. The residences of Big Creek are set back from a horseshoe-shaped bay fronted by a narrow beach known locally for its sandflies—as a result it is usually deserted by day. Trunks of palm trees at the edge of the beach, bent over the white sand, cut a photogenic pose. Residents have clubbed together to build the docks and boathouses lining the water here and there; a paved road, meanwhile, hugs the shore. There are a couple of new backpackers' hostels at Big Creek near Icelar's house, increasing traffic on the road. One of them has a lively bar with a TV screen showing tapes of episodes of *Friends*, one after another, ad infinitum. Despite the sandflies, the beach is the venue for full-moon parties—a marketing trick borrowed from Thailand, an excuse for an extended night of drinking, sessions of trancelike dancing, songs around a campfire if someone has brought a guitar, and maybe a spot of skinny-dipping.

Icelar had the house built to his own specifications: there were two self-contained studio apartments on the first floor and the principal residence on the second level. There was also a basement, which was useful for storing the collection of artwork and artifacts that Icelar had shipped to Bocas from New Mexico. The first-floor apartments could be rented out as and when required, and the second-floor balcony looked out to the bay and caught the best of the breeze. Icelar traveled back and forth between Santa Fe and Bocas for about a year while the architectural plans were made, the plot cleared, and the house, finally, took shape. Each time he returned to the States he stayed with Sharon McConnell in Santa Fe. (As it turned out, soon after Icelar quit Santa Fe for good, so did McConnell.) In Bocas he usually lodged at Cocomo-on-the-Sea, Douglas Ruscher's guesthouse. Ruscher said that Icelar had originally bought into what he expected to be a planned community. "This happened to a load of people. They saw an ad saying 'Buy a lot, you'll save money.' And so all these people bought these lots and there was to be all this infrastructure. There were supposed to be tennis courts, a swimming pool, a weight-lifting room, all these facilities. But it fell through. Every development has been the same, they've all failed. The guys went under. I have not yet seen one development completed in twelve years." Ruscher recalled that someone once, improbably, promised a golf course here in the jungle. The bush in Bocas del Toro is as thick as squares of wheat. "They thought they would build it on the cheap." It's another story to add to Bocas del Toro's long list of real estate fiascos. Ruscher said that Icelar never mentioned to him that he was disappointed when the planned community and all the promised facilities failed to materialize. At least he had his mansion and unobstructed access to it. "In that respect, he came out all right," said Ruscher. Icelar used a shell company with bearer shares, named Iguana Limited, Corp., set up in 2004, to buy the plot in Big Creek, in just the same way as Michael Brown had done for his home in Darklands. In fact, the shell company also controlled the title of another, separate, empty plot, too, that Icelar had bought as part of his investment in Big Creek. The mansion and the empty plot were thus owned by whoever had the bearer share certificates in his possession. Icelar had no wife and no children.

If Bo Icelar's dream was to get closer to the natural world, as his friend Sharon McConnell said, Big Creek was the place. The edge of the plot was marked by broad leaves of sturdy banana plants. Fiery orange-and-yellow bird-of-paradise flowers grew in profusion. Hummingbirds visited from time to time. Beyond the perimeter of Bo Icelar's plot was the jungle, untamed.

"We dated for nearly a year in '95, '96," recalled Sharon McConnell. "It was explosive. Let me put it this way. We broke up after I jumped out of a moving car that Bo was driving." By this time McConnell was almost blind. After a period in her twenties spent working as a cook on private jets, flying with the likes of George H. W. Bush and his wife, Barbara, Henry Kissinger, Al Haig, and Donald and Ivana Trump, McConnell woke up one day in Chicago and could hardly see. Doctors eventually diagnosed uveitis, a degenerative eye disease involving an inflammation of the uvea, the middle layer of the eye. After several years of surgeries and treatments she took up sculpture. "It's the vehicle I use to access my lost sense," said McConnell.

After their breakup, Icelar and McConnell's relationship transformed into something that is practically undefinable, she said: "Our friendship went through a huge change from being lovers to something like being brother and sister. We were very affectionate and very, very close." There was a degree of violence in Icelar's environment when he was growing up, said McConnell. He grew apart from most of his family, including a brother and sister. Later, it was Bo Icelar who introduced the blind Sharon McConnell to blues music. McConnell was soon hooked and started to create life masks of blues musicians. Sometimes she worked with bronze, sometimes driftwood. "I wanted to discover the faces behind the music I love, so I went to Mississippi to map out the visages of the real Delta blues men and women." That's where Sharon McConnell met David, her current husband. They now share a home with McConnell's guide dog, Avatar, in a small town an hour south of Memphis across the Mississippi state line.

The life of the man known to his friends and fellow residents of Big Creek as Bo Yancey was low-key but hardly reclusive. "He was a nice guy," said John Lang, Bo's nearest neighbor in Big Creek. "He could be a little eccentric. If he was sitting here today, I'd say the same." Bo did not like the idea of people interfering in his business. "Especially the US government," said Lang. "If he got annoyed with you, he'd cut you out. His circle [of friends] got narrowed." Lang, a former prison guard from Michigan, arrived in Bocas del Toro two years before Bo. Back in Michigan, he had progressed through the ranks and retired as an inspector, basically a prison's chief security officer, he explained. He wears a chain around his neck with a tiny gold dolphin at the end of it. Like many North American newcomers in Bocas, Lang believes in capital punishment: "Michigan has no death penalty. But I dealt with these people for over twenty-five years. We need it."

Lang said there were two groups in Bocas. He counted them on the thumb and forefinger of his left hand. "First you have the boring, dull people. This is the older crowd living off a pension. They get high on lager and rum. Then, second, you have the other group, the party people." Lang says that they are generally a younger crowd, but there are exceptions. If they arrive married, they don't often stay that way. They use cocaine for their kicks rather than sit around tables playing mah-jongg. Lang doesn't say which group he belongs to, but he lives off a pension and has a beer cooler advertising a Hooter's restaurant in Grand Rapids.

Sharon McConnell and Bo Icelar spoke almost every day on the phone the entire time Icelar lived in Bocas. In early 2009, Icelar needed to have an operation on his right foot. He chose to have the surgery done at a hospital in David. "Bo wrecked his knee right in front of his store in Santa Fe trying to catch a man who tried to steal from him. That caused his right foot to become troublesome," said McConnell. Icelar told only a very small number of people that he was going to the hospital in David. And, as Icelar had the habit of keeping few lights on at his property, even if he was at home a passerby might not be sure of it.

Walter Kawano can't remember the precise moment that he became friends with Bo Icelar. Kawano is a real estate agent, and his ground-floor agency lies at a strategic position in Bocas Town off Bolívar Park, the unofficial center of Bocas, where there are several supermarkets, the town hall, and plenty of places to grab a coffee. He shares his office with two other realtors. Bo passed Kawano's agency each time he came into the town center from his house in Big Creek or if he was headed for the only bank in Bocas or if he had to pick someone up from the airport. Icelar liked to come in to say hello, catch up on local news, and check his e-mails. He walked in with the aid of a stick topped with a carved wooden serpent's head. That was the lasting legacy of his brush with the thief outside his store in Santa Fe, in addition to the pin that medics had fixed in his knee to help him get mobile. In the wet season especially, when relatively few gringos are around to browse property listings and make viewings, Kawano was glad to have Bo Icelar's visits.

On one occasion Bo Icelar and Walter Kawano arranged a trip to Panama City together. For Kawano, it was a trip home. "I introduced Bo to my mom, my uncle, and the rest of my family. They all met him."

In Panama City, Icelar hit it off with one of Kawano's cousins and the two of them had a long discussion about spirituality. Icelar was the exception that proved the rule: in a place where locals and newcomers led largely separate lives, despite sharing the same spaces, Icelar took the trouble to find out about his environment and the people in it. In Kawano, Icelar could count on at least one local who came to regard him as "almost family."

Icelar gave Kawano an antique horse file that makes a nice paperweight. But Kawano seems prouder that Bo donated an old iron cross to the Chitré restaurant on Bolívar Park, a place frequented mainly by locals. They put it on the wall, where it remains. Kawano has another keepsake that reminds him of Icelar: it's a copy of the *Bocas Breeze* from August 2009. Kawano takes the newspaper out of a drawer in his desk. It is kept open at a page where a rectangular display ad, two inches by three inches, reads: *I BUY HOUSES, BOATS AND BUSINESSES. HASSLE FREE AND FAST CLOSINGS*. Below it is a cell phone number, with a dollar sign before and after it. "That's the number Bo called," says Kawano. In the same issue of the *Bocas Breeze* is Holbert's ad for the Jolly Roger Social Club, the one promising that *Over 90% of our members survive*.

If Kawano felt aggrieved that his friend called a purposely anonymous number he found in a local paper rather than use his services as a realtor, he doesn't show it. Icelar's mansion was his biggest asset. Sometimes the thought of the effort expended to save for a home—and Icelar had a mansion in the best location in Bocas—can cloud anyone's judgment. By the first months of 2009 Icelar had decided he wanted to leave Bocas and return to the United States, possibly as soon as Christmas of that same year. His timing wasn't great: housing prices were tumbling in the United States (and in some, but not all, European countries) and the volume of transactions across the United States was also down. On the face of it, this was good news for someone planning to buy a home in the States. But it also meant that people who wanted to sell their home in the United States to move to Latin America were often delayed in making a sale. According to Kawano, Icelar had wanted $470,000 for his house. Douglas Ruscher is one friend who confirmed that Icelar had received a serious "cash offer" of $430,000. But this offer almost certainly came through by the end of

2007, before the worst of the global property crash kicked in, and Icelar was determined to hold out for more. He was far from the only person wanting to sell a house during this period who would come to regret not grabbing an offer before house prices tumbled. There was a further nuance to the sale: the house was too expensive for most Panamanians to consider buying, and it was located in an enclave of wealthy expats. This meant that the natural market for the property was Americans planning to leave the United States—precisely the group most affected by the housing slump. So, when the credit crunch arrived, Icelar's asking price simply didn't reflect the new reality of the market from the perspective of the kinds of people most likely to submit an offer. By the second half of 2009, any deal around $350,000 or $370,000 would have been good business for the vendor. If there was ever a time to be realistic about the pricing, and to move fast if necessary, this was it, because the housing market everywhere appeared to be moving in one direction only.

As 2009 progressed, Icelar's mind became made up. "He couldn't wait to leave," said McConnell. "He would say to me, 'I gotta get out of this place.' The rest of the time, we talked a lot about the blues." The idea was hatched for Bo to move to Mississippi. McConnell said that Bo had tired of the drug culture in Bocas. "He didn't even drink very much alcohol," said McConnell. "Wherever he went there were people taking drugs. There was a kind of pressure to take them, to conform. Bo was a very serious, spiritual being. In any case, he had no tolerance for bullshit." It should have been a big piece of news, then: the prospective sale of Icelar's mansion at Big Creek. Icelar told McConnell that there was this couple who wanted to buy it. Then it turned out that they were going to get a divorce, which cast a doubt on the whole thing. Then the deal, thankfully, seemed to be on again. But Icelar didn't go into many details in their conversations over the phone. "It seemed to keep falling through." By this time, Icelar was truly desperate to get away. "I guess he thought that if he spoke about the sale at length with me, he would somehow jinx it." The couple in question was, of course, William Adolfo Cortez and Jane Seana Cortez.

McConnell spoke to Icelar on the phone on November 29, 2009. It was the last time they would speak. On the same day there was a sighting of

Bo at breakfast time at a café on the waterfront in the center of Bocas. He had a stack of papers with him and he commented to a fellow customer that he was going to sell his house. On November 30, a local handyman showed up at Icelar's mansion on Icelar's instructions. Icelar had asked him to come to paint the house. Surprisingly, Icelar was nowhere to be seen. Holbert yelled at the handyman that Bo Yancey was gone and to get off the property, as it was now his. On the same day, McConnell called Icelar, but her friend didn't answer his phone. Subsequent calls in the following days also went unanswered. McConnell wanted to travel down to Bocas herself to see what she could find out, but she was apprehensive about going with her guide dog to a place she knew nothing about, other than the rather negative picture of Bocas painted by Icelar. Christmas 2009 came and went, and Icelar's US credit-card bills and bank statements were coming to McConnell's house, as they always did. But by January, she realized the credit-card bills weren't being paid, which wasn't like Bo.

In early November 2009 Icelar had known he would be selling the house and started to make practical arrangements. He decided to sell some of his furniture to Scott McAda, who wanted to furnish a property he owned in the Boquete area. Walter Kawano put the two men in touch. Icelar and McAda quickly agreed on a price of $1,000 for the items of furniture. McAda recalls a conversation that took place in the last week of November. "That was when Bo Icelar told me that he was selling his house to Cortez for $400,000: 'I'm selling my property in Bocas and I'm selling to Wild Bill,'" said McAda, repeating what Icelar had said to him. "'I'm getting top dollar.' I immediately thought that was strange. I had heard that Cortez got good prices for real estate." But Holbert, meanwhile, had been chatting with his friend Mike Smith about the planned purchase of Bo Icelar's house in Bocas. Holbert had boasted to Mike Smith that he was paying just $180,000 for Icelar's property. And Mike Smith had told this to Scott McAda.

A day or two later, Holbert called McAda. "He was on the phone attacking me," said McAda. "The thing is, Cortez knew that I knew both figures."

In the period between Thanksgiving and Christmas 2009, Scott McAda started receiving more phone calls from Holbert. Now, the tone had changed. "Cortez called to ask me to go gambling with him at a casino in David," recalls McAda. His immediate reaction was to say no to Wild Bill. "First of all, I don't like gambling so much. I like a drink, but to get to and from the casino I'd have to drive." So McAda turned Holbert down and he expected the matter to end there. But Holbert called again shortly afterward, upping the stakes: "In that second call, he said to me, 'Scott, I've got us a suite at the casino in David.'" McAda is a man with a keen sense of humor, but he speaks plainly. One exchange between the two men that took place sometime in 2008 stuck in McAda's mind: "We were talking about boats with some other people, including Mike and Fran. Someone mentioned the Spanish word for 'spark plug,' and Cortez didn't recognize it." It was a trivial matter, but still a bit surprising. "I said to him, 'Come on, Bill, I thought you ran a bike shop!'" For once, Holbert was at a loss for words. "I was pretty rude at the time," said McAda, "and I insulted his level of Spanish."

Holbert's powers of persuasion had met their match in the figure of Scott McAda. Suite or no suite at the casino in David, McAda turned Holbert's repeated invitation down. "I cut Bill short. I told him I didn't want to go. I said to him, 'Please don't call me again.'"

"I had trouble figuring it all out at the time," said McAda. But with the advantage of hindsight things have become clearer: "Had I gone to the casino, one of two things would have happened. Either Cortez would have killed me, or, more likely, he would have gotten me into trouble with a female. He would have spiked my drinks and I would have woken up in bed with a dead woman."

Meanwhile, increasingly worried, McConnell contacted Daniel Anaya, an attorney in Bocas Town. Anaya was the lawyer who had processed Holbert's purchase of Michael Brown's house in Darklands, meaning that at the beginning of 2008 he had the task of checking that Holbert had in his possession the necessary package of documents pertaining to Latitude 9.10, Inc., Michael Brown's shell company. This comprised all the required bearer shares, the corporation charter, and the undated resignation letters signed by the proxy directors. After he had done the deal with Bo Icelar, Holbert made a new appointment at the offices of

Anaya's law firm. On December 9, 2009, Holbert showed up at Anaya's office with the same kind of package as in 2008: the required bearer shares, the corporation charter, and the undated resignation letters signed by the proxy directors. As he had done with the change of directors of Michael Brown's shell company, Holbert identified himself with a Dutch passport in the name of William Adolfo Cortez. A lawyer working with Anaya drew up a document installing William Adolfo Cortez as the new president and secretary of Bo Icelar's company Iguana Limited, Corp., and declaring Jane Seana Cortez as its treasurer. The change was duly recorded in a central Panamanian register of corporations.

Anaya was twenty-five years old when Holbert came into his office for the first time in 2008. Anaya said that during that period he was the only corporate lawyer in town and worked from a room that was essentially a satellite of a big law firm in Panama City. It was his first position after graduating from law school. Anaya is hardly the stereotypical Central American lawyer: he has dark hair cut to just above his shoulders, and usually wears a polo shirt and skinny jeans to the office. (When I meet Anaya, I think he takes a little pleasure in asking me: "I'm not quite what you expected, am I?") If he's not working, he often takes his surfboard out to the Punch Beach or Bluff Beach on the exposed northeast coast of Columbus Island. Anaya is married to a Swiss woman and they settled in Bocas. When conversation switches to the big waves of Bluff Beach, Anaya visibly relaxes.

Anaya readily gave McConnell the name and cell phone number of the person he said was the new owner of Bo Icelar's mansion at Big Creek. It was William Dathan Holbert—the man most people in Bocas del Toro knew as Wild Bill Cortez.

McConnell called Holbert a first time, but he didn't answer. McConnell left a message saying that she was getting concerned, as she couldn't locate Bo Icelar. Soon afterward, McConnell called a second time, saying that by now she should have heard from Icelar. There was no reason for him to disappear from her life; certainly, he had never done so before. Bo Icelar wasn't the type of man to be afraid of being on his own, but that didn't mean he would just go off and stay out of touch. "It struck me that Bo simply hadn't sold his house to Bill," said McConnell. Then

McConnell called Holbert a third time and laid down an ultimatum. She told Holbert to get back to her by the end of the day; if he didn't, she would call the police. There was still no call from Wild Bill. In the end, McConnell called the US embassy in Panama City and relayed her concerns about the well-being of her friend. She also called Walter Kawano and asked him to file a missing persons complaint locally, which he did on April 24, 2010. In Bocas, meanwhile, the complaint was handled by the office of the *personero*, a kind of low-level district attorney in the Panamanian system. But the police didn't find the story of a disappearing gringo compelling enough to follow up. Icelar went away from home from time to time, this much was apparent. He didn't always let his friends and acquaintances in Bocas know before he traveled. He hadn't exited Panama at a regular border crossing, port, or airport, and could easily be someplace else in the country. For the time being, the police in Bocas left it at that.

Meanwhile, Holbert and Reese turned Icelar's house into party central. Wild Bill held his most boisterous parties on the nights when Reese was absent, but they never became excruciatingly loud. Holbert now favored Latin music, the kind you could dance to; he no longer listened to much heavy metal. But he sought to dominate social events and was often, said his neighbor John Lang, "obnoxious." Lang was invited to parties at Bo Icelar's old house from time to time. "He was always drunk off his ass," said Lang. At one party, with Reese someplace else, Holbert wanted to have sex with a woman. The woman said no. Holbert screamed at her: "You fuckin' bitch, I'll fuckin' kill you!" Lang said that Holbert had the same personality whether he was drunk or sober. "But when he was drunk, he was nastier."

The parties may have looked like a housewarming bash repeated several times over, but readers of the *Bocas Breeze* who were familiar with the appearance of Icelar's mansion might have supposed that they were in celebration of an imminent departure. In April 2010 the *Breeze* carried a large display ad with a photo of the Big Creek house that was now home to Holbert and Reese. It said: *HACIENDA STYLE BEACH HOME—$359K. Newly completed 3 bed 2 bath home in desirable Big Creek Village. Priced 100K below market value. ABSOLUTELY BEST DEAL IN*

BOCAS—LOOK AROUND! The empty plot was also advertised in the same display: *1300 METER BEACH LOT! $69K. Cheapest titled beach lot in Bocas of its kind.* And below the two offers: *MAKE US AN OFFER! OWNER FINANCING? LET'S TALK!*

Wild Bill and Jane had turned into real estate flippers.

Casie Dean hails from Atlanta, Georgia. At twenty-eight, she is the owner and editor of the *Bocas Breeze*, the monthly newspaper published in English and Spanish, paid for by advertising, lying in piles in shops and hotels for visitors to pick up. I pick up a back issue from January 2014. That month, the paper led with a piece entitled "Wed in Barefoot Luxury at Popa Paradise." There was a story asking the question: "Lionfish: Deadly or Delicious?" Another feature was titled "Holistic Healing in Bocas." There were advertisements for lunch deals, secondhand boating equipment, construction materials. Dean and I meet on the rear terrace of one of the hotels that line the seafront in Bocas, jutting out over the water. Dean is wearing a red-checked shirt, faded jeans. She has the habit of fixing her gaze on the motorboats in the water as they arc toward nearby jetties, spewing out exhaust, bringing gap-year tourists back from the best island beaches.

Casie Dean and her husband decided on the island life on New Year's Eve 2010 in Philadelphia, with sixteen inches of snow outside the door. Her husband's family used to own a hotel just outside Bocas Town and she had vacationed there. "It seemed like an all right place," she says. (Dean is a little prone to understatement.) After tying up some loose ends for a business and sorting out the paperwork to travel with a cat, the couple arrived in Bocas in the spring of 2011. As soon as she was in Panama, Dean, an animal lover, hit the ground running: "I saw so many stray, malnourished dogs here. I helped set up a spay and neuter clinic. Basically I became a community activist." Dogs are popular in Bocas, for companionship and security, but they are not always well looked after. Even with the clinic up and running, many wander around town in a daze, so thin you can see their ribs.

Dean adopted a puppy she found in a garbage pile. Island life was as good as they had dreamed it would be. And in Bocas, there was so much to get done. What about providing safe drinking water? Unlike some other places in Panama, the water that comes out of the tap is not fit to drink. Or how about getting medical treatment to remote parts of Bocas with a floating doctor's service?

While she was seeking out the next business opportunity, the *Bocas Breeze* landed on her doorstep. The former owner had had it for six or seven years, wanted to sell up, and approached Dean. "She said that I reminded her a lot of herself when she was younger. She planned to retire but she wanted to offer the paper to me first."

Dean quickly learned the first ground rule of expat life in Bocas: be careful who you get to know, because you can invest time and energy in a relationship and then, without warning, your best friend gets the next plane out. Dean looks out again across the water. A plastic bottle and a piece of foil packaging bob up and down near one of the posts supporting the terrace. "There is something very . . . provocative about life in Bocas," she says. She immediately narrows her eyes as if to let me know that "provocative" isn't quite the right word. But I think I can see what she means.

When they first arrived in Bocas, Dean and her husband leased Bo Icelar's old property, which by then stood empty. The couple were told several times about the history of the place. It didn't freak them out at first. The house had passed to a nephew of Bo Icelar's who had been living in the United States. He came to Panama and put it on the rental market, and Casie Dean took it as a rental for a year. But it hadn't been properly maintained. The plaster was falling off. The garden was a mess. One day, Dean set to work on clearing some weeds. "I was digging and I hit something. I thought: Maybe it's Bill's getaway bag. But it turned out to be a tarpaulin sheet covering a leach field." A couple of Rottweilers kept in the yard of a neighboring property often howled at night. The echoes made them sound like ghosts.

At the beginning of 2012 the *Bocas Breeze* appeared in the island's hotel lobbies and restaurants with another picture of a missing person, this time of a woman named Yvonne Baldelli. Dean and Baldelli only knew each other for a few months, but they were close. Baldelli had recently lost her job at Procter & Gamble in California. At age forty-one and with no children—a medical condition prevented her from having any—she realized there was nothing stopping her moving south to Panama. She and Dean became fast friends—they went to the same bars in the evenings and shared a lot of laughs. But having spent a couple of months making contacts and planning a new bikini business, Baldelli disappeared one day without notice. Dean had learned by now that Bocas' residents sometimes left in a hurry, but she couldn't believe that Baldelli wouldn't even have said good-bye. It seemed that no one knew what had happened, and Dean decided to run a picture of her friend in the *Breeze*. Some of the newspaper's advertisers told Dean: "If there's a murder, it's not good for tourism. So don't put it in."

I want to have a look at Bo Icelar's old house in Big Creek from the outside. I'm in Bolívar Park in the center of Bocas Town. There's a sign in Spanish that says NO DUMPING GARBAGE. FINE $1,000. There is a large pile of trash next to it. I mention to a *gringa* woman while I buy a coffee that I'm looking for a taxi to take me to Big Creek. She tells me, with no evident malice: "Someone has to die to get a good rental because Big Creek is getting expensive." I wonder briefly if maybe the housing market has turned. She also advises me to avoid a taxi driver whom I'm going to call Juan because, she says, he's a rapist. "Make sure you remember the number of his cab." I make a mental note of it and, to my mild surprise, when I start looking for a ride on Main Street, Juan's cab immediately appears. The hand I have raised to flag Juan's vehicle quickly finds its way back into my pocket, a piece of theater that Juan looks at in puzzlement through a half-open window as he drives by.

I find Bo Icelar's residence easily. The mansion is salmon-pink and is fronted by a large, smooth lawn. The clumps of banana plants at the back make it difficult to work out where the plot ends, but from where I stand it looks pretty extensive. Casie Dean and Bo Icelar's nephew did a good job of repairing it. Like his uncle before him, the nephew likes to work out, and he also has a reputation for keeping to himself. I have been told that a young couple from Belgium is now renting out part of the house, but it appears deserted.

When the police forced the front door in 2010 and went inside, they were surprised to find many dozens of Bo Icelar's prized wood, stone, and bronze masks, the ones that he had shipped from the States, and wondered if some of the masks might have been brought into the country illegally, as they later told newspaper reporters. Subsequently, some of these masks seem to have disappeared, perhaps taken by policemen or guards or the forensic team, stuffed into the little backpacks that people around here carry. Many people in Bocas del Toro are superstitious, and I can imagine the police officers averting their gaze from the masks as they took them off the walls and carried them down into the cellar to join the rest of Bo Icelar's artwork.

The sun will soon set abruptly, as it always does here. On the street, banners for Panama's presidential election campaign are nailed to lampposts. The candidates wear smart jackets and shirts without a tie. One has a folded handkerchief in his top pocket. They are supported on their ticket by local politicians, who will serve their mandates here in Bocas. Almost all of these are men in colorful polo shirts, sometimes a baseball cap, smiling broadly. A couple of them give a thumbs-up sign. The local children, dressed in immaculate blue and white school uniforms, are safe at home by now. The Afro-Caribbean ladies you see by day, walking to and from the market, straight-backed, with slow, deliberate steps, using umbrellas as sunshades, are at home, too. This is part of the Bocas that the gringos, for the most part, do not connect with.

Sandi Hodge, a former neighbor of Icelar's and a close friend of Cher Hughes, has offered to tell me her story. When reporters from ABC News came calling in August 2010, Hodge told them that the police didn't know what really went on in Bocas. But then, neither did the expats. Each of them took one another's backstories on trust. Hodge used to own a beauty salon, but what proof did she have? They could all be lying to one another. "Oh boy, did I get crucified after that," says Hodge. "My friends who owned businesses said now no one would come here anymore."

Night falls on Sandi Hodge's balcony and a background noise of crickets and flies is accompanied by the gibberish of a pet parrot and the occasional barking of dogs, one of which—Jack, the Doberman pinscher now yapping at our feet—used to belong to Hodge's great friend, Cher Hughes.

I ask Hodge why she left her salon in Oceanside, California—"a big one making big money." She gestures with a wave over her shoulder at the scenery behind her. I note the beach at the end of her drive; her garden with its Bismarck palm trees and purple-and-orange bird-of-paradise flowers. The climate is so hot that you can comfortably wear a swimsuit day and night, as Hodge is doing now. Hodge has offered me a cold glass of white wine, a Chardonnay. The glass sweats in the hot night.

Earlier in the afternoon Hodge took her young grandson to a surfing beach. "I'm an island girl, I'm a nature lover. I did my time. I did thirty years in the city. I came here because I wanted just to breathe the fresh air. We're not in a big place and struggling to get by. And anyway, how great is this? I have my girlfriends come over. We cook meals together, we swim together." Hodge also stays in Bocas for the sake of her grandson, whom she looks after: "People don't hurt children here." I don't ask her age, but I guess that she is in her late fifties, athletic and healthy. Despite her warmth, she has the look of someone who has learned not to suffer fools gladly.

"There have been so many people who come here and get wrapped up in heavy drug use, alcoholism," says Hodge. "Many have a big cocaine problem, and when they come here it escalates. This can be a tough place." On the streets of Bocas Town, cocaine sells for a quarter of the price in the United States, sometimes less. Hodge says that people retire early, have too much time on their hands, and don't know what to do. They sell up in America or Europe and come to sail or relax in the sun. Then they can't go back. They somehow lose the will to do so. They have burned their bridges.

During this period Hodge often saw Holbert around town. "Sometimes he would be down at the hardware store and he'd say, 'Yeah, I'm great, I'm doing this, I'm doing that.' He was acting big all the time." One day, Hodge gave Holbert a ride back to Big Creek from town. Holbert told her that it was time for him to go back to work, which Hodge took to mean he was going to leave Bocas and return to the United States.

"So I asked him, 'What do you do for a living?' He said: 'I buy and sell real estate. I come in when people are having a rough time and I buy the real estate from them.' And I said, 'Okay, so you're running out of money and it's time to go back.' That's when he turned around and looked at me and said, 'No, I'm totally solvent.'" Holbert's cheeks were quivering and his eyes were narrow, his rage barely under control. He had practically spat the last line at Hodge.

"One day the police came here and they said, 'We're looking for Bo Yancey.' I said, 'He's gone, he's sold his property.' They said, 'Someone's filed a missing persons complaint on him.' I said, 'No, Bo was just weird, a recluse, he could find an issue with everybody, he was trying to sell his property, he wanted to go. He had a breakup with a girl and just wasn't happy here anymore.' When I heard he'd sold up and left, I thought, 'Okay, he's gone, he's had enough.'" Hodge pauses, reflecting. "But he had beautiful masks."

Back in town, a minibus slows down as a couple of laughing local children cross the road. Bocas is no longer "the place no tourist went" that Graham Greene had found all those years ago, and the bus is headed for a beach on the far side of Columbus Island known for its pink starfish. The driver has left the sliding door of the minibus open, hoping to fill an empty seat. Juan, the alleged rapist cabdriver, is leaning against his cab with his lower belly poking out from under his T-shirt, spies a young blond holiday-maker through the open door, and draws the fingers of his right hand together, raises them to his mouth, and makes a loud, exaggerated kissing sound. The blond woman turns her head in Juan's direction and laughs at the apparent comedy of the gesture before resuming a conversation with her friend.

One day just before Christmas in 2009, Wild Bill was in the Barracuda Bar, right on the waterfront, one of the most popular places among the expats. He was carrying a heavy load wrapped in a tarp. Someone called out, "Hey, Bill, what you got there on your shoulder?" Holbert replied,

"Half a cow." Another person spied Jane outside the bar wiping what appeared to be blood from their station wagon. "Now we are quite sure that was Bo," said Sandi Hodge. And there was another suspicious sighting: someone spotted Holbert pulling a heavy bag from his SUV to his boat moored on the jetty across the busy beach road in Big Creek. Holbert is a big man, but he was struggling to carry the bag.

None of the expats put two and two together.

5. "We Are Just Molecules"

It was late June 2015. From a distance, the man sitting on a chair in a room at El Renacer prison in Panama City appeared relaxed in a white, open-neck shirt, well ironed, its tails left hanging outside his pants. But under the glare of a spotlight he looked alert. The television interviewer thanked him for agreeing to talk, promising viewers that the man in the white shirt would "break his silence after so many years." The interviewer wore a dark suit and worked for the Telemetro channel. This interview would be the lead item on the news that night and would soon be discussed in newspaper columns and at dining tables, offices, factories, and bars.

What, the interviewer asked, did the man wish to say to the country?

The man paused and put on a pair of thick-rimmed glasses. Clearly he didn't intend to be rushed. He said he had come of his own free will. He had no personal interests to advance. But he wasn't there to give an interview, he said. He was there to make a declaration.

"That's what I'm going to share with you today," said the man, holding up a sheet of paper with handwritten notes on it, some of them underlined with a red pen. "This is what I'm going to read."

"Right," said the interviewer, gesturing with the open palm of his right hand, "go ahead." The man, age eighty-one, fixed his sight on the television camera.

"My name is Manuel Antonio Noriega. I was the last general of the military era which started on eleventh October 1968. I was a lieutenant in the National Guard at that time. I have been imprisoned for over twenty-five years. . . . Recently I have been thinking about things. I've been talking to members of my family. I've been conversing with the Church. I think it's now the right time to make my contribution to society by closing the chapter of the military era by asking for forgiveness as the last of that group of generals."

In the 1990s other Panamanian military men were accused and found guilty of heinous crimes, including murder. They had done time in jail and been released. Noriega was the only one left behind bars.

"Let me say again that my inspiration is the Lord's Prayer, which was the first prayer I learned at home. And so I ask the forgiveness of anyone who was offended, affected, injured, or humiliated by my actions."

"General Noriega," said the interviewer, "this is a historic moment. Asking for forgiveness means recognizing we are at fault and that we want to change. As part of the asking for forgiveness which we have just heard, what would you say to the family of Dr. Hugo Spadafora?"

Hugo Spadafora had been a swashbuckling physician, and the greatest thorn in Noriega's side. Noriega paused again. "Well," he replied, "these Christian reflections include asking for forgiveness, which is an inherent part of being sorry, which I have just done."

The interviewer wasn't satisfied with Noriega's convoluted answer. "Would you agree to talk with them?" asked the interviewer, referring to the family of Hugo Spadafora.

"I want to maintain the solemnity of what I'm saying, the solemnity of my thoughts and of the spiritual guidance I have received. I don't want to get diverted from the reason I accepted to sit down with you and ask for forgiveness to the people after so many years."

The interviewer asked what, precisely, Noriega had been talking about with his spiritual advisers.

A brief smile crossed Noriega's lips. "I understand your question, but I repeat that I want to keep to the thoughts I have expressed today and which I have just read out."

"I see what you're saying," replied the interviewer. "But I'm a journalist, and that's why I need to ask some questions. Since asking forgiveness and reconciliation go hand in hand, and this month of June marks forty-four years since the disappearance of the priest Héctor Gallego, are you ready to work with the authorities, work with the family, to find an answer to this case?"

Héctor Gallego was a young Roman Catholic Colombian priest sent to Panama's Veraguas Province in the late 1960s. Gallego set up a system of successful cooperatives for poor subsistence farmers, riling a number of local landowners, including a cousin of Omar Torrijos's, Noriega's former boss. The landowners didn't like it that the impoverished farmers had found a way of bypassing their stores and bringing in less expensive goods and produce from elsewhere. One night, a group of men from the National Guard pulled Gallego from a simple hut he was sleeping in on the pretext that he was wanted for questioning. The priest was never seen again, and his body was never found.* Noriega was head of military intelligence at the time, working directly for Torrijos, who called Noriega "my gangster."

Noriega removed his glasses. "Any answer I give to the question that you ask," he said, raising his voice, the "you" now the informal "*tú*" rather than the formal "*usted*"—in the context of an interview in Spanish, a way of talking down to someone—"will mean that I get diverted from the solemnity in which I am asking forgiveness at the altar of my conscience."

"Would you like to go back to your family, go back home," asked the interviewer, changing the subject, "if the government granted you the possibility?" But Noriega wouldn't be drawn into that subject.

"I am a son of the Lord and my strength comes from God."

"Are you at peace with yourself?"

"Totally."

---

* In 1993, a Panamanian jury found three National Guard members guilty of participating in Héctor Gallego's murder. They were each sentenced to fifteen-year prison terms.

It was close to midnight. The girl, Arianne Bejarano, nineteen years old, had been to a party and was crossing a street in the city of San José, Costa Rica, on her way to the restaurant her family owned, where her mother was about to lock up. As she reached the far sidewalk, a male voice shouted from a passing car that the girl was beautiful and that she should go over and talk to him. Arianne strode on and took no notice. But the man in the car wouldn't give up. Arianne's mother appeared and the young woman was happy to get into the car with her, to escape the unwanted attention. But to no avail. Now safe in her mother's car, the man kept asking the girl to step out, that there was something he wanted to tell her. Arianne's mother told the man to stop, that enough was enough. But the man got out of his own vehicle and approached them, offering to take both of them dancing. He had a friend who was riding with him who would happily make up the numbers. He said that he at least wanted to buy Arianne a drink. He didn't drink himself, but he would like to buy her one. He would like to talk to her. Arianne was annoyed but she found it curious that the man had told her he didn't drink alcohol. By now Arianne's mother was getting angry. The man had made a mistake; the girl was her daughter and they had no intention of going out again that night. They owned a restaurant and had just closed for the evening.

The man wanted to know the name of the restaurant.

It was called the Cocina de Leña.

He said he would be there the very next day.

The man wished the women a good night and got back into his own car. He told his friend, there and then, that he would one day wed the pretty girl he had seen crossing the street. A mere three months later, in July 1981, he did just that. In the meantime, the man, Dr. Hugo Spadafora, then forty-one, divorced and with two children from his first marriage, took Arianne dancing and dined regularly at the Cocina de Leña. He sent her flowers, a box of classical music cassettes, and a copy of a book he had written, titled *Thoughts and Experiences of a Physician/Guerrilla Fighter*.

Hugo Spadafora came from a big, provincial Panamanian family with

Italian roots. His father, Carmelo, was a small-town politician with a reputation for probity in a country where holding political office was commonly perceived as a fast and inevitable route to corruption. Hugo Spadafora earned a medical degree at the University of Bologna, graduating in 1964. Returning from Europe to Panama by sea, he threw his passport off the deck rather than go through the indignity, as he saw it, of having to present it to US officials in the Canal Zone—an occupying force—before entering Panama proper.

With Cuba under the control of Fidel Castro and his revolutionaries, and the Cold War in full swing, Spadafora decided to take part in one of the revolutionary movements that were beginning to emerge in the developing world. The plight of Portugal's African colonies filled him with a particular passion. In his first guerrilla adventure, Spadafora joined a makeshift army of rebels fighting for the independence of Portuguese Guinea in West Africa. He amputated limbs and treated horrific burns, returning to Panama a minor celebrity, thanks to newspaper articles he penned on the experience. After National Guard officer Boris Martínez had staged his coup in 1968—and was Panama's short-lived strongman before being removed in turn by Omar Torrijos—Spadafora discreetly traveled to Chiriquí. He helped the rebels there by treating their injuries—these were the same insurgents with whom Peace Corps volunteers John and Susan Freivalds had been confused—and was captured. When he recited the Hippocratic Oath to his National Guard interrogators, they realized that they were dealing with someone a little out of the ordinary.

But this didn't alter the fact that Hugo Spadafora was in prison and his family was naturally worried. Carmelo, his father, wrote to Omar Torrijos in the middle of 1969 pleading for a solution. It was a bold move: Carmelo Spadafora had been a supporter of deposed president Arnulfo Arias, whose followers had rebelled in the Chiriquí highlands. Torrijos, curious, summoned Hugo Spadafora. The young physician explained to Torrijos something of his worldview. The strongman was exasperated, but he warmed to the idealist, too. Torrijos said that he knew just the place he would send him, somewhere he could forget about weapons and have plenty of sick people to heal. That place was Darién, a province of mountainous jungle in the far east of the country. The mainly indigenous population of Darién lacked medicines and doctors (they still do), partly because the place is so difficult to access. Malaria is endemic. The Pan-American Highway peters out in the middle of the province and the only way to get around was by dugout canoe or on horseback. Spadafora was at this time married to his first wife, María Elena, and they had a baby son. The young family went together to Darién, and Spadafora escaped a jail sentence. When the infant became seriously ill, Spadafora requested a transfer. Next came a posting at a hospital in San Miguelito, a wrong-side-of-the-tracks town that functioned as a dormitory suburb of Panama City. Crime was rife, much of it drug-related. With another principled physician, he set up a small private clinic there using part of his hospital salary to buy medicines. But the clinic was always in the red. It wasn't Spadafora's style to get overly concerned about the bottom line.

Spadafora frequently wrote opinion pieces for Panamanian newspapers. From time to time, Torrijos sought out his views on public health matters. Torrijos charmed and indulged the former Chiriquí rebel, helping him forget just how he, the general, had come to occupy the top seat at the table of soldiers who called the shots in Panama, with no free elections in sight. Somehow, Torrijos made Spadafora overlook the systematic graft at the heart of Torrijos's public works projects, financed by massive loans from overseas lenders. Spadafora, meanwhile, was almost as well known for his good looks as his adventurous, if improbable, career as a fighter and a healer.

One night in 1975, Spadafora and María Elena were at a party in a resort on the Pacific coast close to Panama City. The host was a good friend of Torrijos's and there was a rumor circulating that Spadafora was in line for a big promotion, a position in government. Spadafora and María Elena were dancing when a soldier approached him and laid a hand on his shoulder. The soldier had come with a message. Lieutenant Colonel Noriega, Torrijos's head of military intelligence, was asking—ordering, it seemed to Spadafora—the young medic to go over to his table. Spadafora told the soldier that, no, he wouldn't go over to speak with Lieutenant Colonel Noriega, as he, Hugo Spadafora, happened to be enjoying a dance with his wife. The soldier turned around and relayed the snub to his boss. Noriega, angry, quit the party soon afterward.

Torrijos offered Spadafora the post of deputy minister for health. It was quite a turnaround in his fortunes. People said that Torrijos was grooming Spadafora for even greater things. But the workings of the Health Ministry were a disappointment. The place was bloated with members of the National Guard; at best they were incompetent; at worst they were thieves. Spadafora threatened one particularly corrupt Guardsman with the sack. Removing a public official from his or her post was no easy matter in Panama. The file went to the minister, who asked for Torrijos's opinion. Torrijos swiftly rubber-stamped the decision. And so the Guardsman, who, coincidentally, was close to Lieutenant Colonel Noriega, was fired from his post. Noriega retaliated by passing on the message to Spadafora that one or another of his phones was being tapped.

Some of Spadafora's friends warned him about making an enemy of Noriega. But the animosity between the two men seemed to be something that no one—not even Torrijos—had the power to stop. At one meeting, with the general present, Spadafora accused Noriega of being a drug trafficker. He also said that Noriega found out people's secrets so as to blackmail them. Lieutenant Colonel Noriega was, for once, left speechless. No one had dared confront him before in this way. If Noriega's murky business activities were a red flag to the bull that was Hugo Spadafora, friends of the physician wondered about the initial cause of the animosity on Noriega's side. Tall, handsome, popular, Spadafora was everything that Noriega—short, pig-ugly, and socially awkward, and a failed lab assistant to boot—was not. In a country that practically ran on the fuel of rumor, many people also said that Noriega, though a married man with a young family, was bisexual. One medic friend suggested to Spadafora that Noriega might even be in love with him. But there is nothing to indicate that Hugo Spadafora dwelt on such matters. A new adventure was looming on the horizon. The physician was planning to go into guerrilla combat again.

When Manuel Antonio Noriega became de facto ruler of Panama in August 1983, the country was already the murkiest crossroads of the Americas, a place where illegal drugs were channeled to lucrative markets in North America and, gradually and in smaller part, in Europe. In return came the proceeds of drugs sales, piles of cash dollars, mainly twenty-dollar bills that ultimately grew to such great volumes that they needed weighing rather than counting. Noriega's fingers were in many Panamanian business pies, from selling Cuban cigars (he had the sole right to do so, a gift from Castro) to arms dealing and routing embargoed high-tech machinery and equipment from the United States to the Soviet Union. Shrimp from Cuba was repackaged to pass as the product of Panama, to beat the embargo. The sale of mandatory identity cards for the huge fleet of Panamanian-flag ships netted the military millions in profits. Noriega even had an interest in a firm that bought stolen jewelry and metal ornaments and melted them down for resale.

But it was the illegal drug trade, and specifically the clandestine export of cocaine from South America to lucrative markets in the United States, that would make Noriega an exceedingly wealthy man. By the early 1980s, Colombian drug traffickers from the cities of Medellín and Cali had come to dominate the production and trafficking of cocaine, displacing traffickers from Bolivia and Chile. Cocaine is a hugely addictive, euphoria-producing stimulant and, in a booming America, inhaling the drug appealed to sections of the population with cash to burn.* (It is more compact than marijuana, which is also grown in Central and South America, but which has a distinctive smell and is easier to detect.) The gangs of traffickers, criminal clans often termed "cartels," sent the cocaine north by sea and by air, stuffing packets of the white, crystalline powder in commercial shipments of flowers, coffee, furniture, and clothes—and even, on at least one occasion, a corpse—being sent to the United States for burial. They also used their own speedboats and light aircraft to get the cocaine to wholesale markets in the United States, using islands of the eastern Caribbean, such as Jamaica, Haiti, and the Bahamas, as staging posts on the way to Florida. It was a cat-and-mouse game that pitted the US Coast Guard and the Drug Enforcement Administration, or DEA, against pilots flying propeller planes as close to the sea as they dared, to

---

* Although the really big profits were to be made in North America (and Western Europe), Colombia's cartels also targeted urban areas in South and Central America, fueling the appetite for illegal drugs that Hugo Spadafora saw in the slums of San Miguelito.

better escape detection, and men driving fast cigar speedboats as far as the fuel in their tanks would carry them.

But the Coast Guard and the DEA managed to tighten the screw on the traffickers with more effective patrolling of the sea and air approaches to south Florida. The traffickers responded by opening up a new route— or rather, a range of new routes—via Central America and Mexico, and from there across Mexico's largely porous, 1,950-mile land border with the United States.* The indented, island-specked coastlines of the countries in the region offered boundless possibilities, nowhere more so than Panama. And Panama still does, in fact: in the absence of a highway link across the Darién, cocaine is loaded onto cigar boats or light aircraft and makes its way from Colombia to drop points on Panama's Pacific or Caribbean coast or to remote landing strips in the jungle. Much of this cocaine is trucked north into Costa Rica on the next stage of its journey to the United States.

Bocas del Toro is one such entry point. In Bocas, islanders hear the hum of a small plane in the dead of night and know the score. Waterproof packages of vacuum-packed cocaine fall from the sky and are quickly picked up by associates in the lagoon. Inevitably, some drops are botched and product washing up at dawn on a beach will likely enter the cut-price retail market for cocaine in Bocas Town, where gringos are the prime customers. Even those packages that are picked up as arranged will likely "lose" a percentage as a payment to the associates, bringing yet more cocaine to addicts living in the archipelago.

The prostitution, public works, and smuggling rackets that had traditionally lined the pockets of officers of the National Guard were the precursors of a deep involvement in the cocaine trade, with Noriega calling the shots. The United States opened an antidrug office in Panama in 1972, a year before the DEA was set up. The American antidrug agents had their work cut out for them: by then, contraband of all types was rife in Panama, much of it passing through a massive free-trade zone in the unruly city of Colón, at the Caribbean end of the canal. As soon as the 1968 coup

---

* The DEA estimates that 90 percent of the cocaine shipped to the United States now passes through the Central America–Mexico corridor.

was launched, much of the National Guard top brass looked enviously at how portions of the country's upper-class elites—unscrupulous financiers, lawyers, and businessmen—had enriched themselves by facilitating criminal activity, and these Guardsmen wanted a share of the action. They weren't clamoring for pay raises; rather, they wanted to be in a position to extract bribes and make shakedowns. It was logical that giving a helping hand to the Colombian drug barons would happen one day.

In 1979, a representative of the Medellín cartel met with Torrijos and Noriega to negotiate a deal whereby the Panamanians would ensure protection for drug transshipments. But the deal didn't materialize, as the Colombians balked at Torrijos and Noriega's demand of $100,000 per shipment. Within a couple of years, however, Noriega was facilitating money laundering for Colombian drug traffickers and overseeing some drug running of his own with a small group of pilots whom he trusted. (Noriega had access to cocaine: when drug dealers were apprehended in Panama, their product was usually "recycled," entering the drug trade again, only with a different dealer.)

In February 1988, one of these pilots, Floyd Carlton, looking sinister in a black hood to shield his face, testified before the US Senate Subcommittee on Terrorism, Narcotics, and International Operations, chaired by Senator John Kerry. Carlton revealed that he met Medellín cartel chief Pablo Escobar on two occasions on behalf of his boss, Manuel Noriega— Tony Noriega to those who knew him well. After a period of haggling, the Colombians agreed to Noriega's demand of $700,000 for allowing four planes loaded with cocaine to transit through Panama. By this time, Noriega was the official tasked by Torrijos to liaise with US antidrug agents, a role that gave the ambitious lieutenant colonel access to drug intelligence. It proved to be just the start: an arrangement with Escobar, who trusted Noriega about as far as he could throw him, led to the Colombian drug chief and his entourage being given refuge in Panama, at a high price, of course (indeed, a son of Escobar's was said to have been educated in the country).

Manuel Noriega's coffers swelled with income from the drug trade, by the mid-1980s netting him and his underlings around $10 million a month according to some estimates—the only person who knows exactly how much is the elderly man who gave the evasive television interview in the room at El Renacer prison. By this time Noriega had renamed the National Guard the Panamanian Defense Forces, or PDF. A large chunk of the profits from drug deals was distributed in briefcases that were flown by PDF men around the country. The idea was that people Noriega trusted would receive the briefcases for safekeeping.

"Some people here made a lot of money," said a man who worked as Noriega's bodyguard for a number of months in 1988 and early 1989, before settling in Bocas del Toro. The man saw Noriega oversee the stuffing of countless briefcases with US currency. These were then dispatched around the country. "And when it all collapsed, they were left with the cash that Noriega had sent them to look after. Some of them have lived off it ever since."

The cause that initially wrested Hugo Spadafora away from his first wife and two young children was the Sandinista insurgency in Nicaragua against dictator Anastasio Somoza. In mid-1978 Spadafora, tiring of his bureaucratic life as deputy minister for health, assembled a force of some three hundred volunteer fighters. This was Panama's contribution to the struggle to topple the despotic Somoza, and Spadafora left to lead it with the blessing of his boss, Omar Torrijos. While the idealist adventurer Spadafora was risking his life in Nicaragua, Noriega was cynically fueling the conflict by supplying, or helping to supply, arms to both the Sandinistas and Somoza's forces. The capture or elimination of the celebrated Hugo Spadafora would naturally be a big prize for the Somoza regime. One day, Somoza brandished Spadafora's driver's license as evidence he had been killed. But it turned out that there had been a skirmish and Spadafora had had the small misfortune of leaving his wallet behind.

The conflict soon turned against Somoza's men. In July 1979, Somoza fled Managua, Nicaragua's capital city (he was subsequently assassinated in exile in Paraguay). But Spadafora became disillusioned by the way that the new Sandinista government fell fully under Fidel Castro's influence, with the Cuban leader outwitting Torrijos and other regional leaders who wanted their share of clout in Nicaragua. Never a Panamanian version of the bearded Argentinian revolutionary Ernesto "Che" Guevara, Hugo Spadafora evolved from a left-leaning freedom fighter to becoming something approaching a social democrat, according to Amir Valle, his biographer. He joined the resistance to the Sandinistas in the south, where the indigenous Miskitos were engaged in an unequal battle against the new regime in Managua. The most convenient base for the guerrilla medic was in San José, capital of Costa Rica. This was where he spied out of his car window Arianne Bejarano crossing the street. And it was in Nicaragua and Costa Rica that Hugo Spadafora came into contact with the Panamanian airmen carrying arms around Central America and involved in the smuggling of drugs, notably cocaine, into the United States. Spadafora was refined and charming, but he was a man's man, too. The pilots, some of them talkative by nature, all bored when they were not in the air, occasionally gave away information to the inquisitive medic about their operations. One of these pilots was Floyd Carlton, who, several years later in American custody, was a key witness at Senator John Kerry's subcommittee hearings. Spadafora started to log the pilots' movements, flight numbers, and where they were flying from and to. In short, he discovered Noriega's spiderweb of criminal operations.

By the middle of 1985, Hugo Spadafora's dossier on Tony Noriega was nearing completion. The medic used the Panamanian media, beleaguered and subject to a great deal of self-censorship for fear of retaliation from Noriega's thugs, to start his campaign. His most daring article appeared in *La Prensa* on August 10, 1985, an opinion piece titled "The Machiavellian Tuberculosis of Noriega." Earlier, the plug had suddenly been pulled on a radio interview, leaving listeners nothing but the sound of static, when Spadafora launched into a tirade against the strongman. He told acquaintances in Costa Rica that they should prepare themselves for a figurative bomb to explode. His friends worried for him. He was putting himself in grave danger. Surely Noriega would be out to get him? No, said Spadafora: the point was that it was precisely the gravity of the accusations that he made about Manuel Noriega that ensured that Noriega wouldn't have him killed. If he did, it would be clear to everyone that he was behind it. Attack was, in Spadafora's mind, the best form of defense.

Spadafora returned regularly to Panama from his home in Costa Rica. He had a large and affectionate family and, above all, his two children from his first marriage lived there. But even before his campaign against Noriega started in earnest, he was discreet in his movements, preferring not to fly direct from San José to Panama City, as he knew he would be harassed by PDF men on arrival.

On September 13, 1985, a Friday, at the age of forty-five, Hugo Spadafora kissed Arianne Bejarano good-bye and took a small plane to an airfield in the far south of Costa Rica, then a taxi to Paso Canoas, a rough town straddling the Costa Rica–Panama border. The plan was that Arianne Bejarano would fly directly to Panama City the following day. Spadafora chatted amiably with the taxi driver as the car sped through the Costa Rican backcountry, green and moist in the last weeks of the rainy season. At Paso Canoas, he had a simple lunch of rabbit stew and rice, and then walked across the line to Panama and got on a bus to David. The bus took the wide Pan-American Highway out of Paso Canoas, and shortly afterward slowed down at the first of several PDF checkpoints. A PDF man nicknamed Bruce Lee was also riding the bus that day. Lee, who had earned his nickname for his interest in martial arts and his reputation for violence, told Spadafora to step off the bus. After a few minutes of questioning, Spadafora and Lee got back onto the vehicle. At a second checkpoint Lee told Spadafora to step off again. This time, he wasn't permitted to get back on. At about one p.m. that day, Hugo Spadafora was escorted to the barracks in the town of Concepción. The best guess is that he was interrogated and tortured there. Worse was to come.

A group of PDF men took him to the shore. Myriad rutted tracks led through dense banana plantations to the warm, blue waves of the Pacific Ocean, lapping beaches narrow like pursed lips. It was mid-afternoon. Major Luis Córdoba, who controlled Chiriquí Province, and who was the highest-ranking officer present, spoke on an open satellite line to Paris. At the other end of the line was Manuel Noriega.

Córdoba: *We have the rabid dog.*

Noriega: *And what does one do with a dog that has rabies?*

Noriega, the former lab assistant, knew. And so did Córdoba. Dogs suspected of rabies have their heads cut off, so as to be able to run checks on their brain tissue.

First, though, they jabbed sharp objects under his fingernails and beat him in the groin. They stripped him of his clothes, made symmetrical cuts on the inside of each leg, knocking out his thigh muscles. An autopsy found that an object or objects had been rammed up his rectum. He was likely still alive when the military party left the isolated beach and arrived at a PDF building at a settlement named Corozo, in remote bush under a mile from Costa Rica. That was where Noriega's instruction was carried out, most likely with a butcher's knife. Spadafora's headless body was put in a US Mail bag and driven to Costa Rica. The body was dumped a few hundred yards over the border. The head was taken elsewhere and never found. The PDF men opened some booze and had a party at Corozo. Noriega, meanwhile, flew from Paris to Switzerland for a consultation with his dermatologist, who prescribed creams for his acne.

Colonel Roberto Díaz Herrera is a polite, soft-spoken man in his late seventies. We are sitting at a table in a windowless café of a five-star hotel in central Panama City. The colonel is wearing an informal shirt hanging loose over his pants. He isn't wearing socks. Every so often, men and women of a similar age greet him warmly, one or two with a marked deference. Each time, the colonel looks up and smiles, the kind of smile that seems to say how pleased he is to see them. But Díaz Herrera wasn't always known for his perfect manners. In the early 1980s he was Noriega's deputy. In the PDF's gentleman's agreement on succession to the top job, Díaz Herrera, a first cousin of Omar Torrijos's, was due to have a turn heading the military junta after Noriega stepped down. But that's not the way it turned out. There was no chance Tony Noriega was going to let go of the lucrative reins of power of his own accord.

In June 1987, when Díaz Herrera turned fifty, Noriega forcibly retired his potential rival. Shortly afterward, a couple of journalists paid the colonel a visit. The journalists were used to military men being either tight-lipped or spouting platitudes, and when they heard out Díaz Herrera that day, things were no different. But after the journalists left, the colonel had a change of heart. He called the paper. The journalists should come back, he said. Colonel Roberto Díaz Herrera was ready to talk again. This time it would be different.

Noriega had been behind the plane crash that had taken the life of Omar Torrijos, said Díaz Herrera. He had planted a bomb on the plane. Noriega, too, had ordered the murder of Hugo Spadafora.* Elections for the puppet post of president had been rigged.† He described the PDF as a massive racket where all the top military men were involved in one scam or another. With the possible exception of Torrijos's death in the plane crash, these were charges that many, if not most, Panamanians had long suspected to be true. Indeed, in June of the previous year the *New York Times* had run a story penned by Seymour Hersh alleging that Noriega was involved in money laundering and drug smuggling, and was implicated in Hugo Spadafora's murder, citing unnamed sources in the State Department, White House, and Pentagon. But it was remarkable that here was someone who had, until a few days before, been at the very heart of the regime confirming much of Hersh's allegations. (Díaz Herrera didn't speak of Noriega's drug deals and claims to this day that he didn't know about them; he also didn't criticize his cousin Omar Torrijos directly.) Meanwhile, the colonel revealed that his own scam had been to charge fat fees to Cubans and others for issuing Panamanian passports—hence the large, comfortable home in which he was delivering his bombshell.

Within hours, Díaz Herrera's mansion became the focal point for Panama's opposition. Visitors came and went. Díaz Herrera kept on

---

* In 1993, Manuel Antonio Noriega (in absentia) and two other PDF men were found guilty of involvement in the murder of Dr. Hugo Spadafora.

† One often-repeated story concerns Jimmy Lakas, Torrijos's first puppet president. In the mid-1980s, when he had retired from the government, an elderly lady got into an elevator with Lakas and a number of other people. Barely able to control her anger, the lady accused Lakas of stealing $10 million from the Panamanian people. Lakas denied it, smiling at the lady and informing her that he had, in fact, stolen $20 million.

talking. Housewives in Panama City banged saucepans on their balconies, Latin America's traditional urban demonstration of disgust. On the streets, the colonel's allegations against Noriega and the military junta sparked demonstrations that were put down with casual ruthlessness. The regime declared a state of emergency. But the damage to its reputation had already been done. The images of violence perpetrated by Panama's military were broadcast around the world, just as news of Díaz Herrera's outburst had been reported in newspapers in many countries. But the easy living of Panama's elite, and the perception that most of the country's upper class was not resolute in their opposition to Noriega and the iron fist of the PDF, informed some correspondents' reports. The protests of the capital's rich residents were sometimes satirized by foreign journalists who saw white handkerchiefs dangling from darkly tinted windows of expensive sedans. Some members of Panama's upper class even sent their maids to the demonstrations.

With Díaz Herrera's residence surrounded by Noriega's forces, there was an uneasy standoff that lasted a month. He became a prisoner in the home built on the proceeds of the passport kickback scheme. When the inevitable happened, and the house was stormed by Noriega's men, Díaz Herrera was thrown in jail. He was lucky: after six months he was released and exiled to Venezuela, the home country of his second wife. He lived quietly in Caracas and in 1988 wrote a book titled *Panamá: Mucho más que Noriega* (Panama: a lot more than Noriega). The title the colonel gave to his book was still decidedly optimistic.

"I never had the intention of becoming a soldier," said Díaz Herrera. "I came from a family of teachers. I liked reading and writing." Díaz Herrera had a poem published in a local newspaper in his hometown in rural Panama when he was thirteen. A couple of years later, he wrote to presidents and ambassadors around Latin America looking for a scholarship. He had eight brothers and sisters and money was tight. When an offer came from Lima, Peru, he was greatly surprised. It was for a place at Lima's Leoncio Prado Military Academy, an institution whose systematic and cynical cruelties were memorably described in Mario Vargas Llosa's novel *The Time of the Hero*. Tony Noriega was studying in Lima at the same time, at the Chorrillos Military Academy, and the fact they were both Panamanian and had acquaintances in common meant the paths of the two young men occasionally crossed.

"I saw him in the street from time to time," said Díaz Herrera. "He was quiet and isolated, kind of closed in his shell. He didn't want to communicate. He didn't show any emotions."

Back in Panama under Omar Torrijos, the two men climbed up the same greasy pole to become National Guard top brass. But whatever Noriega had, he was never satisfied; he always needed more.

"I had a secretary once who had to go and see Noriega. When she came back, she told me that Noriega had said to her, 'Change sides. You're better off with me.'" On another occasion, Díaz Herrera got an invitation from Tony Noriega to go to a small party he was throwing at a borrowed house with a swimming pool. Noriega told Díaz Herrera not to forget his swimming trunks and asked if he was planning to bring anyone. Díaz Herrera turned up for the party with a blond lady whom Noriega then pursued openly and forcefully, even though he had a female companion of his own sunning herself by the pool that day.

Many years later, Díaz Herrera met a former instructor of Noriega's from the Chorrillos Military Academy. He asked the instructor about Noriega. What was he like? "And this man told me, 'When I observed this *zambo*, I realized that he was made for spying. I felt he was bitter about life. A man not satisfied with himself. So a perfect spy, because in spying you have to be ready to do anything, absolutely anything.'"

Our conversation has taken us through the ups, and some downs, of Díaz Herrera's career. But we keep coming back to the subject of Tony Noriega in spite of the fact that Panama is, as the colonel had claimed, a lot more than him.

"I observed in him a rejection of his body," said Díaz Herrera. "I was short, too, but I didn't let it bother me, even though you can imagine how much I was teased at Leoncio Prado."

The light in the café shines a harsh white. The AC is on to the max. It's a bit chilly. I'm wondering if the colonel is regretting not putting socks on.

There is a pause, then Díaz Herrera talks about the Spadafora case and other disappearances carried out by PDF death squads, including that of a seventeen-year-old girl named Rita Wald, who had become involved in the Panamanian student opposition. Rita Wald was abducted in 1977 and her body, like Hugo Spadafora's head, was never found.

"There is a code of silence. They won't say where the remains are. For instance, they could tell a priest as part of their confession."

Noriega was—is—short and unattractive. Díaz Herrera is five foot four; Noriega is just an inch taller. Tony Noriega was ridiculed for his appearance even as he amassed power. He was the *Cara de Piña*, the "Pineapple Face." Spadafora was well built and handsome. He was a real soldier, too.

"Yes, Spadafora's physical presence would have been an additional factor." To the colonel, the fate that befell Hugo Spadafora is unfathomable. "The head . . . Why cut the head off?"

One day at home in Caracas in exile, the phone rang. Díaz Herrera picked it up. There was a familiar voice at the other end of the line spouting abuse and threats. The colonel put the receiver down. His wife asked him who it was. "Noriega," he replied. Díaz Herrera never heard from his old boss again.

The murder of Hugo Spadafora and Díaz Herrera's allegations put intense pressure on the relationship between the United States and Panama. Apart from a break during the Carter presidency, Manuel Noriega had long been on the payroll of the Central Intelligence Agency (when Ronald Reagan took office with George H. W. Bush as vice president, Noriega's fees were around $200,000 a year). Noriega supplied the CIA with intelligence on Communist Cuba, among other places. His paymasters made the calculation that the usefulness of the information traveling north outweighed the value of the intelligence headed south to Fidel Castro, who was also paying Noriega to spy. Crucially, between 1982 and 1984, when the US Congress passed legislation—the Boland amendments—outlawing assistance to the Contras in Nicaragua, who were waging war against the Sandinista government, US support for the Contras went ahead anyway. But it couldn't have done so without Noriega's efforts to help train Contra fighters in Panama and fly arms covertly to the Nicaraguan rebels.

The empty planes that returned to the United States after dropping off the arms weren't, in fact, empty: Noriega's men stashed packages of cocaine in them. The Americans discovered the ruse, but Noriega was confident he would not easily be exposed. After all, if it was known that he was flying illegal drugs into America, it would also become known what the airplanes and pilots had been hired for in the first place.

And then there was the US Drug Enforcement Administration. Paradoxically, Noriega received letters of commendation from DEA bigwigs. His men regularly paraded drug smugglers before the cameras and were generous with the tip-offs they passed on to DEA operatives. Noriega, in short, knew how to make the DEA look good. In return, Manuel Noriega used the DEA as a kind of sheriff-on-demand, turning over amateur traffickers and professional rivals who had not paid him and his men protection money. He extradited felons to the United States without delay and gave timely permission for the US authorities to board suspicious Panamanian-flag vessels in international waters.

Notwithstanding Noriega's cheerleaders at the CIA and the DEA— and in both agencies he had his detractors, too—Noriega was considered by many a vulgar irritant. To George H. W. Bush on the 1988 campaign trail, Manuel Noriega was a thorn in his side. The word from Bush's campaign team was that candidate Bush didn't recall having met Noriega, until photos of the two men together surfaced to jog a memory or two. Earlier, chasing the Republican Party nomination, Senator Robert Dole of Kansas had challenged Vice President George Bush to explain the "mixed messages" that had long been sent to Noriega. A sample bumper sticker from that period: BUSH/NORIEGA '88—THE CRACK TEAM.

By the first months of 1989, and with President Bush now installed in the White House, brute force meant Noriega's hold over Panama and its people looked stronger than ever. To flank the actions of the PDF and intimidate Panamanians brave enough to demonstrate against him, Noriega set up the so-called Dignity Battalions. These were groups of convicts on early release from jail, aggressive and barely employable youths from the slums, and off-duty policemen. They broke up public meetings not sanctioned by the dictatorship with blows from truncheons and steel rods. Meanwhile, the country was on the verge of collapse: while Noriega and his cronies were squirreling away hundreds of thousands of dollars in overseas bank accounts, the sewer system was failing and diarrhea was rampant. On top of that, there was little street lighting and many traffic lights had stopped working. Teachers and hospital workers received their paychecks only sporadically. Many ordinary Panamanians had, understandably, given up hoping for change.

In May, Panama's electoral tribunal, a body stuffed with Noriega supporters, annulled the result of an election to the post of president of the republic, claiming interference from election observers from overseas. Since the coup two decades earlier, Panama had had a string of puppet presidents that took orders from the military men at the top. The fact that the population voted overwhelmingly for alternative candidates mattered little when soldiers could go from polling station to polling station and vote for the dictator's choice as often as they wished. Former US president Jimmy Carter, one of the overseas observers, publicly declared what every Panamanian knew to be the truth: the vote had been rigged. In Washington, D.C., the House of Representatives unanimously passed a resolution condemning Noriega's actions. Guillermo Endara, the opposition presidential candidate, and his supporters took to the streets of downtown Panama City to protest the rigged vote. The Dignity Battalions were sent in and Endara and dozens of others received a beating. To draw attention to his plight, the portly Endara put a hospital bed in a store window, climbed inside, and went on a hunger strike with a uniformed nurse and the Panamanian flag for company. In July, US forces in the Canal Zone started a series of noisy military exercises that seemed to be designed to remind the PDF where the real power lay, and that Noriega was vulnerable.

The beginning of the end for Noriega came on December 16, 1989, when shots were fired at a private car in which four US soldiers were traveling. The soldiers had been stopped at a roadblock on their way to dinner in downtown Panama City. Their car was surrounded by a crowd of men from the Dignity Battalions and the PDF. The American soldiers decided to flee the scene but, as they sped away, their vehicle was sprayed with bullets. One of the bullets fatally wounded Marine first lieutenant

Robert Paz, one of the American soldiers riding in the car. An American naval officer and his American girlfriend were witnesses to the shooting; the officer was given a severe beating by the PDF men, and his girlfriend was groped and threatened. It appears to be the brutality of Noriega's forces on unarmed young Americans that night that made up President George Bush's mind.

President Bush had something else to consider: some three months before the incident at the roadblock, the United States had failed to give its full support to a coup attempt against Noriega led by Major Moisés Giroldi. A popular and charismatic officer, Giroldi, thirty-eight years old, apparently feared for the future of Panama if Noriega remained in power for much longer. He also reckoned that Noriega knew the game was up, since it was well known within the PDF that Noriega was plagued with depression and panic attacks. Through his wife, Giroldi opened secret discussions with the US authorities in the Canal Zone. At first, Giroldi's coup went well: when Noriega arrived at the PDF headquarters on October 3, 1989, he fell straight into Giroldi's trap and soon realized that the plotters controlled the building. Giroldi's intention had not been to kill Noriega; rather, he wanted him to surrender to the Americans. The United States, meanwhile, blocked two access routes to the PDF headquarters but did not block a third. The forces that liberated Manuel Noriega that day, the so-called Machos del Monte (the Strongmen of the Mountains), stationed at the Río Hato military base northwest of Panama City, took this third route. (Other mistakes: Giroldi's plotters had no reliable radio communications with the Americans in the Canal Zone; Giroldi also failed to call for Panamanians to take to the streets in an unambiguous call for democracy.)

But still Giroldi had time to alter the course of history. Pointing a gun at Noriega, Giroldi called on him to surrender. He tried to reason with Noriega. The country would be better off without him. But Giroldi didn't pull the trigger. Noriega—a witness at Giroldi's church wedding and godfather to one of his children—taunted the younger man. Noriega said, in effect, that Giroldi didn't have the balls to kill him. When the contingent of Machos del Monte arrived and overpowered the plotters, there were no

American soldiers to rescue them. Giroldi paid for his vacillation with his life. In all, Noriega ordered the execution of seventy or more PDF soldiers after the attempted coup.

US support of Giroldi had appeared halfhearted, but President Bush acted according to the statute book, since Executive Order 12333, signed by President Ronald Reagan, was crystal clear: "No person employed by or acting on behalf of the United States Government shall engage in, or conspire to engage in, assassination." The fate of Giroldi and his fellow rebels in their small country in Central America soon faded into the background. In November 1989, all eyes were on the tumultuous changes in Eastern Europe and in particular in Berlin, where "people power" had helped tumble the hated wall. In the republic of Panama, it would take a fully fledged US invasion to remove Noriega and the PDF.

The act that set the wheels of justice in motion was called Operation Just Cause. When the United States attack on the PDF started in the early hours of December 20, 1989, Manuel Noriega was entertaining a prostitute at a club used by PDF officers close to the Panama City international airport. American troops quickly took out the PDF headquarters, a city-center airfield, and various garrisons. Fires raged in the poor, strongly anti-Noriega neighborhood of El Chorrillo near the PDF headquarters, claiming many victims. For three or four days, said a Panama City resident, there was "no God and no law." Twenty-four troops had been lost on the American side, with fifty PDF soldiers dead, according to US estimates. Some three hundred Panamanian civilians had been killed in the fighting and in the fires. (The number of Panamanian victims is still disputed, and some sources place the figure much higher.) Now nobody was safe in their homes. Looting was widespread ("only bookstores were left alone," said the same resident). And Manuel Noriega was on the run.

US Navy SEALs were tasked with hunting down the dictator. Even in peacetime, this wasn't easy. Noriega switched residences regularly, sometimes in the middle of the night. Just to confuse things, another man of Noriega's build—his "double"—made decoy trips around the capital. But now there were enemy choppers in the skies and twenty-five thousand US troops on the ground, preventing his entry into the Cuban embassy, for instance. Plus a $1 million reward had been slapped on Noriega's head.

Tired and running out of options, Noriega made contact with José Sebastián Laboa, the head of the nunciature, the Vatican embassy. Laboa, who was known as the nuncio, felt he had little choice but to let him stay at the nunciature, traditionally a place of refuge for all. The nuncio sent a priest to pick up Noriega from the parking lot of a Dairy Queen fast-food restaurant in downtown Panama City—the agreed rendezvous point. It was December 24.

Frustrated that Noriega had eluded them, US forces put pressure on the Vatican to have Noriega handed over. Laboa, too, wanted Noriega to turn himself over to the Americans, just as a number of other PDF top brass, who had briefly sought refuge in the nunciature,* had already done. The US forces decided to try to blast out their onetime informer. Rock songs were played at high volume yards from Noriega's room: "Another One Bites the Dust," "Born in the U.S.A.," and "I Fought the Law (and the Law Won)." A machine gun was trained permanently on Noriega's window from the building next door. If he looked out he could see it. And on December 25, Noriega got an idea of the fate that might await him if his fellow Panamanians got to him before the Americans did. Romania's loathed dictator Nicolae Ceauşescu and his equally loathed wife, Elena, had been court-martialed and summarily executed after trying to flee from their angry countrymen. Noriega spent a lot of time watching television in his room. The images of the lifeless bodies of the Ceauşescus slumped on frosty ground in faraway Romania had been broadcast around the world. Meanwhile, outside the gates, crowds were shouting abuse at Noriega. Some demonstrators were brandishing pineapples, referencing the old "Pineapple Face" gibe, but this was no joke. With his own wry humor, the nuncio asked Noriega how much longer he could stand the company of the nuns serving at the nunciature. Laboa told Noriega that he wouldn't throw him out of the building, but that his best option would be to defend himself in an American court. Watching it all was Enrique Jelenszky, twenty-four years old, a lawyer helping out at

---

* Before starting his hunger strike, Guillermo Endara had also taken refuge from the Dignity Battalions in the nunciature. Coincidentally, when Noriega took refuge in the nunciature in a bid to evade American forces, he was assigned the same bed that Endara had slept in six months earlier.

the nunciature, who found himself conveying messages between the nuncio and the American troops outside his door.

"It was surreal," said Jelenszky. "I remember watching a live CNN broadcast with the nunciature as the backdrop and there I was sitting inside the same building. . . . Noriega was lost in his thoughts in those days. He was sad and appeared as if he had . . . shrunk. That's the word that comes to mind."

Jelenszky spoke to Noriega from time to time. "I talked with him out of compassion, not curiosity," said Jelenszky. Noriega talked about philosophy, religion, world politics. The young man listened and then got up and carried on with his chores.

One day—Jelenszky thinks it was the twenty-sixth of December—the young lawyer walked past Noriega's bedroom. As ever, Manuel Noriega was watching television. The image on the screen was of children skating happily at the rink at Rockefeller Center in New York City. Outside, as at all times, an American soldier had a machine gun trained on his window. Guillermo Endara had been sworn in as the new president of Panama. Noriega had lost power and he would never get it back.

"I asked him if his days were long," recalled Jelenszky. Noriega gestured at the TV set with the images of the smiling children and their parents skating in Manhattan, and then at a Bible. The young man encouraged the older man to find a good side in all of it. You can always find a good side, whatever the situation. Noriega heard Jelenszky out and his gaze returned to the television screen. He looked up at Jelenszky again.

"Noriega then said, 'Life goes on. We are just molecules.'"

Noriega walked out of the nunciature on January 3, 1990, and surrendered to US forces. He was bundled into a waiting helicopter. His next place of residence was a jail cell in Miami, Florida. After a lengthy trial in the same city, he was convicted on eight counts of drug smuggling, money laundering, and racketeering and sentenced to forty years in prison, reduced to thirty years on appeal. While Noriega waited for the days to pass in his bare, air-conditioned American prison cell, the wheels of justice were turning elsewhere. In September 1993 Noriega was tried in absentia for the murder of Dr. Hugo Spadafora. He was convicted and sentenced to twenty years in prison. Subsequently, in March 1994 Noriega was found guilty, again in absentia, of the murder of Major Moisés Giroldi, and was sentenced to another twenty years in prison. In 1999, a Paris court also found him guilty of money laundering. France requested his extradition, a remarkable turnaround for the country that a decade and a half earlier had awarded him the Légion d'honneur. Noriega fought the extradition, but lost, and was sent to jail in Paris, once his favorite European capital city, in April 2010. Finally, Manuel Antonio Noriega's journey ended where it had started. On December 11, 2011, Noriega was extradited to Panama from France, a convicted murderer, another jail cell awaiting him.

The untangling of Noriega's financial affairs was a huge challenge for President Guillermo Endara's administration. Hundreds of millions of dollars in overseas bank accounts were traced. But the families of PDF men who had amassed riches during the dictatorship stayed wealthy, and the recipients of the briefcases stuffed with cash for safekeeping had a happy windfall when a defeated Noriega was flown out of Panama on an American jet. One Panamanian opposition leader quipped that the Americans had taken away Ali Baba but left the forty thieves.

It was marginally easier to make an inventory of Noriega's real estate. He owned two plots in Bocas del Toro, including a discreet, one-story house on land adjacent to an outpost of the Smithsonian Tropical Research Institute in Big Creek, near Bocas Town. His main home in Panama City was the hacienda-style residence in the Altos del Golf section; there was also a bunkered mansion on a forty-five-acre plot in Playa Blanca, near the Río Hato PDF base (the one that used to belong to the US Air Force); another house in Panama's Azuero Peninsula used as a location for parties and equipped with cameras for covert filming and subsequent blackmailing; a villa in Spain; a château in the French countryside; an apartment in central Paris; and more homes in the Dominican Republic, Israel, and Venezuela. Noriega also owned various stores and had a major interest in a hotel chain. In Potrerillos, near Boquete, Noriega owned a country residence, later bought by an American couple. The couple found that the house needed some work. "It was like Austin Powers gone bad," said the American woman owner, "everything was so gaudy." In the garden stood Noriega's Japanese-style outbuilding, a place for barbecues in the form of a pagoda. "This was a party place, a kind of sex orgy house," said the American woman matter-of-factly. Inside, the ceilings were made of paneled wood; a carved staircase was a work of art of sorts. It is said the cool marble floor was a gift from Fidel Castro. The walls were twice as thick as those of most homes. From the garden there was a narrow, distant view of the Pacific Ocean.

With Noriega long gone, there was still "a lot of evil" in the house, the woman said: unexplained noises when nobody else was around; her cat, pressed low to the floor, hairs standing on end, for no obvious reason. A shaman came to help. "There was a bad vibe and it took a while to go."

Noriega owned yet another property, this one also in Potrerillos, used exclusively for voodoo rites (the building is now part of a school). The American woman pointed out a gap in a wall near the carved staircase. It's where the safe used to be. For many years, Noriega employed a housekeeper here, who looked after the place when he wasn't around, cleaning up after the dictator and his cronies. When Noriega was sent off to America, the housekeeper took his chance. He dynamited the safe and blew the door off. The cash and valuables that were inside, rumored to be significant, were now his.

6. Where Is Cher?

Cher Hughes and Keith Werle's wedding was a day to remember. The guests came from far and wide: friends of the couple from Florida, Hughes's family and close friends from Missouri, Werle's buddies from the film world in California, and expats and Panamanians. They gathered on the western tip of Solarte Island, a mile from Bocas Town, at a place known as Hospital Point. The service was held on a grassy clearing in the jungle perched on a low bluff where, in 1899, the United Fruit Company had built a hospital to treat its workers. In the early twentieth century, yellow fever and malaria were the two big scourges. The facility closed its doors two decades after it opened and Solarte Island became a backwater—in fact, a backwater of a bigger backwater—until the expats and the tourists came in the 1990s.

In the middle of the clearing in the jungle, Hughes and Werle made their vows. Hughes, white petals in her long blond hair, her veil swept back over the straps of her wedding dress, was beaming. It had taken an age to iron out the creases in her silk dress. But it was worth it. She looked, said her sister, Diana Motlik, who had flown in from St. Louis, Missouri, "absolutely gorgeous." Werle, the groom, wore a dark linen suit. He stood straight-backed, clean-shaven. Hughes's father, Walter Hodecker, was not able to travel and so it fell to a man named Mike Cooney, a close family friend, also from Missouri, to give the bride away. Both Hughes and Werle had been married before, but few doubted this was a love match.

Hughes had gotten dresses in pastel shades sewn for around a half-dozen little girls who lived on Carenero Island, where she ran her rental property, the Casa del Sapo. These were some of the local children she regularly invited for movies and popcorn. Hughes was childless but loved kids. The wedding ceremony over, the little girls got into a boat and sang songs they had rehearsed. The boat carrying the girls pulled away from shore past clumps of mangroves, their roots bent this way and that like arthritic fingers. The sun was now setting. "You could hear the voices of the little girls even when they were a long way off," said Motlik.

A short while later the adults followed the singing children from Solarte Island across Bocas Lagoon to Carenero Island. Bocas' own Ken and Barbie had tied the knot. A barman was getting the drinks ready. Tables and chairs were set out at the water's edge. Guests were thinking through the amusing toasts they were about to deliver. It was almost time to party.

Cher Hughes first heard about Bocas del Toro from friends while she was living in St. Petersburg, Florida. When Hughes and Keith Werle made their first trip to Bocas in 2000, the couple were blown away by the place: the beauty of the islands, the climate, and the smiles of the Panamanians. They wanted to make a fresh start, and Bocas was just what they were looking for. In 2002, Hughes, in the year she would turn forty-five, sold her thriving electric sign business and took her nest egg to Panama. Hughes wanted more time to unwind, but this was not going to be a full-blown retirement; that wasn't really her style. Hughes bought land on Carenero Island and elsewhere in the archipelago, including a tiny tadpole-shaped island just off Darklands. On Carenero, the couple built and operated a property with rental units they called the Casa del Sapo. The property was two separate houses, one on the water and the other just behind the footpath that ran along the shore on the leeward side of the island. Keith Werle, three years younger than Hughes, was a carpenter and had the ideal skill for Bocas, where wood is the default building material. But Hughes had long wanted to live on an island—her own island. That was the plan for the speck of an island she purchased in Darklands. All of Hughes's assets were put into a shell company with bearer shares. Hughes chose the name Caribbean Sun, Inc., a near echo of Southern Exposure, the name of her successful sign business in Florida.

Sandi Hodge thinks back to the day she sat on a log on the grassy ridge of Hughes's private island. You could see the blue of the Caribbean on three sides; on the fourth was the looming, green mass of Darklands. This was the spot on the island that caught the best breezes and where the rains of the wet season drained away fastest. "It was before they even started building the house," said Hodge. "Keith pointed out where the kitchen, the other rooms, and the yard would be, and it all came true." Werle built much of the house with his bare hands. The dwelling was a modern construction with a huge deck. Tall palm trees arched above and, down below, there was a sheltered cove. The water was so clear, you could float on the surface and see the pebbles at the bottom yards below you. The couple moved out of the Casa del Sapo and made this their main home. From their bespoke house on the little island off Darklands, Hughes carried on running the rental at a distance, and Werle earned a living as a building contractor.

When the Darklands house was built, Hodge sometimes would sleep over. Hughes was a careful homemaker and had the best of everything— fine linens and soft towels and a top-of-the-range Jacuzzi-style bathtub. The women loved to go "jungle shopping." They would visit a friend who had every type of flower and plant on his land, bringing their boots, shovels, and buckets. They looked for spiky, orange strelitzia blooms to fill their vases and cut fragrant white ginger flowers. Hodge is a strong woman but where Hughes led, Hodge followed. They became young again, laughing like banshees, throwing themselves into the cool water. Hodge would be falling asleep in Hughes's place in Darklands and, suddenly, there would be a shout in the night: "Come on, let's go!" The two women would call a boatman and set off on a moonlit search for armadillos.

"It was heaven," says Hodge, "and I got to go on Cher's dream with her."

Hughes and Werle lived a mile and a half from the Jolly Roger Social Club. They were some of Holbert and Reese's most regular guests at the bare-bones bar run by the pair they knew as Wild Bill and Jane Cortez. The two couples had a casual, boozy friendship. Their homes were close by in an isolated and peripheral part of the archipelago and there were fewer newcomers there than in Bocas Town. Geography threw them together, but they ended up seeing a lot of each other out of choice.

In fact, the first time Hodge met Holbert was at a party at Hughes's house. Holbert and Reese had offered to take care of the food—"Bill was going to do a pig roast"—but didn't show up in time. "Later that night, Bill and Jane came." Their late arrival wasn't a big problem, since the residents of Bocas are relaxed timekeepers. "Bill was very boisterous, loud and kind of obnoxious. At one point he fell off his chair. And Jane just sort of sat there," recalls Hodge. "She had nothing to say." Holbert and Reese then left with another couple who were passing through Bocas del Toro and had been invited to the dinner. They were staying on their yacht across the calm waters of the archipelago, and Holbert said he would give them a ride in the Browns' old boat after making a short stop someplace else. But Holbert forgot to reset the navigation system when they were leaving, so he had no idea where he was going. Speeding along in the inky night, Holbert crashed into the couple's yacht. All four of them were taken to the hospital.

Unfortunately, Hughes's marriage didn't survive the change of pace in Panama, and she split from Werle in September 2009. Her husband left the home on the island off Darklands, starting a new relationship with a young expat woman in Bocas Town named Melissa Martz. Hughes found herself living alone in the house on the island they had designed and built for their life together. People started to say that she was going off the rails. These were not easy times for Hughes, particularly as Werle's new girlfriend was an acquaintance of hers. Expat social life in Bocas can be claustrophobic; the gringos in town who have come for the long haul tend to congregate in the same half-dozen drinking spots. Hughes saw Werle and his new girlfriend frequently in Bocas, and it upset her. Disheartened,

Hughes told one Panamanian friend that her 12-gauge sawed-off shotgun—which she kept in her bedroom for safety—and her dog, a Doberman named Jack, were her only friends. She also started to see less of Sandi Hodge, who had meanwhile offered a self-contained rental unit at her own home in Big Creek to Keith Werle. Hodge wanted to help Werle out, as he was short of a place to stay. Hodge considered both Hughes and Werle to be friends and intended to keep it that way. But offering accommodation to Werle put a strain on the two women's relationship.

"I don't know if you are my friend anymore," Hughes told Hodge in the late fall of 2009. "I don't know who I can trust."

In November 2009, the month that Bo Icelar disappeared, Cher Hughes had been in St. Petersburg, Florida, spending some time with her youngest sister, Judy Barber, who was going through a rough patch in her own marriage. Hughes was feeling particularly down when she left Panama for the States, but seeing Barber cheered her up. The two women visited some favorite old haunts, including the Don CeSar at St. Pete Beach, a pink palace of a hotel recalling the heyday of carefree Florida tourism. Hughes told Barber: "If anything happens to me, I want you to bury me on my island." Barber said she would, that it was a promise, and conversation quickly turned to lighter matters.

Back in Bocas in December, Hughes e-mailed her sister to say that she had seen Werle in a bar again and had later called him. But the phone call soon turned into an argument: *He has turned everything around and everything is my fault now*, wrote Hughes. *I am exhausted with his tricks.* Barber tried to encourage her sister: *Hey, hang in there*, she wrote back. *It will get better. I filed for my divorce yesterday at 8 am when the office opened. Believe me after all we've been thru it'll get better . . .*

There were also some practical problems in Darklands for Hughes to contend with. She was hit by electricity outages and the TV was broken. Sometimes the freezer failed, too. But eventually Hughes managed to get things fixed. That boosted her confidence a little, but the isolation in the onetime dream house was intense. *I am sooooo lonely . . . it's horrible. Last night cried myself to sleep again*, Hughes told Barber in an e-mail. Hughes texted Werle to let him know that she was *on a beautiful island and in the middle of a nightmare fairytale.* She badly wanted to reach out to her estranged husband. But Keith Werle had gone, and the split appeared permanent. Cher Hughes would have to get on with her life without Werle.

The sisters phoned and e-mailed, and they longed to see each other again in the flesh. When they were together, they could put their worries largely behind them and find something to laugh about. Barber told Hughes in mid-December that she had gotten hold of a passport application form and had filled it out immediately. The following year was to be Barber's first vacation in Panama, the first time she would see Cher Hughes's piece of paradise. Big sister Hughes was naturally delighted at the news. In any case, Cher Hughes wasn't someone who would mope around for long. Her depression was lifting. She spent Christmas with five of her girlfriends and the deep blue sky of Bocas cheered her up, too, as did an outing to see *The Rocky Horror Picture Show*, and a diving trip. She wrote Barber: *I'm just wanting to do stuff . . . don't care what it is but I am doing it.*

On New Year's Eve 2009, at a party hosted by a wealthy American businessman with a large, secluded mansion on the outskirts of Bocas Town—a key fixture on the Bocas social calendar—Hughes appeared to be back to her old optimistic and vivacious self. She hugged her expat friends warmly as the crowd cheered when the clock struck midnight. Life was getting better. On January 5, Barber told Hughes that her passport had come through. Meanwhile, there was news from Mary Wittmeyer, the sisters' aunt, a woman several years older than Hughes who was close to both sisters and had babysat them back in St. Louis. Wittmeyer got in touch to say she would come on the trip to Panama, too. *Can't wait till you girls come here*, replied Hughes.

By early 2010, Cher Hughes had settled on a plan: she would sell the Casa del Sapo, her rental unit on Carenero Island, and use the proceeds to buy a new home in Panama City. Hughes no longer spent much time at the Casa del Sapo and the day-to-day administration of the rental units was carried out by a young American woman named Maria Hudson. Hughes and Hudson had a professional relationship, but they were friends, too. Hudson told Hughes that she was worried because on two or three occasions there had been attempted break-ins at the rental. Nothing had been stolen, but the intruder had attempted to force open Hughes's filing cabinet. One night, a neighbor caught sight of a man with what looked like blond hair speeding off from the Casa del Sapo in a motor-boat. It was clear that the rental property was increasingly difficult to defend, especially since it was two separate buildings, and one of these would inevitably be left unprotected since Hudson couldn't sleep in both buildings at once.

Cher Hughes had made another decision, too. She would sue for divorce from Keith Werle.

In this period, with Werle gone, Hughes grew closer to Wild Bill Cortez and his wife. Hughes defended Bill Cortez when some people expressed surprise that she could be friends with someone so vulgar and uncouth. She also opened discussions with Holbert on the sale of the Casa del Sapo. By then, Holbert had moved into Bo Icelar's house in Big Creek, but Cher Hughes and Bill Cortez still partied all the time—Hughes needed the company, and Holbert wanted to close on the deal. It was clear that money wasn't a problem for Wild Bill. He told people that he had just sold an eighteen-hundred-acre property outside Cancún. Before that, the peas-ants, as he called them, would pay him rent, "like a feudal system," one expat recalls him saying. Holbert, still only thirty years old, said he had been approached by someone wanting to sell him a bank in the Cayman Islands. He also told folks that Jane had inherited a big country house in Ireland. Holbert and Reese both bulked out during this period. Holbert's appetite was voracious. He would regularly go into an expat-owned butcher store in Bocas and buy $200 or $300 of meat at a time, "and only the best cuts like prime rib-eye," according to the owner. Meanwhile, at parties at the Jolly Roger Social Club, Holbert would fire bullets into the air to get people's attention. He stopped charging for food and liquor. There was ample cocaine for guests to snort at the tables, but Holbert preferred drink. He wasn't too choosy, either, dumping rum, vodka, whis-key, and any random firewater into the same cup. No mixer; the joke was that Bill's mixer was whatever other spirit he had on hand. "Our Lord is liquor," Wild Bill shouted into the night across the still water of the lagoon. "We've gotta drink so God is within us!" And nobody at the Jolly Roger was allowed to puke any of it out. It was Wild Bill's bar and Wild

Bill's rules. The idea was that all of Holbert's guests at his bar would get wasted, and stay that way.

When Bo Icelar had opened discussions with Wild Bill Cortez on the sale of his mansion in Big Creek, Icelar's realtor friend Walter Kawano was mildly surprised that Icelar did not seek him out for his advice. Six months later, when American expat realtor Mark Johnson, who was a good friend of Cher Hughes's, found out that Holbert had made an offer for the Casa del Sapo, he asked Hughes if he could see the numbers. But, like Kawano, Johnson didn't manage to find out precisely how much Wild Bill was offering.

Cher Hughes had a wide social circle, including a couple of local Panamanian women friends who were younger than she was. One, Leiza Serrano, ran a long-term parking lot in Almirante where Hughes used to leave her red Dodge Ram pickup, since there was no road access to Darklands. Another, Shariel Binns, was a soft-spoken woman from Bocas Town with an engaging smile who turned heads. It's easy to imagine that Hughes saw in Shariel Binns, who was in her mid-twenties, a younger version of herself. Hughes asked Binns to help her find a suitable attorney in Panama City. There was to be no turning back on getting a divorce from Keith Werle. The idea was that the two women would visit the attorney together. Hughes was more than capable of looking after herself, and she spoke workable Spanish, so Binns was primarily included in the trip for moral support. Moreover, Binns was planning to be in Panama City at the same time as Hughes. On March 12 or 13, 2010, Hughes drove to David to get her Dodge Ram serviced and flew from there on an Air Panama plane to the capital, where she met Binns. Hughes had her eye on a penthouse apartment on the seafront Avenida Balboa (Binns later told investigators that Cher had said it had a "spectacular view"), but the deal fell through. Binns accompanied Hughes to the office of an attorney named Petra Soriano. Hughes explained to Soriano that she wanted a divorce, and the reasons for wanting it.

After several days in Panama City, Hughes and Binns returned to David to pick up her vehicle and drove back across the mountain to the Caribbean coast. One boat ride later, both women were at Hughes's house in Darklands. On March 18, Hughes went to the Toro Loco bar in Bocas

Town, and the following day she e-mailed Judy Barber several pictures of the Carnival celebrations there.

In the days immediately before the beginning of Lent, local men dress up as devils and parade up and down the main drag, bending their bodies forward and backward, splaying their arms, stamping the tarmac. They wear huge papier-mâché masks with white fangs, topped with red feathers. Sometimes they have the number "666" sewn into their black shirts. Tourists take photos, music booms from loudspeakers. Young local women leave the crowd to dance with the devils, gyrating slowly or grinding suggestively. Men approach the devils and stare them out, usually with a bottle of beer in their hands. Grilled meat is flipped on barbecues lining the road. The devils are such a familiar sight at Carnival time that only the youngest local children hide behind their mothers in fear. Hughes, in a red top and black skirt, had pictures taken hugging two Carnival devils, grinning. *I wanted you all to see that I am fine and hanging with the devils . . . Love you all, Cher.*

On March 20, Hughes had been invited to a party at the nearby Hacienda Cortez. As Binns was staying at Hughes's place, clearly she would go to the party as well. In relaxed Bocas, bringing an extra person to a party was something you didn't need to flag to your hosts in advance. But Binns was surprised to find out that the party was not really a party at all. They arrived to find that it was basically just Bill and Jane Cortez waiting for Hughes. This was no problem, but the two women were tired and after several hours returned to Hughes's house on the island. The next day, a Sunday, another expat offered Binns a ride back to Bocas Town. Taking the ride would mean leaving her friend. Binns worried for Hughes, who was in a delicate emotional state after meeting the attorney in Panama City. She knew that Hughes was about to embark on negotiations with Wild Bill over the sale of the Casa del Sapo rental place. Binns tried to persuade Hughes that she should stay with her; after all, Wild Bill and Jane lived in a big house and Binns could simply go into another room while her friend discussed terms with Holbert. But Hughes told Binns there was "no need" for her to stay. Consequently, Binns accepted the offer of the ride back to Bocas Town for Sunday, March 21. Binns left some clothes and also her ID card—an oversight—at Cher Hughes's place.

Shortly after she left Hughes's island, Binns realized what she had forgotten. Hughes told Binns she would get her friend's things back to her in a day or two, and not to worry.

Holbert and Reese employed two young indigenous men at Hacienda Cortez to cut the grass and the weeds, feed the goats and hens—what was left of Michael Brown's experiment in self-sufficiency—and clean the house and the speedboat. These were David Machuca, who worked as a night watchman when Holbert was away and was paid $115 every two weeks, and Rolando Morales, who earned $110 every two weeks, but was married and never slept on the property. Morales later told the police that one afternoon in May (likely a typographic error in the police report— Morales almost certainly meant March), he and his wife, Basilia, were on their way to church in their dugout canoe when they saw Holbert driving Hughes's boat with Cher Hughes in it as it approached the dock below her house. Morales recalled that his boss was wearing a red T-shirt and cut-off jeans and wore his hair tied back; Hughes wore a white T-shirt, casual shorts, had her hair untied. Morales made no mention of Reese. Had she stayed behind in Hacienda Cortez? Was Reese somewhere else entirely, a day after the curious "party" with the single guest?

Later that same day, Sunday, March 21, Holbert and Hughes returned to Hacienda Cortez. Night fell quickly, as it always does in the tropics. Holbert and Hughes drank, quite possibly heavily. Then Holbert invited Hughes to look at some sloths that had made a home in the trees behind his house. When you shine a flashlight, their eyes glow in the dark. They make a long, high-pitched call that echoes through the forests. Lower down, the moist ferns and banana leaves are home to hundreds of thousands of insects. Hughes was little over a mile of dark water away from the house she had built in her own patch of paradise. And then, she disappeared.

By the final week of March, people were starting to wonder exactly where Cher Hughes was. Things simply didn't add up. First of all, Hughes had told Shariel Binns that she would get the clothes and personal belongings Binns had left at Hughes's house in Darklands back to her early the following week, but when Binns tried to reach Hughes on her cell phone there was no answer. A plastic surgeon from Panama City had also called Binns to inquire about Hughes's whereabouts, saying that he had expected to hear from her, but that she hadn't been in touch. Meanwhile, Leiza Serrano was due to help Hughes out with some administrative red tape having to do with the license plate of her Dodge Ram. The two women had arranged to meet up on March 25, a Thursday, to get this done. Hughes, most surprisingly, didn't show. And then there were her dogs, her beloved Jack, a Doberman, and also Feldman, a shih tzu. It was unthinkable that Hughes would take off and leave them behind without making careful arrangements for them. But it soon turned out that this was what she had done.

Leiza Serrano's brother, Miguel Ángel, drove his boat over to Cher Hughes's island to investigate. He moored his boat and climbed the steps as he normally did but, to his surprise, he saw Jane Cortez at the top. "She told me I couldn't enter and that the property didn't belong to Cher anymore, but to her husband," said Miguel Ángel. Jane Cortez appeared to get a bit angry and said that Cher Hughes had gotten sick and had gone off to Panama City. Miguel Ángel walked back down the steps to the wooden dock, and there was Jack whimpering and appearing to chase his own tail, looking distressed. Something was evidently not right.

That same week, Holbert strolled into the Casa del Sapo, Hughes's rental on Isla Carenero. "I'm your new boss," he announced to Maria Hudson, the woman Hughes had hired to run the place for her. Hudson saw that Holbert was carrying Hughes's iPod. "I asked him why he had it," Hudson later told investigators. "He said she [Hughes] had left Bocas in a hurry. He gave me the impression that Cher had had a nervous breakdown from getting divorced, so she had sold up and moved away quickly." Holbert took down the sign with "Casa del Sapo" on it and replaced it with a much larger one that said: *CASA CORTEZ SHORT & LONG TERM APARTMENT RENTALS—A Delightfully Wicked Place.*

Then, miraculously, Cher Hughes appeared to send some news. It was a text message sent on March 25 to a large group of friends and family from her cell phone. The message said, in effect, "I'm fine, don't worry about me, I met a guy and went off on a sailboat with him." Keith Werle was one of the people who received the message, and he was immediately perplexed. Despite their differences, the couple spoke often, but Hughes had suddenly stopped answering her phone. Also, the cell phone message was strange in two ways: it wasn't written in Hughes's usual style, and Werle's estranged wife didn't much care for sailboats. If a boat didn't have a fast motor, Hughes didn't really see the appeal. So why had she gone off on one?

Two days later Wild Bill went to see Keith Werle. Holbert told Werle that he had bought everything—the rental on Carenero Island, the island in Darklands, and two other plots of land in the Bocas archipelago that Hughes owned. But Holbert also still had many, if not all, of Hughes's personal possessions. It brought to mind something similar that Werle had seen several months earlier. Wild Bill Cortez had asked Keith Werle to come over to Bo Icelar's mansion in Big Creek. Wild Bill told Werle that he had bought the house from Icelar (calling him Bo Yancey, as he was known then). Wild Bill wondered if Werle, a contractor, would be interested in doing some jobs on the property. Werle agreed, and the work took around ten days. All the time, it seemed strange to Keith Werle that so many of Icelar's belongings were still there in the house he had supposedly sold to Holbert.

And now, Holbert was telling Werle bluntly that if he wanted to recover any of his estranged wife's things, he would need to wait until she got back. Werle knew that Hughes had wanted to sell the Casa del Sapo. But she had never said that she wanted to part with the island in Dark-lands—it had been her dream home, after all. Werle asked Holbert for proof that he had indeed bought all of Hughes's properties. There was none. Holbert just muttered something about Hughes demanding the deal be kept secret, saying that it was a condition of the sale that he shouldn't discuss the details with anyone—Keith Werle included. Both Werle and Hudson thought the situation was very strange, but neither went immediately to the police.

At the beginning of April, Holbert and Reese hosted a housewarming party at Hughes's property in Darklands. But the guests who moored their boats at Hughes's dock and trekked up the pathway cut into the steep slope of her island soon realized that this was not going to be one of Wild Bill's better parties. In fact, it was a pretty muted affair, despite all the drink on offer. The guests knew Cher Hughes had disappeared. But her clothes and shoes, kitchen utensils, toiletries, books, pictures, and music CDs were visible everywhere.

Back in the States, Diana Motlik, Cher Hughes's other sister, was clear that something was badly wrong. Like Werle, the text message was a give-away to her: "She would not have gone off in a sailboat as she didn't like them," wrote Motlik in an e-mail. Also, her sister was simply too savvy ever to announce to the whole world that her house was empty. Most of all, it was unthinkable that Hughes would go off when she knew that Judy Barber was five weeks away from flying to Panama to see her sister's island paradise for the first time. When Barber e-mailed Hughes to say that she would be arriving with Mary Wittmeyer, their aunt, on May 2 rather than the day before, as originally planned, and asking a couple of practical questions about internal flight connections from Panama City to Bocas del Toro, Hughes—who usually answered her e-mails promptly—failed to reply. Wittmeyer and Barber didn't want to go to Bocas if Hughes wasn't there. Instead, with their leave booked and space in their diaries, the two women flew to Las Vegas. Ignoring the casinos, they put their heads together to figure out what to do next in the search for Cher Hughes.

Mary Wittmeyer found out Holbert's number and called him: "Bill Cortez told me on April 29, 2010, he had bought all Cher's properties and belongings a month earlier," said Wittmeyer. "He wouldn't give me the name of the lawyer as he had signed a confidentiality agreement, and was afraid he would be sued if he gave out any information. . . . He said he'd got a great deal and paid half price as Cher was desperate to leave the country. He also said that if Judy and I came to Bocas del Toro, he would take us in his boat to look for her, but it was a waste of time because Cher was in Panama City." It sounded odd, even disturbing. Wittmeyer wasted no time in dialing the US embassy in Panama City to file a missing persons report. But Wittmeyer felt palmed off by the embassy staff: "They were saying, 'Don't worry, it happens all the time,' and 'She'll probably contact you soon.' It was like I was looking for some surfer kid."

Wittmeyer was torn. On the one hand, she knew that someone must have seen Hughes if she was in Bocas; on the other, she spoke little Span-ish and it felt like looking for a needle in a haystack. But Hughes's father,

Walter, was one of several people who encouraged Wittmeyer to travel to Panama to try to find her. This time it was Diana Motlik who would travel to Panama with her, as Judy Barber had run out of vacation days. To help find out what had happened to Cher Hughes, Wittmeyer contacted a former air force intelligence officer named Don Winner who ran a popular blog called Panama-Guide.com with items of Panamanian news in English. Winner lived in Panama City and had good contacts with the authorities there. Most of all, Wittmeyer could tell that Winner was fired up and keen to help.

Back in Bocas, people were now figuring out that Cher Hughes wasn't the only expat who had disappeared. With Wild Bill and Jane now effectively living on three properties—Bo Icelar's house in Big Creek and Cher Hughes's place in Darklands, as well as at the house the Browns used to live in—John Lang started to have concerns about his friend and neighbor, Bo Icelar. But Lang's worries were tempered by the knowledge that Icelar would often leave on trips without letting him know that he was going anywhere: "Bo was strange and secretive, so it was odd and not odd at the same time." Lang came to the conclusion that Icelar had "just taken off and left." But Lang's suspicions mounted when he got a call from the US embassy, acting on the report filed by Sharon McConnell. The embassy told Lang that he was registered as Bo's contact in case of emergencies. This suggested that if Icelar was going to go away for an extended period, he would have let Lang know, however secretive he might be. At the end of April, Icelar's Panamanian realtor friend Walter Kawano filed a missing persons report on Icelar at the police station in Bocas. The local police started asking questions and interviewed Sandi Hodge, who also lived in Big Creek, to see if she had any idea where Icelar could be. Apparently, though, Bo Icelar didn't switch the lights in his house on very much, so you often couldn't tell if he was home or not. When the police had gone, it dawned on Hodge that there were two people she knew—Cher Hughes and Bo Icelar—whose whereabouts she didn't know.

In early June, John Lang received a call from an FBI agent asking him to make some inquiries. Specifically, the agent wanted to know where exactly Bo's things had been shipped, and to whom. "I was asked to check the whole paperwork of the shipment," said Lang. But Holbert refused to show him, just saying that Icelar's things had been shipped to Panama City. Holbert refused to give Lang any more details. Then Lang spotted something inside Icelar's mansion that gave him a start: it was the carved cane that Icelar used for walking. Since the operation on his foot, Icelar had needed a cane to get around. It had "Mexico" carved into the handle, and it was the only cane Icelar had, to the best of Lang's knowledge. And there it was in the house that Holbert said he'd bought from him. If it was unthinkable that Cher Hughes would leave Bocas without making arrangements for her dogs, it was equally difficult to imagine Bo Icelar leaving on a long trip without his cane.

On June 11, a Norwegian woman friendly with Hughes filed a missing persons report with the police in Bocas Town, noting that the last time she saw Hughes was at the Toro Loco bar on March 18. Keith Werle, meanwhile, went to the Bocas police station on June 24 and reported his wife missing, noting that they were separated but they often talked on the phone, and that Bill Cortez had acquired their properties but he had seen no document to prove it. The police checked recent airline manifests for planes flying out of Bocas and the lists of passengers for the Taxi 25 shared motorboat service to Almirante. There were, it was true, other ways that Hughes could have left Bocas, but these searches threw up no sign of her name. Meanwhile, the *Bocas Breeze* published photographs of Hughes and Icelar, asking readers to come forward if they knew where they might be. Icelar's picture was grainy; he looks uncomfortable in front of the camera and his hand is clutching a cane—the same one Lang spotted when he paid a call on Holbert. Cher is smiling broadly with bright pink lipstick, blond hair pinned back, head turned coquettishly.

As it turned out, shortly after John Lang had asked for the paperwork on the shipment Holbert had supposedly made on behalf of Bo Icelar, he and Laura Michelle Reese quit town. Another reason for their departure was likely an altercation Holbert had at the Riptide Bar, an expat watering hole housed on an old, rusting shrimper brought down from Florida. The Riptide was moored to a dilapidated floating jetty on a plot off the road from downtown Bocas to Big Creek, and it was—after his own Jolly Roger Social Club—the bar Holbert frequented the most. Mark Johnson, the realtor who was friendly with Cher Hughes, had in the meantime gone to Panama City on business and took time out to inquire as to Hughes's whereabouts. He drew a blank with each lead. There seemed to be no way that Hughes had bought an apartment in the capital. Johnson frankly doubted Holbert's story of the cut-price sale of all of Hughes's properties in Bocas and, one evening at the Riptide, he told him so. Wild Bill had been drinking assiduously and quickly got angry, threatening to throw Johnson off the shrimper. But, in the end, it was Holbert who took flight.

The couple left Bocas del Toro as quietly as they had arrived. Holbert drove Hughes's red Dodge Ram over the mountain to Boquete and rented a house from an Irish expat in a small subdivision called Emerald Drive, paying a $900 deposit and $900 rental for the first month. But after a couple of weeks Holbert called the Irishman to say that he had to travel to the United States because his brother-in-law had cancer. Holbert asked for the $900 deposit back, and the Irishman gave it to him. Otherwise, the Irish expat didn't notice anything strange about the couple, except that the day they left the house he saw that Jane was crying. The Irishman put this down to her brother having cancer.

Before fleeing, Holbert had fired Maria Hudson at the renamed Casa Cortez and rushed to put in a new manager, an American woman named Renay Hallman. From Boquete, Holbert called Hallman to say he was going to come back over the mountain to "give Keith a kick in the ass for talking bad" about him—although he didn't tell Hallman precisely what Werle had been saying. He never did come back over the mountain, at least not for many, many months. He also called Hallman from the David branch of PriceSmart, a large discount store, to see whether she thought that the towels they had on sale there were a good value. He didn't buy the towels, though.

One evening in June, Holbert and Reese drove to Mike Smith's house in David, which was under an hour's drive from Emerald Drive. Smith was at home, but his wife, Fran Tilbury, was at their other place in Split Hill in Bocas del Toro. Holbert drank a whole bottle of white rum that night. Mike Smith went to bed, then woke up at three a.m., having to pee.

"That's when I find Jane sleeping in my bed," said Smith. "And I can't find Bill."

Smith grabbed the pistol he always keeps under the mattress. It looked like Wild Bill had just gotten into his vehicle and left. Smith called Holbert on his cell phone, but he didn't get through. Then he sent Holbert a text message: *You can't leave your wife.* Meanwhile Reese was in a state, screaming, "I'm afraid to go with him!" The turn of events had made Mike Smith understandably uncomfortable, and he kept calling Holbert's cell number. When Holbert finally picked up, Smith told him, "This is not right." About forty-five minutes later, Holbert reappeared at Smith's gate. Reese reluctantly left with Holbert, and they drove off into the night.

The next morning, Mike Smith received a call from Reese. "I'm sorry for last night," Reese said to Smith, "but it's kind of funny, don't you think?"

Mike Smith did not find it funny at all.

Mary Wittmeyer and Diana Motlik arrived at Tocumen International Airport in Panama City on July 11, 2010. It was the middle of the rainy season, and when the women stepped out of the cool arrivals hall the air enveloped them like a hot, moist rag. They checked into a Marriott hotel in the city that Wittmeyer knew from occasional layovers in Panama in her career as a flight attendant. The next morning the women met Keith Werle, who had flown in from Bocas, and Don Winner, the expat blogger. Winner had set up a meeting at the attorney general's building with assistant attorney general Neftalí Jaén, a lawyer with the reputation for being particularly well connected, and drove the three Americans there.

"This is not a runaway," said Wittmeyer, placing a photo of her niece on the table in the meeting room opposite the smartly suited Jaén. "Cher Hughes has been the victim of a crime. Can you help us find Bill Cortez?" Jaén took the matter seriously enough to send the group to the state prosecutor's office. After phone calls and e-mails, this was the first time the women had met Don Winner. "I was sold on him," said Wittmeyer. "He told these guys that he knew how important they were. He knew exactly how to handle them. He implied that the authorities were at fault for not running background checks on Holbert when he opened his motorbike shop [Vikingo Motor Sports, in Volcán]. At the same time, he knew how to grease them up a little. Don Winner was seriously cool."

Meeting with the prosecutors, Wittmeyer again placed Cher's photo on the table and made the same plea to them that she had made to Jaén. The officials consulted briefly and the lead prosecutor told the group that the investigation needed to be upgraded. "I don't usually cry," said Wittmeyer, "but that's when I broke down. I fell apart. I wanted to hug him [the prosecutor], but he just looked away."

Werle told the Panamanians that the man he knew as Bill Cortez kept an AK-47 assault rifle on his property. He accused his former friend of murder. "I'm signing my own death warrant doing this," he later told Wittmeyer and Motlik. By telling the authorities that Holbert had an unlicensed firearm on his property, he gave them the grounds to apply for a search warrant.

The trio's work for the day wasn't quite done. All three made individual statements to detectives the same afternoon. The first impression of the police station was not auspicious. It was located next to a busy underpass. You needed to have a key fetched to use the restroom. Keith Werle— who had left Bocas in a hurry and was wearing shorts—was told he wasn't dressed well enough to use it and had to leave the building to relieve himself elsewhere. But Wittmeyer got a good feeling when she met the homicide detectives, men from Panama's Dirección de Investigación Judicial who were tasked with investigating serious crime: "I knew they were thinking, 'Hey, something's wrong here.'"

Werle made his statement first, telling the officers about the unusual text message purporting to be from Cher, saying that she had left on a sailboat, and finding out from Holbert that he had bought all of Werle's estranged wife's properties. Werle was asked if he had anything else to say. "I want to know what happened to my wife and where she is. [. . .] I would like to add that Wild Bill moves about Bocas del Toro with a firearm."

Wittmeyer had spoken with Sharon McConnell, Bo Icelar's friend, just before her trip to Panama and the women had compared notes. She and Motlik both told the police about the strange disappearance of Bo Icelar (who went under the assumed name "Yancey" in Bocas): "I also have been informed that Mr. Bo Yancey disappeared on November 29,

2009, in circumstances very similar to those of my niece, and what they have in common is that Bill Cortez was buying their properties," said Wittmeyer. Like Werle, both women identified Holbert as the man whom the authorities needed to track down.

Motlik said: "I fear very much that not only has Bill Cortez taken all my sister's possessions, including her money, he has also done her harm or has killed her."

"It was exhausting, but it was exhilarating, too. Finally we felt like someone had listened to us," said Wittmeyer. At the US embassy in Panama City, Werle and the two women were introduced to FBI agent Paris Johnson. Agent Johnson also listened carefully to what they had to say, and his manner was consoling, too.

In fact, just about everyone had listened to Hughes's estranged husband, her sister, and her aunt, and taken note of what they said. But by mid-July, Wild Bill and Jane Cortez had long left Bocas. After the strange incident at Mike Smith's house in David, Holbert and Reese headed off into the highlands. They drove through Volcán—Holbert got out of his car to buy a lottery ticket at a market—and made a right turn in the center of town to take the road to Cerro Punta, Panama's highest settlement. In the Las Nubes section of Cerro Punta, a place of market gardens and swirling mists, no more than a hamlet really, the couple unlocked the door of a modest, two-room chalet. A few days later, a local workman found an empty bottle of Seco Herrerano rum that had been tossed onto the grass in the small yard. Also in the yard someone had dug a ditch in the soft ground, the soil freshly turned. Holbert had bought the property from Shariel Binns's American husband a couple of years previously. Apart from Binns and her husband, few people knew he owned it.

The couple likely stayed in Cerro Punta for no more than a week. They then backtracked into Volcán and crossed into Costa Rica at Río Sereno in the dead of night, showing no papers. They ditched Cher Hughes's red Dodge Ram before they left Panama. (In 2007, Holbert and Reese had made the same backwoods border crossing, but in the opposite direction.) In Costa Rica, the couple rented a new vehicle and a vacation cabin, and invented new names for themselves. With the FBI involved alongside the Panamanian detectives, the hunt for Wild Bill and Jane Cortez had become international. Their pictures appeared on local television, first in Panama and then Costa Rica. For William Dathan Holbert and Laura Michelle Reese, it was time to move on again.

It can't have been easy for Keith Werle to go back to the house he built with Cher Hughes, but at least he had the dogs for company. When Holbert and Reese had fled, they left Jack and Feldman to fend for themselves. But Jack was agitated and wouldn't stay still. Several times he got into the water and swam across to the Hacienda Cortez, the house Wild Bill and Jane Cortez had abandoned.

It took a week for the homicide detectives in Panama City to organize the paperwork to obtain a warrant to search Hacienda Cortez. On July 19, an advance party comprising the Bocas del Toro local district attorney, the *personero* Virgilio Morales, and two police officers, Nelson Berchi and Ronny González, was dispatched from Bocas Town to Darklands to inspect the property. As the three men arrived at Holbert's floating dock, the skull and crossbones logo of the Hacienda Cortez struck an immediate, ominous note. The men saw several large concrete blocks on the dock and noted this down in their report. Fifty yards up the slope of the yard, the varnished wooden walls of Hacienda Cortez gleamed in the sunlight. The PVC window frames and line of solar panels on the roof marked this out as a home built by someone with a comfortable budget. Inside the house they found a big plasma TV and a chocolate-colored sofa, but not much else in the way of furniture. The place gave off a bad smell and there was fungus on many of the surfaces. The smell got worse when the men opened the door of the freezer—the power had been cut and the trays of beef and chicken inside were rotting away. They saw discarded syringes and vials, and boxes of pills; cigarette butts littered the floor here and there. The policemen soon discovered two cartridges they recognized as being the type used with an AK-47 assault rifle, just as Keith Werle had predicted. They also found a sawed-off shotgun, a .38-caliber Ranger revolver made in Argentina, a rifle, and lots more ammunition. *Personero* Morales made a list and stored it all away as evidence.

Hacienda Cortez had a living area with a kitchen facing the water;

behind this there was a narrow corridor with four bedrooms, two on either side. One of the bedrooms contained a pile of canned food and soaps and shampoos; in another there was a safe with the door open. In one of the other two bedrooms, lying on a bed, were Cher Hughes's passport, checkbook, credit cards, bank statements, purse, and cell phone. There was also a filing cabinet with papers and documents strewn around it. The people who lived there had surely left in a hurry.

The afternoon sun was casting long shadows by the time the *personero* and the police officers encountered David Machuca and Rolando Morales, the two local workmen employed by Holbert and Reese. These workmen passed on some news: On two occasions, the first toward the end of the previous year, 2009, and the second several months into 2010, Bill Cortez had asked Machuca and Morales to dig two holes in the ground. Each hole was three to four feet deep and five to six feet long. The workmen told the police officers that they had dug the holes on a rise behind the Hacienda Cortez. You got to it by going through a gate in a rickety fence behind the house. From a distance, it looked like there was no way through the jungle, but, when you got closer, you could see a rough path that led into the bush. It was somewhere near there that Wild Bill habitually asked Machuca and Morales to dump his trash. Only, in the case of these two holes, it was Wild Bill Cortez who had dumped the garbage himself, several bags of it, in fact, and threw in some topsoil without any help from the workmen. No one appears to have asked the workmen why they didn't find this strange at the time. On the other hand, it would be highly unusual for laborers in Panama to question their paymasters.

The next day, July 20, a larger, beefed-up group of around a dozen police officers, including forensics experts and detectives, made the forty-five-minute trip across the lagoon from Bocas Town to the Hacienda Cortez. First to disembark was a police sniper who quickly took up a position on the fringe of the yard (Holbert and Reese were still on the run and almost certainly armed). The policemen met Keith Werle, who presented his passport as ID. A policeman took note of the passport number. By now it was eleven a.m. The atmosphere was muted, tense. In view of the concrete blocks found on the floating dock the previous day, a police diver had been brought along. He searched the silty water around the dock but found nothing unusual. Jack, Hughes's Doberman, was there, too, and he couldn't keep still. He immediately ran to the back of the house and barked. A blue Toyota Hilux pickup stood next to the gate on a patch of ground littered with rotting coconut husks. Still Jack barked. *Personero* Morales and a couple of the detectives opened the gate and walked up the muddy, rutted path that led to the garbage dump that Holbert's workmen had described the day before. Jack followed, yapping all the time, excited. After about three hundred yards they came to a small clearing. This was where Wild Bill disposed of his trash.

The policemen looked around them. In such a remote place, there was a wealth of flora. From a distance it was all green, indistinct, looking pretty much the same. But closer up, things were different. The officer tasked with writing the report of the day's activities noted that there was "a great variety of trees." You didn't have to know the names of the scaly trunks and giant ferns to be momentarily struck by the raw beauty of such a place. Just a few steps away from the clearing behind the Hacienda Cortez there might well be ground where no human being had ever trodden.

The *personero* pointed to a rectangular patch where the dirt had been disturbed. A couple of policemen started digging. The other officials found some shade under a mango tree; it was now noon and the sun was fierce. After a few seconds, a flash of tarp appeared, bright blue. "We observed a package wrapped in a blue plastic material, tied up with a piece of sticking tape. We cut the tape and took off the material. We then saw a corpse in an advanced state of decomposition." The person lying in the shallow grave had been killed with two bullet shots to the head. Strands of long blond hair showed as the skull was uncovered.

The men called for Keith Werle to come up the path into the bush from the Hacienda Cortez. They called for bags, too. He identified his wife from her breast implants and dentures. Werle was "devastated," said an expat who saw him later that day. Forty-five minutes passed. Then, some five yards away from the first shallow grave, the policemen found another ditch of similar dimensions. They called for more bags. It contained a second skeleton; this time, it was impossible to work out the gender. But from its appearance it was clear that this other corpse had been lying in the ground for many months.

The news spread by cell phone, text message, and urgent knocking on neighbors' doors. The group of policemen arrived back in Bocas Town as the sun was setting. By nightfall on July 20, many expats in Bocas had found out about the gruesome discoveries at the Hacienda Cortez, right next to the Jolly Roger Social Club, where Wild Bill Cortez had promised that *Over 90% of our members survive*. Later that same evening, an angry group on Carenero Island pulled down and smashed the sign announcing the Casa Cortez that Holbert had put up on the wall of Cher Hughes's Casa del Sapo rental property, the one that promised it was *A Delightfully Wicked Place*. They left the splintered remains of the sign on a nearby beach and set them alight, sparks fizzing and darting in the humid summer night. After a day or two digesting the news from Darklands, some of the people who were friendly with Holbert and Reese wondered how close they came to being their victims, too. Others worried that Holbert and Reese might find a way back to Bocas to kill again.

The nightmare that Wild Bill and Jane Cortez had created, however, was a long, long way from its conclusion.

Cher Hughes set up Caribbean Sun, Inc., as a Panamanian *sociedad anónima* of the most discreet type—like Mike Brown and Bo Icelar and many hundreds of other expats did—by having bearer shares issued. But in September 2009, Hughes had taken a precaution. With the help of an attorney in David, she set up a private interest foundation also named Caribbean Sun. The purpose was, in effect, to ring-fence her four properties—the rental on Carenero Island, the house on the island, and two other plots of land in the Bocas del Toro archipelago. Private interest foundations of the type that Cher Hughes used had existed in Panama since 1995 and took their cue from a similar setup on the statute book in the Alpine microstate of Liechtenstein. One Panamanian law firm described the private interest foundation as a *flexible vehicle for use in estate planning and asset protection*. It's common in Panama before a divorce for one party—the one with the principal assets, often real estate—to discreetly place her or his assets in a foundation. In Hughes's case, her properties were "donated" to Caribbean Sun and she made herself the foundation's soul beneficiary. Moreover, in Panama, there is no need to write a separate will to dictate what will happen to the assets owned by a foundation in the event of the death of the beneficiary—you simply include the relevant information in the charter. This is precisely what Cher Hughes did: should she die, the assets of the Caribbean Sun foundation would pass to her father, Walter Hodecker. Hughes's foundation became a legal entity once the charter was recorded at the Public Registry Office, which took a matter of days. Hughes's action had the intended effect that her husband, postdivorce—if there was to be one—would not be awarded a share of any of her principal assets. There was an unintended effect, too: a future sale of any of the assets—Casa del Sapo, for instance—would require undoing Hughes's Caribbean Sun foundation. Not a difficult thing, just not as simple and as fast as handing over a bunch of bearer shares.

It is very likely that none of the expats in Bocas del Toro knew about the existence of the Caribbean Sun foundation. When Keith Werle spoke with the detectives in Panama City on July 12, he told them that he and his wife "jointly" owned the four properties in Bocas del Toro via a shell corporation. For his part, barman Wild Bill Cortez did his best to find out everyone's secrets at the Jolly Roger Social Club. He knew that Cher Hughes had set up a Panamanian corporation with bearer shares to buy her properties. He assumed that Hughes had left it that way. But when he emptied Cher Hughes's filing cabinet onto the bed of the rear bedroom at the Hacienda Cortez, he didn't find the bearer share certificates he was expecting. By then, it was too late.

At her house in Big Creek, Cher Hughes's friend Sandi Hodge ponders something, likely not for the first time: the value of Cher's Darklands home was only worth what someone was prepared to pay for it. It's the lesson of real estate punts the world over.

"Cher and Keith built a beautiful oasis there. We would go there on weekends and have a great time. But there are only so many people who want that isolation," said Hodge.

7. Darklands

After fleeing Bocas in early June 2010, and eventually crossing the border into Costa Rica, Holbert and Reese had
planned to lay low. The problem was, their faces were all
over the local television and newspapers. In the middle of July the pair
pitched up in a resort town about an hour out of San José and rented a
cabin. But the owners recognized them and called the police. Holbert
and Reese had a narrow escape and, with the manhunt in full swing—
Interpol had been alerted and the FBI was giving chase—they decided to
switch countries again. Part of Costa Rica's border with Nicaragua to the
north is the broad, meandering San Juan River. On July 26, Holbert and
Reese stole a powerboat on the Costa Rican bank by dumping its owner
into the water, and headed for the Nicaraguan side. However, they were
spotted by a group of Nicaraguan soldiers who knew that the pair were trying to enter their country illegally before they realized exactly who they
were. Confronted by a line of machine guns, Holbert and Reese surrendered. When questioned by the Nicaraguan authorities, Wild Bill
and Jane claimed to be Dutch nationals. They had thought up some
new names for their purposes. They were dressed in T-shirts, short pants,

and flip-flops, every inch the guileless tourists who had lost their way. But their story didn't wash for a minute. They were handcuffed and taken away to a nearby police station. The law had caught up with Wild Bill and Jane.

On July 29, 2010, William Dathan Holbert and Laura Michelle Reese were deported from Nicaragua and flown in a light aircraft to Panama City. The plane touched down at Albrook airfield, Panama City's domestic airport, as day was about to turn into night. It had just stopped raining. Reese emerged first from the plane and descended the short steps onto the runway, slowly, unsure, like she was dipping her toes into a hot bath. Then she was ushered to a waiting police car, looking down all the time, perceptibly shaking. Holbert came out next and glanced over at a couple of photographers who called out his name, holding their stares. He then held his head high, back straight, nose pointing up to the sky as he, too, was taken away. His body language was arrogant, even imperious. Both Holbert and Reese were admitted to police custody, the blinking lights of the capital city blurring as their vehicle sped off.

Ariel Barría, then spokesman for the National Police, recalled that, in the days that followed, "we were all amazed to see how the detainee behaved. He waved and smiled at the cameras as if he were a rock star, that's the only way we had to describe it, even though the circumstances were so tragic." The precise circumstances of the unfolding drama in Darklands were what Panama's prosecuting attorneys wanted to uncover. There was some urgency, too; the local media was sensing a big story, calling the police and the state prosecutor incessantly. The following day, July 30, was a Friday, and at three p.m. deputy state prosecutor Ángel Calderón faced a relaxed William Dathan Holbert in an interrogation room at the state prosecutor's office. Laura Michelle Reese would have to wait her turn to give her account of events to Calderón and his team. Holbert told Calderón he spoke and read Spanish, but the prosecutors had already hired an interpreter for the session, which was the usual routine when non-Hispanic detainees were being interrogated.

First there was the question of who this man was, in fact. Holbert was announced as William Adolfo Cortez, but when asked for confirmation of his name, and other personal details, he gave the impression of wanting to level with the investigators: "My name is William Dathan Holbert, I am thirty years old. I got married in Costa Rica in 2006 near the city of San José, but I don't remember what the place was called exactly. I was born on September 12, 1979, in Hendersonville, North Carolina, in the United States." Holbert gave the names of his mother and father and his US social security number. He said he earned a living from farming.

"Why the name William Adolfo Cortez?"

"I chose the name thinking that Panamanian people would prefer a Latin name to a gringo one, and I wanted to fit into society. [. . .] I found a man on the Internet who sold camouflage passports. The idea of these passports is that a citizen of the US or Israel can carry one and if they are kidnapped by terrorists, no one will find out that they are American or Israeli."

Holbert bought a fake Dutch passport in his new name for $600. The man who sold it to him was very secretive and there was no way of knowing from which country he was operating.

"If you have any tattoos, tell us where they are and what they are."

"I have four. I have the American Confederate flag tattooed on my chest on the right-hand side. I have a cross on my left shoulder, a wild boar on my right shoulder, and a lightning bolt on my back." Holbert briefly took off his shirt to show his tattoos. He was asked the color of his skin. He replied, "White." Holbert spoke slowly, politely, deliberately. When Holbert put his shirt back on, he told Calderón's team of his life in Darklands. His farm, by which he meant the Hacienda Cortez—tending his cattle, growing bananas—earned him around $1,500 a month. He supported one other person economically: his wife.

Calderón cut to the chase, as the formal record of the interrogation indicates: *Once the identification of the detainee was completed, he was informed that he was being accused of the crime of murder.* Holbert was read his Miranda rights; he was free to remain silent if he so wished. An attorney, Javier Racine Gómez, had been provided to Holbert by the state and was present. *Any person who has been arrested must be informed immediately and in a form that is understandable, the reasons for their detention, and their corresponding legal and constitutional rights. Persons accused of having committed a crime have the right to a presumption of innocence until they are proven guilty in court . . .*

Holbert told the investigators that he and Reese had both entered Panama illegally in 2007, via a little-used border crossing close to Río Sereno. He had hopped on a bus and went to David, bought an SUV, and went back to the border to fetch Reese. This was as easy as walking along a track. "It was the middle of the night and there was no one around." The year's lease on the house in David cost him $3,200; he was carrying $50,000 in cash, he said, which were the spoils of a fraud that he had committed in the United States. Tiring of David, the couple went to the Chiriquí highlands. That's when he saw Michael Brown's ad on Craigslist and called him. "We arranged that he would pick me up in Chiriquí Grande [a small port southeast of Darklands] so that I could visit the property. I found out that this man had been a drug trafficker in the past. He told me this himself. I came to the conclusion that he was a desperate man, like I was. My first thought had been to rob him because he told me that he had a lot of money. But I changed my mind when I saw his property, which was in a remote, beautiful place, and that was when I decided to kill him and his family, too."

Holbert said that he had seen Michael Brown's nest egg, which was around $90,000 in cash. Brown had owned his assets through a shell corporation. He explained to Holbert how a shell corporation with bearer shares worked and that "whoever was holding the shares was the owner of the corporation." Brown's shell company, Latitude 9.10, Inc., held the property on Darklands that had been advertised on Craigslist. "If I killed him," said Holbert, "the shares would be mine and so would the property."

Holbert hatched a plan on the third day of his stay with the Browns. He asked Michael Brown to show him a well that was at the rear of the house. When they got to the well, Holbert shot Michael Brown with a single bullet to the head. "I had bought the gun in a bad part of David. I asked a man selling drugs if he could get a weapon for me and after thirty minutes he came back with a new gun that was still in its box. I don't remember the make or brand but I remember it was made in Argentina and it was a piece of garbage. It was of a very low quality and made of the kind of metal you would use to make pots and pans. It felt like aluminum."

Holbert assured the investigators that Michael Brown "died in an instant and he didn't feel a thing."

"What I want to say to you is that it gives me no pleasure to kill people. Actually, it's a difficult decision to make and it's difficult to do."

After Holbert had shot Michael Brown, he walked back to the house. "Then I said to his son, whose name I can't remember, that his father wanted him to bring a shovel and help out. I told him that I would go with him to his father. The young man was about eighteen years old. I took him near to where his father was and I shot him in the same place, and also in the back of the neck. I then returned to the house and Brown's wife was in the garden, working and bent over. I shot her in the same way that I had shot the father and son."

To make sure they were all dead, Holbert shot Michael Brown, his wife, Manchittha Nankratoke (Nan, for short) Brown, and their son, Watson, in the neck for a second time. The Browns kept a pickup truck on their farm and Holbert threw the three corpses into the back of it. He drove into the bush along a rough track behind the house. He stopped and dug two shallow graves. He put Nan Brown and Watson in one and Michael Brown in the other. Their bodies would stay where they were, gradually decomposing, until they were discovered two years and seven months later. Holbert drove back to the house and found some soap and some bleach to clean the truck. Then Holbert said he got drunk and— when he woke the next day—made the journey back to Reese in Volcán in reverse, using the Browns' motorboat to get to Chiriquí Grande. Back with Reese, "I explained to my wife that we had a new house."

Holbert said he thought that he and Reese moved into the Browns' residence on New Year's Eve of 2007. For the next two years the couple lived a "trouble-free" life. The Browns' home was spacious and there was plenty of money, too. Apart from the $90,000 in cash, there was another $225,000 in a bank account with HSBC in Hong Kong that Michael Brown had controlled. "I found information on the account when I went through Brown's documents, which were in a filing cabinet. That's where I found the passwords . . .

"I made a request to HSBC for a new [debit] card with a new PIN, since I didn't have the PIN of the old card. I sent the request to Hong Kong, because if I had sent it to Panama City, I would have been asked for identification." Holbert got the card in a package at the office of an express mail service in Bocas Town. "All I had to say was that I was picking it up for Michael Brown. These things are very easy in Bocas." Holbert then bled Michael Brown's account dry with systematic withdrawals up to the daily maximum at the ATM in Bocas Town. With part of the money, he stocked his new bar. He bought a powerful motorboat. The rest of Michael Brown's money was spent on day-to-day living expenses.

Holbert and Reese took off for occasional trips to the Chiriquí highlands and other parts of Panama. "When we left, I would tell my friends that we were visiting relatives. It was a lie, but it stopped them asking more questions about my family."

Holbert told the investigators that he wanted to confess to a number of other crimes. "I bought an AK-47 from a woman named Ann who had anchored her sailboat in front of my house. She told me she was short of money and that is why she was selling the weapon." Holbert paid her $600 for the AK-47—coincidentally, the same amount that the fake Dutch passport cost—and it came with a thousand rounds of ammunition. "I also bought a rifle from a delinquent in Bocas Town who went by the name of Bobby. [. . .] These weapons are in my house, in the house that used to belong to the Browns, in the main bathroom under a dropped ceiling. The gun I used to kill the Browns is in parts lying around the house."

Around May or June 2009, Holbert and Reese started to fight. She was drinking too much and so was he. At that time, Holbert was spending a load of money and was away from home a lot. "We came close to getting a divorce, but the biggest complaint she [Reese] had was that she was stuck on a farm in the middle of nowhere. So I put an ad in the *Bocas Breeze* that said that I bought houses. At the beginning, my intention was honorable. A man called Bo Yancey [Icelar] called me to see if I wanted to buy his house. But he wanted over $400,000, which wasn't a reasonable price, so I turned him down."

The purpose of the ad in the *Bocas Breeze* was to find people who really needed to sell their homes, people who were desperate to sell. In September and October 2009, Holbert came across Icelar at various parties and get-togethers. A deal might still be on.

"I got the impression that he [Icelar] was in a witness protection program that had something to do with the Mafia, judging from what he said. So I decided to kill him because I thought that his death would be attributed to the Mafia in the United States."

In November 2009, Holbert said he invited Icelar to his house so that he could meet with Holbert's attorney. "But the story about the attorney was a lie. I went in my motorboat to Bo's house in Big Creek to fetch him, and on the way from there to my house, when we were in the boat out in the lagoon, I shot him in the neck. I used a thirty-eight-caliber revolver, which I also bought from Bobby." Of course, Icelar was carrying the bearer shares of his shell corporation. In anticipation, Holbert had instructed his workmen to dig a hole in a small clearing in the bush about three hundred yards behind the Browns' house. "I threw Bo's body into the hole and covered it with a thin layer of dirt. On top of this, I threw in household garbage." The following day Holbert asked his workers to fill in the hole with more dirt. Reese wasn't in the house when Bo Icelar was shot and buried, said Holbert, as he had sent her off to Boquete or someplace else to go shopping.

Holbert and Reese now had two houses. The pair lived mainly in the house in Big Creek they had stolen from Bo Icelar. They quit drinking for about six weeks and, during this time, Holbert made some improvements to the Icelar property with a view to flipping it. Eventually, however, they returned to Darklands: "It was where I liked living the most." It was in 2008 in Darklands when Holbert and Reese met Cher Hughes and her husband, Keith Werle. Holbert digressed to describe a couple of boozy parties where some of the guests, including Keith Werle, came to blows. Eventually, Werle left Hughes for an acquaintance of hers. That hurt Hughes. Calderón's report of the interrogation makes no mention of what the officials from the state prosecutor's office made of Holbert's slice of Bocas expat life. Eventually, the detainee's story changed gear: "Around the middle of March 2010, Cher mentioned that she wanted to sell her property [the Casa del Sapo rental place]. This might have happened at her house, or it could have been at my house, as she started to visit with us frequently.

"One time when she came to see me, she confided that she didn't want to carry on living. She was a tall woman but because of the effect of drugs, she weighed under a hundred pounds. As she had got to that point, I decided to kill her and take what she owned."

On the night Holbert killed Hughes, "I think my wife was staying at Bo's house or maybe she was elsewhere, as we were going through some problems in our marriage." Holbert killed Hughes execution-style and drove in the Browns' old pickup to a new hole he had instructed his workers to dig. Holbert covered Hughes's body in a blue tarp and tossed it into the hole. He covered it with a layer of dirt, just as he had done with Bo Icelar's corpse, then some household garbage. Subsequently Holbert asked his workers to fill in the hole with more dirt. Holbert dispatched a large gray plastic cooler, of the type you can wheel around, on a plane to Panama City. The cooler contained some of Hughes's clothes and personal belongings. "I did this to cover my tracks."

With his account of the Bocas del Toro murders complete, Holbert had something to say about Laura Michelle Reese: "My wife is innocent of all these crimes and didn't have any knowledge of the crimes I committed. I have always acted alone, as is my habit. If there is any justice in the world, she will be released.

"I moved to Bocas Town and worked in the hotel I got from Cher," said Holbert, this despite "becoming lazy [. . .] and unhappy." At nights, Holbert got into the habit of getting drunk in an expat bar called the Riptide. "I did nothing to take over [formal] ownership of the Casa del Sapo. I just took physical possession of it along with the rest of her assets. Then a time came when I started to realize that I really missed my wife, and so I went back to the farm, which is where she was living." Holbert and Reese had two parties in Cher Hughes's house: "I don't remember the dates, but I don't think they were successful. Then we decided to go on vacation in the way that we used to every three months or so, in order to get away from everyone we knew. We rented a house in Boquete in a subdivision called Emerald Drive from a friend of ours called Tom Byrne, who is Irish."

Holbert told the investigators that on June 11, 2010, he got a call from a friend in Bocas who informed him that the police were looking for him. "I told my wife that we had to escape and we went to Costa Rica that same night." The pair moved from place to place in Costa Rica, not staying for more than three or four days in the same motel or rental. On July 23 or 24, Holbert said that Reese caught a glimpse of their photos on the TV news.

Reese was "very upset and afraid," said Holbert, "because they were calling us serial killers."

By the time Calderón's team wound up the interrogation it was 8:25 p.m. William Dathan Holbert signed the confession in his spidery handwriting. He was given an ink pad to make a thumbprint, which he put next to his signature. The confession was filed away with a sketch that Holbert made of the layout of the former Brown house. It showed the main residence and a housekeeper's cottage near the shore. At the top of the map was a stream marking the boundary of the property. Between the stream and the residence were two fences. Holbert marked a path that snaked from the residence as far as the stream. On the left-hand side of the path, between the second fence and the stream, two Xs marked the spots where Holbert had buried Hughes and Icelar. Close by, on the right-hand side of the path, an X marked the grave shared by Nan Brown and her son, Watson; another X indicated where William Dathan Holbert had buried Michael Brown.

On July 31, 2010, Ángel Calderón questioned Laura Michelle Reese, who was then twenty-seven years old. After Reese had confirmed her identity and her rights had been read out, she complained to Calderón that she had been "unjustly imprisoned" and that her detention was "very stressful." Reese spoke and understood little Spanish and, once again, the prosecutor's office provided an interpreter. She also complained that the Nicaraguan police who had arrested her on the San Juan River had stolen her wedding ring. Calderón informed Reese that she had been detained, like Holbert, on suspicion of involvement in the murders of three members of the Brown family, Bo Icelar, and Cher Hughes. But her interrogation then took quite a different turn from Holbert's a day earlier. "What does William Dathan Holbert do for a living?"

"I don't know."

"Where did his money come from?"

"I don't know."

"What about the [stolen] credit cards and checkbooks found at the house? Where did they come from?"

"No idea."

Reese said she had no information to share about where the family who lived in their house in Darklands had gone. She also didn't know how much her husband had paid for the Browns' property or who owned the jewelry—necklaces and bracelets belonging to Cher Hughes—she was carrying when she was arrested.

"What do you have to say to the fact that five bodies were dug up on your property?"

"Nothing."

"If you're American, why do you travel on a Dutch passport?"

"I haven't seen any of those documents, so I can't tell you." Reese could not remember where she entered Panama from Costa Rica with Holbert, nor what documents—if any—were shown. Reese said that Holbert had decided she should call herself Jane Seana Cortez. She'd had nothing to do with it, she said.

Reese signed her short statement in a looping, girlish script. She was obliged to take part in another interview on September 22; by this time both she and Holbert had been transferred from the police cells to jails in Panama City. This second interview also yielded no useful information; Reese merely stonewalled her interrogators again. As with the longer, more voluble statement made by Holbert on July 30, and his subsequent depositions, Panamanian prosecutors would have the task of separating fact from fiction. Crucially, they would have to come to their own understanding of the extent to which Reese had been involved in the killings.

On July 30, 2010, the same day that Holbert was being interrogated by Ángel Calderón, an Air Panama plane was touching down at the Bocas del Toro airport. A large gray plastic cooler with wheels was unloaded from the hold. With it was a letter addressed to Virgilio Morales, the *personero* (municipal district attorney) in charge of the Bocas del Toro archipelago. The letter was from an Air Panama executive and explained that the cooler had originally been flown from the Bocas airport to Albrook airfield in Panama City on March 29, 2010. It weighed ninety pounds and the cost of freight was to be paid on delivery at Albrook. But no one had picked it up. Air Panama staff had become suspicious and contacted the authorities in Bocas del Toro, and the decision was made to send the cooler back where it had come from.

The police in Bocas forced the cooler open. Among other things, it contained forty-one blouses and tops, thirteen pairs of trousers, shorts, an overcoat, underwear, bikinis, and five pairs of shoes. There was a framed photo of a yacht with two people on board; another photo showed three women wearing swimsuits. There was a crucifix and a Bible. In another frame, there was paper with a prayer printed on it: *God, grant me the serenity to accept the things I cannot change, / The courage to change the things I can, / And the wisdom to know the difference.*

After Holbert's confession was made public—and particularly after Holbert and Reese were carted off to jail—Panamanian journalists scrambled to find out more about this odd pair. In the wake of their arrest, and given the rumors, hearsay, and few hard facts emanating from Bocas del Toro, the local media did not quite know what to make of Holbert and Reese. First of all, there was the color of their skin. In common with many other Latin American countries, Panama's prison population is almost totally poor and dark-skinned. The perception was, and still is, that white people can buy their way out of trouble, not necessarily by bribing policemen or judges (although this happens, too) but more commonly by employing cunning lawyers to find loopholes to endlessly delay cases from ever coming to trial. In Panama, the statute of limitations for criminal proceedings is six years for offenses that entail up to six years of imprisonment. For offenses that entail more than six years of imprisonment, the period is a time equal to the maximum prison sentence imposed for that offense. The court system is chaotic and—like much of the state sector—underfunded. Long delays in criminal trials are par for the course.

Locally, the developing Wild Bill and Jane case gave support to a view commonly held in Latin America: that cold, ruthless multiple killers—whether serial murderers like Ted Bundy and Jeffrey Dahmer, or the protagonists of random, mass shooting sprees such as those at Columbine and Sandy Hook—are a product of the United States and other English-speaking countries, or at least of developed, but non-Latin, societies.* American movies and TV shows, from *The Silence of the Lambs* to *Dexter*, only serve to confirm this prejudice. Conversely, Latin Americans enjoy movies and television shows that help them forget their troubles. The fantasy world of the *telenovela*, the Latin soap opera, broadcast throughout the Spanish-speaking countries of the Americas (and in Brazil, too), offers a saccharine viewing experience almost wholly devoid of the often gritty reality of everyday life. Given that all of Holbert's known victims had come from overseas, ordinary Panamanians with no personal or professional stake in the affair tended to think that the case had nothing to do with them. It only concerned Panama insofar as the crimes had been committed on Panamanian territory. This was particularly true of Panamanians living outside the archipelago of Bocas del Toro. One waiter in David, clearing away cups of coffee from tables at breakfast, shrugged his shoulders and said, "It's just a story about gringos killing gringos." This was a typical view. Meanwhile, Holbert wasted no time in learning how to work the unofficial prison system. There was only the smallest chance that underpaid guards were going to hand over the keys to the main gate of a penitentiary to an inmate offering a large sum of money, but bribes regularly bought significant favors in jail. Cell phones or drugs could also be floated over the walls of the prison attached to helium balloons or even just thrown over. Or prison guards at visiting time might just decide to look the other way. Holbert had his own computer and access to the Internet, and maintained his own Facebook page;

---

* Serial killers do exist in Latin America: A man named Silvano Ward, dubbed the "Panama Strangler," murdered three women in Panama City between 1959 and 1973. He was sentenced to thirty years' imprisonment, served his time in jail, and was released. Meanwhile, in December 2014, a man thought to be one of Brazil's most prolific serial killers admitted to murdering forty-two people in the course of a decade. Twenty-six-year-old Sailson José das Graças said he began stealing purses and then "started thinking about killing."

he had a cell phone; for periods he had a cell to himself. Eventually, he even sponsored a prison's soccer team by buying their jerseys.

There were persistent rumors in Bocas that Holbert had cash buried somewhere on Darklands. One scenario was that Holbert had bled dry the bank account held by Michael Brown at the HSBC bank in Hong Kong by torturing him to reveal his passwords and PIN before he killed him (in his confession, he said he found the passwords written down in a notebook). One night at the Jolly Roger Social Club in 2008, Holbert appeared rather flustered and asked his guests if they had any idea why his money access card, which had been working the previous week, was suddenly not working anymore. Nobody knew for sure, but someone said, "Call your bank and see if they might have blocked the account. They'll probably ask you a few security questions and issue you a new PIN." Holbert mentioned to his guests that his account was with a bank in Hong Kong, but since Michael Brown had generally been very discreet about his assets and savings and where they were, none of Holbert's buddies were likely to smell a rat. In another scenario, Brown had another overseas account containing more of his life savings, and Holbert had bled this one dry, too.

What we know is that Brown kept money in the Hong Kong account and transferred funds at regular intervals to a local, Panamanian, account also at the HSBC, from which he made cash withdrawals. He did this by writing checks to himself. Brown's Panamanian account usually had between $5,000 and $30,000 in it. But soon after Holbert murdered Brown, he almost got caught. An HSBC bank statement shows that in January 2008, Holbert wrote a check to transfer the amount of $15,900 from Brown's Hong Kong account to the Panamanian account. The bank official dealing with the transfer spotted that something was not quite right and reinstated the money with the note *firma incorrecta* (signature not correct). But no alarm seems to have been raised, and Holbert tried again with a new check for the same amount on February 8. Right from the beginning—and surely fearful that his source of "free" money might dry up—Holbert took the calculated risk of transferring much larger amounts from Hong Kong to Panama than Brown usually did. From February 8, 2008, when the transfer of $15,900 finally went through, until

April 2 of the same year, when he transferred $43,610, Holbert made a total of $162,710 available for systematic ATM withdrawals on Brown's HSBC account in Panama. As he told investigators on July 30, 2010, he withdrew cash from the single ATM in Bocas Town—or other ATMs in Almirante or in Changuinola—up to his daily limit. This pattern continued until either the money ran out or the account was blocked; the figure of $225,000 that Holbert gave to the investigators might have been the total of the cash that he was able to get out of local ATMs before his activity was halted. It was not necessarily the case that Brown had $225,000 in his HSBC account in Hong Kong—he might have had more. What we do know is that, when he was arrested, Holbert had left just $508.78 in Brown's HSBC account number 100340471 in Panama.

Because of Michael Brown/Salem's criminal past, and the ultra-discreet way in which he felt he needed to live his life in Bocas del Toro, compared to Bo Icelar and—especially—the sociable and vivacious Cher Hughes, when the story of the murders in Darklands broke, much less was known about him and his family. Gradually, this situation started to change. As early as July 22, 2010, a man who preferred not to identify himself made a statement to an officer named Wilmer Santamaría at a police station in the city of Changuinola, the provincial capital of Bocas del Toro. The man told Santamaría that he was "a friend of the Brown family." He said that he still maintained contact with Marco Brown, Michael Brown's son from an earlier relationship, but that the last time he had seen the other members of the Brown family was three to four years previously. This had happened at their home in Darklands. Since the anonymous witness said that he had seen the Browns on a Sunday— and that William Dathan Holbert was also present—it is likely that this was either December 16 or 23, 2007; both these dates fell on Sundays that year. The man related that he was leaving the Browns' house, after spending the weekend with them, just as Holbert was arriving. The two men were introduced, Holbert as "Bill Cortez." That is when Michael Brown took the anonymous witness to one side and told him that Bill Cortez had offered to buy his property for $750,000. Brown went on to explain why he was selling: he and his family had spent a long time in the bush and his younger son, Watson, was growing up, so it would be a good idea to spend time "in the city" (the witness did not specify which city). Brown added that he was having some problems with his other son, Marco. The anonymous witness had no further contact with the Browns after that day. The witness assumed that Brown and his family had left the country. Sometime later, the witness bumped into Holbert and Reese, who went under the names Bill and Jane Cortez, at the Romero supermarket in Changuinola. The witness asked Holbert about the Browns. Holbert told him that he had indeed bought the Browns' property but that he had no idea where the Browns had gone. Subsequently, the declared figure of $750,000, which Michael Brown said that Holbert had offered him for his property, might also have led to Holbert's unmasking if one of Michael Brown's friends or associates had contacted the police after becoming suspicious.

On September 2, 2010, a young woman named Leanne Brown, who carried a Dutch passport, made contact with the authorities in Panama City. She was Michael Brown's daughter and said that she was presently living in Cuba and studying medicine in that country. Leanne Brown was interviewed at the state prosecutor's office by an official named Julio Villareal. Leanne Brown showed Villareal a photo that she said was taken sometime before November 2006. "I know this," said Leanne Brown, "because Marco lived in Panama up to November 2006." The photo showed a smiling, long-limbed boy of African American or Caribbean descent standing to the right of a white man of late middle age. The man was visibly happy and relaxed. In front of the man was a woman of Southeast Asian descent and a shy-looking boy who appeared to be the son of the two adults. The group seemed to be standing on farmland; in the background there were trees and broad banana leaves. Leanne's father, half brother, and stepmother were in the photo and were now dead; only the tall boy—Marco Brown—was still alive. Leanne Brown told Villareal that in January 2008 her mother (Michael Brown's former wife, who was Jamaican) and her brother, Marco, had been trying to contact her father, and Marco had been trying to get in touch with Watson.

When Marco noticed that Watson wasn't replying to his e-mails, he contacted several friends of his father to see if they had had news of him. Marco had the password to his father's e-mail account and saw that he had been in contact with someone named Bill Cortez. On reading the exchange of e-mails, Marco thought that his father had sold the property. Prompted by Marco, one of Michael Brown's friends delved deeper into what had become a worrying mystery. He saw that the Brown family home had been put up for sale on the Internet by a man calling himself Bill Reese. This, of course, was Holbert. But the asking price was much lower than the price ($750,000) that Michael Brown had supposedly sold his Darklands residence for. The same friend sent an e-mail to Bill Reese saying he was interested in buying the property. He got hold of Bill Reese's phone number and then called him pretending to be Michael Brown's brother. He asked Bill Reese/Holbert where the Brown family was. Bill Reese said the same thing to Michael Brown's friend that he had said to the anonymous witness: they had sold up and left quickly. Almost certainly Michael Brown's friend did not relay his suspicions to the police.

Leanne Brown told the Panamanian authorities that the choice of remote Darklands as a place to live had taken its toll on her father and his family. "There are always problems between parents and children. Marco got to an age when he didn't want to live in Bocas anymore. There wasn't much to do there," said Leanne Brown. Marco left for Jamaica, his mother's home country, and enrolled in an information technology course there. But Michael Brown gave his elder son an airline ticket with an open return date so he could fly back to Panama whenever he wanted.

Julio Villareal asked Leanne Brown what her father did for a living.

"My father retired very young and always wanted a small farm with horses and so on, so he moved to Panama and worked his farm."

"How did your parents meet?"

"My parents met in Jamaica in the 1980s. I think it started like any other relationship might start. I was born in 1986 when my mother was nineteen. My brother [Marco] was born in 1989, but very soon after they separated. He [my father] moved to Thailand and St. Maarten, I don't remember in what order, we went when we were very small. My parents remained in contact. I remember asking my father [about the split] when I was about fourteen, and he replied that my mother was very young and she couldn't handle the situation, that he loved her, but that he liked to travel a lot and my mother didn't." Eventually, Leanne Brown returned to Jamaica when she was sixteen. Although Watson Brown, Michael Brown's son with his Thai wife, Nan, was born in 1990, according to his Dutch passport, he looked noticeably younger than his half brother Marco, who was born the previous year. Leanne Brown also said that her father had asked Marco in early December 2007 what he would do if he gave him $100,000, because he had helped build the house in Darklands and it was his share of the sale.

"Did Michael Brown have any enemies?"

"No, not that I know of."

"Did he have any relatives?"

"I don't know where they are, but I do know they are in the United States. My father hadn't talked with them in years."

"Did your father acquire another nationality?"

"My father was a Dutch citizen. That's all I know. I think my father was born in the United States, but he left when he was very young. Then he settled in St. Maarten and became a Dutch citizen."

"Do you know if your father, Michael Brown, was known by any other name?"

"I just know his name is Michael Brown, maybe they call him Mike."

Leanne Brown gave a blood sample to identify her father. The probability of paternity was recorded as 99.46 percent. Later in September 2010, DNA taken from one of Watson's teeth showed a 99.05 percent match with Leanne. Watson's DNA showed a 99.96 percent match with Nan Brown's DNA, demonstrating maternity. In due course, the three death certificates were issued.

As a young man, Michael Brown/Salem had a long criminal record. He was charged with burglary and grand larceny in Florida in 1961 and again in 1964. The following year he resisted arrest; grand larceny again in 1967; then "fugitive flight escape" in 1968. All this was in Florida. There was a count of armed robbery in Atlanta, Georgia, the same year, and in 1969, also in Atlanta, "robbery by use of weapon." In the 1970s there were multiple counts of possession of illegal drugs; two escapes from the custody of the Miami Dade Police Department; and one count each of kidnapping and of attempted homicide. In 1988 there were two counts of importing narcotics (LSD and cocaine), this time in Darwin, Australia.

To become a resident of Panama, Michael Brown presented to the authorities a *Certificate of Good Conduct from the Island Territory of St. Maarten, N.A.* (Netherlands Antilles). The document, dated November 18, 2002, certifies that *Michael Watson Brown is registered in the registers of population of the island of St. Maarten, N.A. This certificate is issued in connection with the VIETNAMESE AUTHORITIES.* At the bottom of the document it reads: *Signed in the name of the Lt. Governor by Derrick E. Holiday, Chief of Police* (the title was written in Dutch).

Derrick E. Holiday was convicted of forgery and fraud in St. Maarten in March 2009. He appealed to St. Maarten's Supreme Court, which upheld the conviction. Holiday was sentenced to a one-year suspended sentence, two years of probation, 180 hours of community service, and a three-year ban from the St. Maarten police force. Meanwhile, Michael Brown's Dutch passport (Nan Brown and Watson also had Dutch passports) records his place of birth—improbably—as Antigua. All three Brown family passports give the relevant issuing office as *Ambassadeur te San Jose* (Ambassador to San José). The Browns had this much in common with the man charged with killing them. William Dathan Holbert's fake Dutch passport made out to William Adolfo Cortez also had *Ambassadeur te San Jose* stamped on the document as the issuing office.

Time has hardly removed the evidence of Holbert and Reese's passage through Bocas del Toro. A small red Mazda covered in dust and dirt is parked outside a police station opposite the airport terminal in Bocas Town. It used to be Bo Icelar's. The license plates have been removed and there is nothing lying on the seats. Close by, men and boys are spilling out of a gate to a soccer field after the referee's final whistle. Their long shadows dance across the turf. Meanwhile, Holbert's old cigar boat bobs up and down in the water behind the main police building on the seafront. Another motorboat is stranded outside of town on a patch of marshland. Locals say it was driven inland in a ferocious storm. That one belonged to Cher Hughes.

Vessels of all sizes ply the narrow sound between Columbus Island and the neighboring island of Carenero so often that the water is barely ever clear. Right now a tottering three-story party boat is returning from a far-off beach. Flags fly from its mast, and kids lie out on deck like so many lizards in the sun, others drinking under the thatched roof of the onboard bar.

I go over to Carenero to take a closer look at the Casa del Sapo, which was Cher Hughes's short-term rentals business. I walk past a couple of pastel-colored hotels, one of which adjoins a red and white lighthouse that might well have been constructed as a real estate feature. The Casa del Sapo is one of several residences built at the water's edge next to the hotels. It's the perfect location, facing Bocas Town across the water. Unlike the other structures, it is made of unpainted wood stained a dark red, Scandinavian style. Three or four air-conditioning units poke out close to windows with white frames. There is some laundry hanging out to dry on the deck, which juts out over the water. One of the windows is ajar. Some-one has rented the house and moved in, perhaps unaware of its history.

Behind the facade of the hotels and the expat residences there is third-world poverty: a couple of fires have been lit to burn coconut husks and other refuse; hens dart across the muddy spaces between the simple shacks of the island families; children are wearing rags. But it feels pro-vincial in a nice way, too, because there are no cars here and everyone says hello to people they meet on the narrow dirt path that connects the dwell-ings, offering a smile. This doesn't happen as much in Bocas Town.

The sun, low in the sky, finally breaks through the clouds and I see that the Casa del Sapo and the waterfront mansions and the two hotels have been angled to catch the sunset views. The narrow strip of beach they sit on is so white, it could almost be made from chalk, except where the lap-ping tide has left black lines of spilled engine oil. In the water, long tresses of seaweed and algae are gently pushed and pulled this way and that.

Over in Darklands, the Jolly Roger Social Club is smaller than I had imagined it. The place is also a ruin. Pretty much everything in the bar that wasn't bolted to the floor or one of the walls has been taken away by souvenir seekers. These days, a urinal screwed to the wall is the only thing left that could feasibly be wrenched off. The floorboards have been attacked by termites and are close to collapsing; it would be dangerous to climb the stairs to the second floor where Holbert and Reese offered a couple of rooms for rent. Most of the paint has peeled off the upper-floor balcony. A few discarded beer bottles lie in corners. Perhaps the structure is still used by someone as a venue for parties. In the kitchen, the stove where Holbert did his greasy cooking has been ripped away and the cupboards are smashed up. The U-shaped, tiled bar where Reese served drinks and stared into the distance is still there. It was probably too big to move. The wooden boards closest to the water are covered by an encroaching slime, like a moist green moss. Meanwhile, the Browns' old house is being guarded by three policemen working two-week shifts. They cook their meals on the open, upper floor where, years earlier, Marco and Watson rode their skateboards. They sleep in hammocks in the same space where they eat. The policemen are bored but friendly. One tells me the place gives him nightmares. He heard some noises in one of the bathrooms one night, when no one was inside, and that gave him the creeps. On the first floor, the inside of the house looks like it has been set on fire. On a ledge in the kitchen there is an old, discolored can of Hershey's cocoa—this is pretty much all that is left. Holbert's flags and his skull and crossbones HACIENDA CORTEZ sign have long been removed; an old DO NOT CROSS police tape flutters in the breeze.

The house that Cher Hughes and Keith Werle built on the island is visible from the Browns' old dock. I think of Jack the dog swimming across this mile and a half of still sea to lead Werle and the police to Hughes's grave. A couple of small indigenous children, a boy and a girl, are playing outside the boathouse that guards access to Hughes's former home. Inside the boathouse there are a stove, a couple of mattresses, clothes hanging out to dry. The only sounds are the tame waves lapping against the shore. Dina lives in the boathouse with her four children. "These two kids are the ones Cher never knew," says Dina, who doesn't give me her last name. The two children Cher used to spoil now go to school, so they are not at home. "When Cher was here, my first two were the ages of these here," says Dina, pointing at her younger children. Does she miss Cher? Dina nods.

A steep stairway cut into a slope above the boathouse leads up to the main residence. The sun beats down, and climbing the twenty or so steps is enough to make you sweat a little. From the outside, the property looks like a new home that has been subjected to a sudden, accelerated aging process. A wide deck, flecks of varnish here and there, has been taken over by termites. It is strewn with corn husks and home to half a dozen hens. A wooden bench with room for two people, constructed like a swing, looks out over a secluded cove. But a couple of the planks are missing so it is no longer functional. The geography of the location becomes apparent: the house is on the brow of a hill and has views of the sea on three sides. Bushes and banana trees give the property privacy, and the deck is out of view of the boathouse. There is a profusion of plants with purple flowers. The water in the cove below is translucent, achingly inviting on such a hot day. An island a hundred yards offshore has a guest cottage. The kitchen is open-air; inside the house there is a bedroom, dressing room, and bathroom with a large, sunken tub. This is what there is—it is a home designed for two people. The bedroom has piles of bedclothes, terminally damp in the moist, salty air. The terra-cotta floor tiles are cool. In the bedroom there is a book on Rottweilers, a picture book of Ireland, another with paintings from the Louvre museum. Photos are on display everywhere: speedboats, sunshine, sea. Maritime charts with the beginnings of mold. There is a decorative bottle with glass geckos climbing over it. Dina looks around impassively. This will never be normal, but it is a situation she must live with. She has little choice unless she leaves her home on the dock. On the top of a low bookcase set against a wall in the bedroom, there is a framed picture of Cher and Keith on their wedding day, smashed. Momentarily, the shards of glass in the frame catch a ray of sun passing through the large window.

A hen has gotten into the bathroom and is clucking around a collection of toiletries. It gets shooed out with a loud flap of its wings. The sunlight outside is almost blinding. But there is something else to see, quickly. Adjacent to the house are two gazebos built in a style common in Central America—essentially, huts with no walls and a roof of bamboo thatch. These have a social function and are used for entertaining. Outside the first gazebo is a stone sundial inscribed with the lines, *Grow old along with me! / The best is yet to be.* In the second there is a pile of cassette tapes: the Beach Boys, Buddy Holly and the Crickets, Chaka

Khan, a homemade mix tape with I LOVE YOU written on it. Also, a book, dusty, its cover faded: it's *The Path Between the Seas*, a history of the building of the Panama Canal, by David McCullough. A Madonna cassette tape is broken, its shiny, narrow tape in ribbons falling onto the floor. The person or persons responsible for taking Cher Hughes's life killed her for all this.

On July 30, 2010, William Dathan Holbert confessed to killing three members of the Brown family, Bo Icelar, and Cher Hughes. On September 20, 2010, Holbert admitted to Panamanian investigators that he had been responsible for the death of American lawyer Jeffrey Arlan Kline, too:

"At the beginning of 2006 there was a fight in the province of Bocas del Toro between Jeffrey Arlan Kline, a US citizen, and myself, which resulted in his accidental death. It was self-defense. [. . .] Shortly after I arrived in Costa Rica, I don't recall when, but it was in 2006, I traveled alone to Bocas del Toro to see what it was like."

Holbert said he had met Kline at the Best Western hotel in San José, the capital of Costa Rica. One thing led to another, and Holbert and Kline found themselves on a boat "close to Isla Colón in Bocas del Toro." In Holbert's account, "Kline started taking cocaine and offered it to me. But I don't do drugs and this upset him. An argument started and he got violent and hit me several times. He was a huge man and while we were fighting he fell over and hit his head on the boat's anchor, which penetrated his head and killed him. I was horrified but I couldn't alert the authorities as I was a wanted man in the United States." Holbert went on to tell the investigators that he returned in the boat to Costa Rica to bury Kline's body, insisting nonetheless that the death had occurred in Panamanian waters.

A man named Raymond Stuart Davies doesn't remember it exactly that way.

On April 29, 2011, in a communication marked "Urgent," Laura Monge Cantero, an official at the Costa Rican attorney general's office, issued a formal request to her counterpart in Panama for assistance in gathering evidence from a vital witness to the disappearance of Jeffrey Arlan Kline. A report appended to the request set out the scenario that the Costa Rican authorities considered most likely. In short, William Dathan Holbert and Laura Michelle Reese had murdered Kline and then dug a hole in the patio of the house they were renting at Playa Negra, just outside Puerto Viejo, the town on Costa Rica's Caribbean coast that had been their first stop in Central America. They had tossed Kline's corpse into the hole and poured concrete over it. For the Costa Rican authorities, there was no doubt that Holbert and Reese had acted together. The communication to Panama's attorney general's office said that Raymond Stuart Davies could likely help the Costa Rican authorities in their inquiries. A mobile phone number attributed to Davies was included in the letter.

On August 1, 2011, Raymond Stuart Davies was interviewed by Panamanian investigators in the city of David. A retired engineer from Cardiff, Wales, Davies was fifty-six at the time he gave his statement. He had lived in Puerto Viejo between 2005 and 2008, running his own motorbike rental shop, but subsequently moved to western Panama "because there are a lot of thieves in Costa Rica."

Back in 2006, Davies and Holbert had been friends, at least for a while. This was despite, rather than because of, Holbert's rather off-putting "Ku Klux Klan–style" shaved head. Davies estimated that Holbert packed around 250 pounds at the time, with Reese—whom Holbert introduced as his wife—then weighing approximately 145 pounds. Davies did not remember precisely when he met Holbert and Reese, but it is likely that it was in late February or early March 2006. Holbert introduced himself as "Bill" and was not using "Cortez" as a surname. Reese, meanwhile, used her real name, Michelle—she had yet to start calling herself Jane. Davies explained that Holbert and Reese briefly quit Puerto Viejo, and then returned. "They frequently rented motorbikes from me," said Davies, recalling the period when he got to know the young American couple particularly well. "This was about five to seven weeks before Jeffrey Kline disappeared."

Davies had a house with four bedrooms and was living alone at the time, so he offered Holbert and Reese a room to rent. It was a casual arrangement; when Davies was not attending to his motorbike business he liked playing billiards with Holbert. After three or four weeks, Holbert and Reese left Davies's house with plans to rent a new place in San José, a six-hour drive away. Money was apparently not a problem: Holbert had boasted to Davies that he had made $60,000 from the sale of some gold.

Davies's account was given in English with an interpreter on hand to relate the Welshman's account to the investigators in Spanish. This may account for an error that appears to have slipped into the statement: when Davies is quoted as saying that Holbert and Reese were away for "about five or six months," it is likely that he said "five or six weeks." At any event, for a while Davies heard nothing more from the pair. But one day Davies came home and was surprised to find Holbert cooking a meal. Reese was there, too. Holbert explained to Davies that he had rented a "very luxurious house" in San José and set up a secondhand car business there. Davies pricked up his ears: "I was interested as I had worked in that line of business." Bill produced a bottle of vodka. The mood was relaxed and Davies and Holbert started a game of billiards. The two friends picked up where they had left off when Bill and Michelle left for San José.

"That's when Bill said he wanted to kill people who weren't productive, people with terminal illnesses, bad people, people who weren't needed. His wife repeated what he said. He took off his T-shirt and I saw he had a lot of tattoos, including a swastika. Bill tried to persuade me that killing people was normal. Then I asked him if he meant what he was saying. He cleared his throat and coughed and changed the subject saying, 'I don't want to talk about it.'"

Raymond Stuart Davies told Holbert, "You're not normal."

Holbert replied, "Everyone has his own opinion."

The atmosphere had become tense. "His wife was like a parrot on his shoulder," recalled Davies, "repeating what he said and backing it all up. They sounded just the same."

Despite the embarrassment of that night, Holbert and Reese stayed on at Davies's house. A few days later, Davies needed to travel to San José to buy some motorbikes. Holbert suggested that he would go along as well; he was also thinking of buying a motorbike. Reese stayed behind in Puerto Viejo. In San José, Davies bought two motorbikes and loaded them onto his pickup, but Holbert didn't buy any. Later, they went to an evening happy hour at the bar of the Best Western hotel where they were staying—a low-rise place with a casino attached, a drone of vehicles passing by, just off the Pan-American Highway.

There was an overweight man sitting at the bar, recalled Davies, "and Bill went up to him and sat very close to him. We got our drinks and started talking with the man. He told Bill that he had just got off the plane. He was dressed very formally in a black jacket and pants. He handed us his business cards, which showed he was a lawyer. Then I asked him why he was there. He said he had come to Costa Rica to start a new life as he had had some problems in his marriage. I asked him where in Costa Rica he was headed, and he replied, 'The Pacific side.' I told him that he would need a lot of money because all the properties on the Pacific were very expensive. In fact, he would need a huge amount of money so as to make an offer nobody could refuse. I was trying to help him so that he wouldn't make an unwise investment and lose all his money.

"That's when the man told Bill and me that he had over a hundred thousand dollars. I said that with that amount of money he would have more chance of investing on the Caribbean side of the country, because it was still being developed."

Davies told the investigators in David that Holbert then said to the man, who had introduced himself as Jeff, that he could stay in the house where he was staying—meaning Davies's house—as there was a room free next door to his. Davies did not object, and Jeff suggested that they all meet again in the morning. Jeff, of course, was the troubled Illinois attorney Jeffrey Arlan Kline. That same day after breakfast, a matter of hours after Kline had met Davies and Holbert, the three men drove back to Puerto Viejo in Davies's pickup. Holbert stepped out of the vehicle a few miles before they reached Davies's house, so Kline and Davies entered the property without Holbert. "I put the man in a room next to Bill's room," said Davies. Kline's room and the room where Holbert and Reese were staying were in a separate part of the house from where Davies slept, and they shared their own entrance.

According to Davies's statement, nobody had previously rented the room that Kline was going to occupy. There was a bed with a mattress but no sheets or pillows. Davies went to fetch bed linens, leaving Kline alone in the room. When he returned, Davies started to make up the bed. "I was only gone for a few minutes to get the sheets and a towel. I came back and lifted up the mattress to fold the sides of the sheets underneath. That's when I saw a large amount of cash.

"I said, 'That's a lot of money.' Jeff said that it was $10,000 that he had brought with him. I told Jeff that it wasn't a good idea to carry around so much money and that he should deposit it in a bank. I told him that I knew the local bank manager and that I would go with him to the bank the next day to help him open an account."

That night, Kline asked Davies for a restaurant recommendation. Davies suggested an Italian place near the beach. Jeff was going to ride there on a motorbike he had rented from Davies. "Jeff asked me if I had time to go down to the restaurant for a beer or two. I had some errands to run and in the end I got to the restaurant at about five p.m. I saw that Jeff was sitting there chatting with Bill and Michelle." Davies had a drink with Holbert, Reese, and Kline and left the restaurant at about seven p.m. But Davies was worried that Kline might be drinking too much and told him so: "Jeff didn't know the way back to the house. He needed to take it easy." Davies made his way home; Holbert, Reese, and Kline stayed on at the restaurant.

At around midnight Davies saw an ambulance outside his window. Kline was getting out of it. He appeared a bit drunk. "I asked him where the motorbike was. He said he had crashed on a bridge and fallen into a river." Kline had been taken to the hospital but had been released after a couple of hours since he only had minor injuries.

After the accident, it turned out that Kline didn't have his room key with him, so Davies went to a storeroom where he kept copies of the keys to the bedrooms. The problem was, the key to Kline's room had disappeared. "I told him that he wasn't going to be able to sleep in his room that night and that he would have to sleep in an armchair on the landing," meaning until the problem of the missing key could be sorted out.

The next day Davies managed to recover the motorbike from the river and took it away to get it repaired. Davies assumed that Holbert and Reese had spent the night in a cabin close to the beach since they had not come back to the house the previous night. "I told Bill and his wife what had happened to Jeff, and that Jeff had ten thousand dollars in cash hidden under his mattress. I also told them that Jeff needed to open a bank account as soon as possible."

The following day Davies went to work in his motorbike rental shop. A little later, Kline came in. "I asked him how he was feeling, He said, 'Not very well. Someone robbed me.' I said, 'What do you mean?' Then Bill turned up and asked him the same question. Bill said to him, 'I hope you don't think it was me who robbed you.' Jeff said, 'No, I think someone got in by opening the door and took all my cash.' I jumped on a bike and Bill asked me if he could come, too. When we got to the house there was no sign that the door had been forced. Bill said, 'I think Jeff has gone crazy. He was using cocaine and I think that made him crazy.'

"I think Bill wanted to brainwash me into thinking that Jeff was a drug addict and that there had been no robbery at all. We went back to the bike rental shop and I said to Jeff, 'I don't understand, the door wasn't forced. Isn't it possible that you had the money on you when you had the accident and crashed into the river?'" Kline replied in the negative. He said to Davies, "I'm not stupid. Anyway, there was too much money to carry in the pockets of my pants."

Davies convinced Jeff that, despite losing most of his cash, he still needed to open a bank account, and that $20 or $30 was all that you needed to open one. But Davies still had to fix the bike that Kline had crashed, and couldn't leave his shop. So Holbert went to the bank to help Kline open an account, saying that he also had an account at the same bank. Years later, Davies came to the conclusion that "that's when Bill realized how much money Jeff had, and found out that Jeff intended to transfer $100,000 from the United States to Costa Rica."

Although Kline had rented the room in Davies's house for a month, he left early. About a week after Kline arrived in Puerto Viejo, Holbert and Reese moved out of Davies's place, too, and rented a cabin on Punta Uva Beach owned by some Italians. Because they had become friends, Jeff rented a cabin on the same beach as Holbert and Reese. In Puerto Viejo, like in Bocas del Toro, over the border, people's living arrangements can be very informal. You can get a good deal offered over a drink. Moving on is as simple as packing your suitcase and jumping into a cab. A couple of weeks after setting up a temporary home in the cabin at Punta Uva Beach, Holbert and Reese moved out and rented a house in Playa Negra— Black Beach—instead. But Holbert and Reese kept in touch with Davies and Kline. "One day Jeff and I were invited to a barbecue on the beach [Playa Negra]. But I didn't go as I suddenly needed to travel to San José. Two days later I got back to find out that Jeff had had some kind of fit and that they [Holbert and Reese] had called an ambulance to take him off to the capital."

Holbert and Reese gave Davies an account of what happened. It seems the episode of getting Kline to get into the ambulance had a comic side: "They were both laughing about how they had had to force Jeff to put his shirt on, implying that there had been a scuffle." But Davies noticed that Holbert hadn't even as much as a scratch on him. "That made me suspicious because [Kline] was a big man." Where was the evidence of this scuffle? Their conversation that day was cut short because Holbert appeared to be in a hurry. "He said, 'I've got to go to the bank and sort something out urgently.'" Later, Holbert and Reese told Davies that Kline "might have been using cocaine because [prior to being taken off in the ambulance] he was hallucinating and was going crazy." Holbert and Reese left for San José a week or so later, but they kept in touch with their former landlord. "From time to time they called me saying that when I went to San José I should stay with them," said Davies.

Davies's statement doesn't give a precise date—it was probably in the middle of 2006—but it turns out that Davies did take Holbert and Reese up on their offer. Holbert and Reese were staying in a rented house in Belén, a pleasant, artsy community around thirty minutes from downtown San José. Davies arrived at about three p.m. and accepted the beer that Holbert offered him. Then the Welshman noticed something unusual.

Beside the house there was a dumpster full of sand and between ten and fifteen sacks of cement. The property had an electric gate and high walls. Davies wondered what Holbert was planning to build, and why. Davies gestured at the dumpster of sand and the sacks of cement. "I asked him, 'What's that for?'" Holbert gave Davies to understand that he was constructing a new security feature. "He said that it was to make sure that his dogs wouldn't escape. I said to him, 'But you don't have a dog.' He said, 'I'm going to get one.'"

When the news broke in July 2010 that an American couple had been apprehended on the border between Costa Rica and Nicaragua, Raymond Stuart Davies—like the great majority of expats—saw the images and recognized his old friends Bill and Michelle, even though Bill now sported long, curly hair. Davies then remembered how Jeff, Holbert and Reese's erstwhile drinking buddy, had disappeared in unusual circumstances. He called the authorities to let them know.

A couple of weeks earlier, police officers in Bocas del Toro sifting through the piles of papers and documents left behind by Holbert and Reese in Darklands found some business cards. There were several cards for Dr. William Reese, MD, Holbert's incarnation as a fake shrink, and another, genuine business card. This one had the name of an attorney-at-law printed on it. It was the card that Jeffrey Arlan Kline— fresh off the plane and still dressed in his North American business suit—had given to Holbert at the happy hour at the Best Western hotel in San José.

One thing you learn if you spend any time among the expats of Bocas del Toro is that cell phones and speedboats don't mix. Salt water, ubiquitous in Bocas, makes many a cell phone a casualty of everyday life. There is a simple way to protect your phone, though: you put it into a ziplock plastic bag. They are sold just about everywhere; all of the Chinese markets in Bocas stock them, for instance. The thing is that people often forget to take this simple precaution.

But two cell phones were working on the afternoon of May 5, 2010, which fell on a Wednesday. They belonged to Holbert and Reese, and the phone company gave the police a copy of the text messages the couple exchanged. The night of May 5 would mark one of the last parties the couple would throw. But it would be a small one. Their social circle was already disintegrating. The couple's days of freedom would soon be curtailed.

Holbert to Reese: *So now what do I do? We may b finished. Our shit is sour, but I truely hate being alone*

Reese to Holbert: *Is everything going ok? Luv u!*

Reese to Holbert: *I just remember well need booze and some kind of mixer for the party, sorry i forgot to put it on the list!*

Holbert to Reese: *Fuk u bocas aint eat shit. This iz a product of ur bullshit. I am 2 old n tired for ur shit anymore, but i luv n mis u 2*

Their game was up.

8. When Scott Met Bill

Scott McAda's fifty-second birthday party on September 30, 2010, was going to be a typically informal Bocas get-together: steak and drinks with friends and neighbors on McAda's fifty-eight-foot Hatteras moored just off Split Hill, the island next to the Darklands Peninsula. McAda and his wife, Belinda, were preparing the food for the party when he got a call from Don Winner, the American expat blogger. "I distinctly remember Don saying, 'Scott, you'd better be sitting down for this one.' It turned out that Don had heard from a North Carolina TV station that Holbert had called mentioning me as being the head of some criminal gang."

The news rather put a damper on the birthday celebrations. McAda called the TV reporter, Russ Bowen of WLOS, the ABC affiliate for Asheville, North Carolina, and found out more about Holbert's allegations. In a nutshell, Holbert had told Bowen that McAda was a kind of Mafia boss transplanted to the Caribbean who had ordered the killings of the Brown family and Bo Icelar. Holbert's story, as relayed to Bowen, involved blackmail and a large dose of casual violence; Wild Bill was not denying that he had pulled the trigger, but he had claimed to Bowen that McAda had ordered the deaths. In a varied business career before moving to Panama four years earlier, McAda had owned five radio stations in the United States and had broadcast on them, too. McAda knew that it was essential to get Bowen quickly on his side to nip Holbert's story in the bud, which is precisely what he did. But Holbert's call to the TV station in North Carolina was just an opening salvo. Things were about to get worse for Scott McAda.

Still, the McAdas' guests were on their way and there was no chance of canceling the birthday party. "Our friends wondered why I looked so preoccupied," recalled Scott McAda. "So I told them." No one could understand why Holbert had singled out McAda—least of all, McAda himself. "I certainly knew the man who everyone at that time called Bill Cortez, but I didn't party with him or socialize with him," said McAda. "Apart from anything else, he was much younger than me. In fact, Holbert was a similar age to my two sons." Age difference or not, the two men were oil and water: for a Bocas expat, Scott McAda is unusually eloquent and reflective, a self-made man who decided on early retirement, entirely comfortable in his own skin. McAda is broad-shouldered, of average height, and keeps his gray hair neat and short. Belinda, his wife of twenty-seven years, wears her blond hair tied back; her bronzed face and arms tell of a love of the outdoors. In a gringo community where assumed names and embellished pasts were the norm, Scott and Belinda McAda were different.

Scott McAda first met Holbert in late 2008 when McAda sold him a floating dock. Several weeks after the dock was installed, Holbert still owed McAda $300 for the labor of a mechanic whom McAda had taken to the Browns' old house in Darklands, which is where Holbert and Reese were living. It was a bill that Holbert should have paid himself, but he said he forgot—"maybe intentionally, to give him a reason to visit," says McAda today. Subsequently, Holbert called McAda and said that he wanted to drop by his house with the money. McAda's main residence at the time was in Boquete. McAda gave Holbert directions to his home and the $300 debt was paid. The two men got talking, casually, after Holbert had given McAda the cash. "I told Bill Cortez that I was from a law enforcement family and that my stepfather, the man who raised me and was the best man at my wedding, had served for twenty-eight years as a special agent for the FBI, and that I was very proud of him."

Holbert left McAda's home abruptly that day and McAda did not hear from him again until he joined Mike Smith and Fran Tilbury—who in the meantime had become firm friends of Bill and Jane Cortez—for food and drinks one night at Holbert's Jolly Roger Social Club. But the boozy get-together took an ugly turn when, as McAda recalls it, Holbert started spouting "ridiculous stuff like he was a god and that people would bow to him. I challenged him and told him he was full of shit and that he might be able to scare some people with that crazy rhetoric, but it did not scare me." Could that rather public dressing-down have given Holbert a reason to bear a grudge against McAda? On another occasion when Holbert was ranting about his "Satanic power," a shooting star fell to earth behind his back. Scott McAda was glad Holbert didn't see it; the young man was "nuts" and he would only have interpreted the shooting star as some kind of sign. On top of that, "I was also the person who found out the two vastly different figures that Cortez was supposed to be paying Bo Icelar for his house," recalled McAda. "I told him back then that he was known to be a bottom-feeder, making low-ball offers on properties to people who were desperate to sell. He didn't like that at all."

Holbert's call to Russ Bowen at WLOS in Asheville was a significant departure from the confession he had made to police in Panama City on July 30, 2010. Speaking of Bo Icelar, Holbert had said in his initial confession that "I decided to kill him because I thought people would assume that it was the United States Mafia who had murdered him. My intention was to steal his assets and to have a house closer to [Bocas] town so I could be happier and my wife could be happier. I took the shares to my attorney, Daniel Anaya, who is innocent of any crime. . . ." Holbert made no mention of Scott McAda or any other expat in his extended statement of that day. His deeds were, he said, his own responsibility and no one else's. And despite the evidence from Raymond Stuart Davies that Laura Michelle Reese had been involved in the plot to kill Jeffrey Kline in Costa Rica in 2006, Holbert claimed that all his killings—starting with Kline and ending with Cher Hughes—were carried out without Reese's involvement or knowledge.

Holbert's new twist on his confession might have received its first airing as early as September 8, 2010. The district attorney's case papers contain a memo for the file from a police officer in Bocas Town named Francisco Orocu, who wrote that he had received an anonymous tip-off that same day from a "very credible source." The source had said that there was "a large quantity of money hidden in a cavity under the bathroom tiles" in Bo Icelar's mansion in Big Creek. According to the source, the money "comes from drug smuggling" and that it concerned, in some undefined way, "weapons to be sold to Colombian insurgents." One possible anonymous source is of course Holbert, who had more of a reason than anyone for planting a lead with authorities (and had access to a phone in jail).

The threat posed by Holbert's call to reporter Russ Bowen had proved relatively straightforward for Scott McAda to diffuse, but the days immediately following the McAdas' party on the Hatteras were the calm before the real storm.

On October 5, 2010, which was a Tuesday, a news bulletin on the Panamanian Telemetro channel aired an off-the-cuff interview with William Dathan Holbert filmed at La Joya jail in Panama City. The footage showed Holbert making a brief statement accusing McAda—in very vague, superficial terms—of being the kingpin of an expat cartel, ordering the man widely known as Bill Cortez to carry out the killings of the Brown family and Bo Icelar. McAda recalled that several of his Panamanian friends called him as soon as Telemetro had run the Holbert item. "The calls started coming in, and it was Walter Kawano [the Bocas realtor who had filed the missing persons report on Bo Icelar] who was the first to phone, I think. They were all saying, 'Scott, what's going on? Have you seen the TV news?'" (Most gringo expats do not tune in to local television programming in Spanish, preferring to get their fix of national news stories from sources like Don Winner's English-language Panama-Guide.com blog—if they bother with it at all.)

Incredulous at Holbert's intervention, Scott McAda—accompanied by his friend Walter Kawano for support—set out almost immediately for the office of District Attorney Luis Martínez in David.* Martínez, a smartly

---

* In the Panamanian system, the district attorney is both investigator and prosecutor. The DA can recommend the dismissal of a case under investigation if it appears there are no grounds for an indictment.

dressed middle-aged man with short, graying hair, was the lead prosecutor for Panama's third legal district—which comprised the provinces of Bocas del Toro and Chiriquí—and had been tasked with handling the investigation into Holbert's crimes. McAda was anxious to see what was going on and was determined to clear his name. With his lawyer present, McAda told Luis Martínez that he had nothing to hide and would naturally cooperate fully with their investigation. Scott McAda also wanted to respond to Holbert directly and in kind. "I was keen to appear on television and the reporters wanted to interview me," said McAda.

McAda's attorney couldn't locate a Telemetro office in David so he approached TVN, which has a studio in David covering news stories in western Panama. McAda, who speaks fluent Spanish, took his opportunity to rebut Holbert's accusations, which were broadcast nationwide later the same day. For his part, DA Luis Martínez had received McAda politely—starting at that first meeting, and for as long as their paths crossed, DA Martínez adopted a scrupulously level, neutral tone with him—but Martínez had not seen Holbert's Telemetro statement. Still, the DA had access to the details of Holbert's new allegations because these had already been made to the authorities. Unknown to Scott McAda, on September 20, Holbert had claimed to Panamanian deputy state prosecutor Ángel Calderón that there was a "massive criminal conspiracy" linking the murders of the Brown family, Bo Icelar, and Cher Hughes. "There are many people involved and their activities include murder, drugs, pedophilia, human trafficking, money laundering, arms trafficking, fraud, fraud by attorneys, and the smuggling of pre-Colombian art and artifacts." Holbert portrayed himself in his new account as a hapless minor player in an unlawful enterprise masterminded by Scott McAda.

Holbert said his links with McAda went back to his first days in Central America in 2006. He told Calderón's team that, while in Puerto Viejo, "Scott McAda called me and told me to meet a friend of his in the Hotel Best Western Irazú [in San José, capital of Costa Rica]. That was the first time I met Mr. Jeffrey Kline. Mr. Kline was a partner of Mr. McAda. I had the order from Mr. McAda that when I was trafficking the illegal immigrants, I should take Mr. Kline with me. . . ." Holbert told the prosecutor that McAda had masterminded fifteen illegal immigrant trafficking operations in a three-month period and that on the fourth or fifth trip he (Holbert) had gotten into a fistfight with Kline and had accidentally killed him. Holbert said that McAda knew he had killed Kline, and McAda could—and did—use that knowledge against him.

There was more: in 2007, when Holbert was operating as a fake psychiatrist in Boquete, "Mr. McAda asked me if I was looking for work, I was out of work, I was broke, the profession of false psychiatrist paid nothing . . . and he suggested that I assassinate Mike Brown and take his job of trafficking people and immigrants as his partner." But McAda was "blackmailing me . . . he knew I was wanted in the United States. Mr. McAda told me that Mr. Brown was sick, that he had cancer of the spine." At some point while he was a guest at the Browns' house in Darklands just before Christmas 2007, Holbert asked McAda what to do about Brown's wife and teenage son, a minor, and McAda said, according to Holbert, "Kill all three of them."

Holbert also stated that McAda "wanted Mr. Icelar dead. I have worked very many times with Scott McAda in various illegal activities. I was morally weak and I accepted [the job of killing Bo Icelar], which I regret. I had made a reputation for myself of being a businessman who bought and sold things. So I went to see Mr. Icelar to arrange to buy his property. We agreed that on a certain day he would come to my house, so he would meet my lawyer. This was all untrue as there was no such lawyer. [. . .] Mr. Scott McAda offered me $100,000 to carry out the contract killing of Mr. Icelar, but there was only $8,000 in cash [in Bo Icelar's house]. That's why Mr. McAda suggested to me that Mr. Icelar's properties be transferred to me to cover the payment for the killing. I wasn't happy about this because I didn't want real estate. I wanted cash. The truth is that Mr. McAda and I planned the killing together. It seems that Bo Icelar was stealing from [McAda] and that's why Mr. McAda wanted Mr. Icelar dead. But I can also imagine that it might have been Mr. McAda who was stealing from Mr. Icelar. What is for sure is that they were up to something unlawful. [. . .] Bo Icelar had a lot of boxes on the first floor of his house containing pre-Colombian artworks and African art. After Mr. Icelar's death, I was given instructions that these boxes were the property of Mr. McAda."

At his interview on September 20, the investigators even gave Holbert time to mount an attack on his treatment in prison in Panama City, which was duly recorded in the file: "The current state of my detention at the hands of Panamanian justice amounts to torture. . . . There's no soap or toilet paper and I can't wash my clothes. . . . The treatment is a violation of national and international law and also contravenes the human rights treaties to which Panama is signatory." A prison guard had asked Holbert for money in return for "basic privileges," claimed the former Wild Bill, taking the moral high ground: "Corruption is not an acceptable cultural difference. Bribes have no place in a fair system."

Holbert was not quite done with his new story, however. The accusation of arms trafficking—apparently to or from Russia, and first raised on September 20, 2010—was fleshed out by Holbert in a statement given to District Attorney Luis Martínez on February 3, 2011. By this time, Holbert and Laura Michelle Reese had been transferred from the penitentiary in Panama City to the prison in David close to where Martínez was based. Holbert claimed that Scott McAda's son Wes, a university professor who had spent two years as a graduate student at Moscow State University, had supplied Holbert with the weapon to kill Bo Icelar. "And something that is extremely important," continued Holbert, "is that Mr. McAda's father was an FBI agent in the United States. He [McAda] said he had links with the CIA. . . . About three days ago I was informed that he [McAda] had put a $50,000 price on my head. This amount of money is sufficient to bring a hit man in from overseas. . . ." Holbert also claimed that McAda had a house in Colombia that he used as a base for his crime network. The district attorney, as ever, read out to Holbert a summary of his rights and obligations before he was invited to make his statement on February 3, 2011. These included the provision that "anyone [who] has confessed in good time, or has revealed the identity of the perpetrators, accomplices and accessories of the crime, and has provided sufficient evidence for their case to go to trial, will have the right to have his sentence reduced by half, or for the sentence to be suspended according to Article 2139 of the Judicial Code." Holbert's motive for implicating McAda could hardly have been spelled out more clearly.

Shortly after Holbert's February 3, 2011, statement, McAda received a summons to appear at the courthouse in David. The policemen delivering the summons lingered at the gate of McAda's comfortable house in Boquete. "I invited them in," recalled McAda. "But they were kind of apprehensive. It was as if they thought I was a gringo version of Pablo Escobar." At the courthouse in David, McAda was informed by Luis Martínez that he was being charged with the murder of, and robbery from, the three members of the Brown family and Bo Icelar—on the basis of an accusation made by a self-confessed killer. McAda would have to report to a police station every two weeks and was forbidden from leaving Panama. It made little sense: if he was being accused of the same crimes as Holbert and Reese (with the only difference being that Holbert had not implicated him in the murder of Cher Hughes), why was he not being sent to prison, along with Wild Bill and Jane Cortez? Under Panamanian law, suspects are only freed on bail when they are charged with crimes for which a prison sentence of not more than four years applies. Here, the maximum custodial sentence was four terms of thirty years each. McAda was thankful not to be locked up, but the DA's "country arrest" decision appeared to contravene Panamanian law. McAda asked his local attorney for an explanation, but the lawyer told him he could not understand it, either.

It was again McAda's turn to react to Holbert, but how? His attorney suggested the little-used option of a *careo* (pronounced ka-RAY-oh), a face-to-face meeting between McAda and his accuser in the presence of the staff of the district attorney's office, with Holbert's lawyer and McAda's own lawyer also in attendance, together with a court interpreter. (DA Luis Martínez put his signature to the report of the first and also the second *careo* with Holbert, but McAda has no recollection of his attending either meeting.)

Shortly after two p.m. on May 13, 2011, Scott McAda took his place in a brightly lit meeting room at the provincial courthouse in David, a sprawling complex on the outskirts of the city. "When you go through the main entrance you see a table selling religious trinkets. There are crucifixes on the walls, and pictures of Jesus," said McAda. As a young man, Scott McAda had wanted to become a preacher. But he started to doubt his faith. He struggled with those doubts for ten years until he became an atheist. Unsurprisingly, then, the religious imagery jarred with McAda's conviction of how a court should present itself. William Dathan Holbert entered the room in handcuffs and manacles, watched over by three policemen, and sat down opposite McAda.

"I expected Holbert to back down when he saw me in person," said McAda. "But he didn't. He actually raised the stakes."

At the opening of the *careo*, Holbert and McAda were asked in turn to confirm that they agreed to take part. Both men said yes. The various declarations made by Holbert while in custody implicating McAda in his crimes were read aloud. Holbert was the first to take the floor: "How can it be that my innocent wife is still in jail while the men who have masterminded these crimes walk free? [...] I have tried to speed up justice, so as to reduce the cost to the Panamanian taxpayer, by helping the investigation as much as I can. The thanks I have been given are the shameless lies peddled by some officials of the Panamanian justice system in declarations made to the national press." Holbert said that various investigators had said that, among other things, he adored Satan, ate human flesh, and had killed over fifty people. "They also said that I'm a racist and that I tortured my victims before killing them."

Holbert then abruptly altered his tone and spoke slowly and deliberately: "I want the truth to be known. I am a Christian and I have an active relationship with Jesus Christ. I have never eaten human flesh. I have never tortured a creature on God's earth. I love people of all races and customs. I love the beautiful people of the Republic of Panama.

"My question today is this: How is it possible for justice to be served when public officials make such irresponsible and untrue declarations with the intention of becoming famous?

"As far as my crimes are concerned, I want to state the following. In a criminal organization, when you receive the order from your boss to kill someone, it's not a simple request you can turn down. It's a shadowy world where sharks eat other sharks. I recognize that my own selfish decisions have brought me to the situation I find myself in. But I never meant to hurt anyone. Violence is a horrible thing and I am not a violent person. [...] I am full of remorse for my crimes and I have asked Jesus Christ for forgiveness for my sins, big and small. I am totally committed to the process of rehabilitation." Holbert was careful to distance himself from the confession he had made on July 30, 2010, the day after he was sent back to Panama from Nicaragua: "I am not confident of the truthfulness of any statement I made from the moment of my arrest in Nicaragua up to the time of my transfer [from Panama City] to Chiriquí." In other words, he wanted the DA to know that he had not acted alone in the way described in his confession of July 30, 2010.

Through the court interpreter, McAda was asked to respond to Holbert's claims. "Mr. Holbert, you have stated that we met for the first time in 2006. Can you please tell me where we met and in which month? I would also like the accused to look at me and tell me if my appearance has changed in any way between the time he claims we first met and the present day. My next question: How did Mr. Holbert communicate with me? If he used a cell phone, what number did he dial? If he used e-mail, what address did he use? [. . .] Regarding the boats that he says were used to traffic Chinese people, what exactly happened on those boats and does anyone else know of their existence? [. . .] Also, Mr. Holbert claims that I gave him instructions to kill the Brown family sometime around Christmas 2007. Where was I when I gave him these instructions, and how did I give them to him?"

The interpreter asked Holbert if he had anything to say. Holbert's words were again measured, delivered in a rather imperious tone. "I bear no ill will to Mr. McAda. Whether or not he is found guilty of his role in these murders is no business of mine. Whatever happens, it won't alter my life. There is no reason for me to lie and I reiterate my statements. But I feel too intimidated to respond to his questions. I'm behind bars. Here I am in a room with a man who has put a contract out to have me killed. It's very stressful. He is a very dangerous man and I'm afraid of him. I thank the Lord that neither Mr. McAda nor his attorney are my judge or my jury. [. . .]" Holbert then described Mike Smith and Fran Tilbury, the regulars at the Jolly Roger Social Club, as "dear friends" who had nothing to do with McAda's gringo cartel. "Thank you for giving me this opportunity to cooperate with the Panamanian justice system," he concluded.

"Holbert came across as by turns cocky, by turns the hammy actor when he said he was afraid of me. That's when he put on a show of looking physically afraid," said McAda later. "But when the DA's people in the courtroom weren't paying attention or weren't looking at Holbert, he would wink at me. It was just weird."

The fundamental problem, said McAda, was that under the *careo* procedure his questions to Holbert did not need to be answered one by one. One of McAda's questions turned on the fact that McAda had worn a beard all the time that Holbert had known him, starting a few months before the period in 2008 when he met Holbert for the first time and sold him the floating dock, up to the day of the *careo*. But in 2006 he had been clean-shaven. Had Holbert known McAda then, he would have been aware of this. The invitation to make long, rambling statements that was the heart of a *careo* made it all too easy for Holbert to disregard McAda's questions. So, what was the point of it all? The official record of the *careo* of May 13, 2011, concludes thus: *It was observed that the participants did not come to an agreement as regards the differences between their various statements. This authority has given them time to talk and come to an agreement. However, the time allotted to the participants ran out before they could reach any such agreement. This careo is therefore now closed. [. . .]* Clearly, the face-off had been set up as a dispute resolution mechanism. Holbert had not been put on the spot in any meaningful way. And the DA's team had run out of time. As it happened, the thirteenth of May was a Friday. As the sun dropped in the sky, the court staff were just about to begin their weekend. Holbert's accusations against Scott McAda had had a concrete effect, and it was beginning to hurt: by court order, McAda was unable to leave Panama and could not visit his sick mother in the United States. McAda wasn't locked up in prison, but his freedom was restricted. And he appeared no closer to clearing his name.

Daniel Anaya, the Bocas attorney who had processed Holbert's "purchase" of Michael Brown's and Bo Icelar's shell companies, was also fingered as a crooked lawyer by Holbert in September 2010 in his new version of events—this despite the fact that the former Wild Bill had explicitly absolved him of any involvement in his crimes in his confession of July 30. "I know of a case of fraud committed by Daniel Anaya, on the orders of the [cartel] bosses," Holbert told investigators. "The two occasions that Anaya was involved were in the transfer [of ownership] of Hacienda Cortez and Latitude 9.10, and the transfer of the property belonging to

Bo Icelar. It was McAda who paid the lawyer. I did speak to [Anaya] and collected documents from him, and passed documents to him, but I have no memory of ever paying him." Anaya came under the same suspicion as McAda for the same crimes, and also had to report to the police every two weeks.*

Holbert, by mid-2011, had become an enthusiastic letter writer: "I am horrified by the illegal way the authorities are abusing me, when these authorities are supposed to be protecting me and rehabilitating me. I now need psychiatric therapy because of the serious and violent abuse that I must deal with [. . .]," penned Holbert in his cell in a handwritten missive to DA Martínez dated June 14, 2011.

"I'm a man," he wrote, "not an animal."

In 2011, Holbert had three sets of criminal charges against him, as did Laura Michelle Reese. These were the murder of, and robbery from, Michael Brown, his wife, and his son; the murder of, and robbery from, Bo Icelar; and the murder of Cher Hughes. The cases were, in legal terms and as far as the DA was concerned, separate, and would thus go to trial separately. Any custodial sentences handed down to Holbert and Reese—the latter of whom professed her innocence of all charges—would be served consecutively. In the first *careo*, the scope was limited to the accusation that McAda had masterminded the murder of the three Browns. But McAda had also been accused by Holbert of having ordered Bo Icelar's killing. McAda could therefore request a second bite at the cherry in the form of a new *careo* on the subject of the murder of Bo

---

*Keith Werle was also accused in statements made by William Dathan Holbert to the authorities. Holbert said that he and Werle had come to an agreement whereby he would kill Cher Hughes for a sum of money. In Holbert's version, this would have enabled Werle to take over his estranged wife's assets. On September 20, 2010, Holbert told investigators that he was having a drink with Werle on the porch of his (Holbert's) home when "Keith revealed that he knew that I was a hit man; after a long conversation, Keith Werle hired me to kill Cheryl Hughes. We agreed to the sum of $50,000. I executed the contract [but] I was never paid in full. . . . It was decided that I would assume control of the hotel [the Casa del Sapo] since I had the reputation of being a real estate investor in Bocas del Toro." Keith Werle repeatedly and strenuously denied any involvement in his wife's murder, and Holbert's accusations against him were soon discarded by the Panamanian prosecutor.

Icelar. He filed his request and a second *careo* was scheduled for September 6, 2011, at nine a.m.

The participants were broadly the same, although Holbert had a new attorney—Claudia Alvarado, an elegantly dressed, soft-spoken lady in her fifties who had spent the earlier part of her career working in the prison service. As a lawyer, she had a reputation in the province of Chiriquí for providing legal defense to the hardest cases: young men accused of homicide, violent drug runners, and the like. Her youngest son had been teased at school about his mother's decision to be Holbert's attorney. People in David wondered why she had taken on Holbert—and Reese, too—as clients. Alvarado was a patient listener, had impeccable manners, and was a committed Christian. A comment on her Facebook page read: *JUSTICE in the hands of men and women is weak, but is great when we kneel before God.*

In the period between the two *careos*, investigators had been tasked by the DA to interview a wide range of witnesses, ranging from the estate agents Walter Kawano and Mark Johnson, to Scott McAda's wife, Belinda, and the workers he employed at his properties in Boquete and Split Hill in Bocas. Crucially, Daniel Anaya found the receipt that showed that Holbert had indeed paid for the transfer of Bo Icelar's shell company, and staff at his office confirmed that they had never seen Scott McAda, which disproved Holbert's claim that Anaya and McAda were engaged in the same criminal venture. Fran Tilbury, the regular at the Jolly Roger Social Club, and a friend of McAda's, told investigators that McAda had a pistol, but only for his own protection. "He's a brilliant man," added Tilbury, "a friendly person, easy to get along with. . . . In fact, he's such a good person that people sometimes take advantage of him."

The procedure in the second *careo* was identical to that of the first. But this time, Scott McAda was invited to speak first. He had come prepared with a statement to read out. "I requested the first confrontation with Mr. Holbert three months ago because I wanted to ask the detainee, in person, why he named me in his ridiculous, concocted story of lies. Naively I thought that if I confronted him face-to-face he might tell me the truth. But Mr. Holbert stuck to his lies. [. . .]

"In my first *careo* in May, I asked the detainee many questions and he did not provide one answer to any of them. Today, I will not ask the detainee any questions, because it only feeds him information for new lies. The people who the detainee himself described as his 'dear friends,' Mike Smith and Fran Tilbury, both testified against Mr. Holbert stating that nothing he ever told them was the truth, that he and Laura Michelle Reese were professional liars [. . .] and also that Laura Michelle Reese had to have known about Mr. Holbert's actions. It would be impossible for her not to have been involved. Furthermore, Mr. Holbert cannot produce one honest witness to verify any of his wild stories. Not one.

"I, on the other hand, can produce hundreds of people; Panamanians, expats living in Panama, and foreigners who know me well. . . . When William Dathan Holbert was a juvenile in the United States I was a respected broadcaster with five radio stations. When Mr. Holbert was running from the law in the United States in 2005 and 2006, I was serving as honorary squadron commander at Eglin Air Force Base in Florida. [. . .] I was honored in this way because of my service to the state of Florida and many years of service to the community in charitable activities. When Mr. Holbert was killing innocent people in Costa Rica and Panama, I was finishing a fifteen-year career with one of the largest companies in the world, WNC Satcom Group, a division of Acer computers, which has nearly twenty-eight thousand employees worldwide in thirty countries. I was senior vice president of WNC Satcom Group. I had indirect responsibility for over nine hundred employees in my division. This job is what originally brought me to Panama.

"All of my properties in Panama were purchased with money that I earned and paid taxes on. I have provided my tax returns to the authorities. [. . .]

"My wife and I love living in Panama. We have had the same employees for five years and they have all made declarations. I am wishing for the day when our lives return to normal."

McAda, in this second *careo*, was able to trip Holbert up conclusively: "I do not own a house in Colombia, as he states in his declaration. I have never been to Colombia and my passport records verify that fact.

"All of the stories about importing illegal Chinese aliens and arms from Russia are absurd lies that the detainee invented. Another false claim made by Mr. Holbert is that I put a $50,000 reward on his head. I did no such thing. I don't want Mr. Holbert to be killed. I want him to live a very long life in prison without the possibility of escaping so that he has many years to think about what he did. . . . I have no doubt that if he escaped, he would kill again. Mr. Holbert also accused my son Wes of involvement in his crimes. My son Wes is a university professor of linguistics in China. He lives in China but he has nothing to do with importing illegal Chinese immigrants.

"Mr. Holbert has said that he has cooperated with the authorities in order to receive lenient treatment; in reality, he has misled the authorities by telling malicious lies about me and about others. He has lied about his wife's involvement in the murders. . . .

"I understand why he intentionally attempted to mislead the authorities, but he picked the wrong person to implicate in these crimes."

Holbert countered. He said that Scott McAda owned a lot of real estate for someone living on a pension of $50,000 a year. "I know a lot about Mr. McAda because we are close friends. I am not going to answer Mr. McAda's questions. It is not for me to answer each of Mr. McAda's questions. I'm not a judge and it's not my job to find him innocent or guilty, but I would be happy to answer each and every question if it's the prosecutor who asked me. The opinions of Mr. McAda and his friends are worthless. I forgive Mr. McAda for all the lies he has said about me. I have a clean record in the United States and in Panama and I can prove it. I don't have any gringo friends, only Panamanians, people of different colors. Mr. McAda is a madman. . . .

"I am really afraid of being in the same room as this man who has ordered the killing of many people and me, too."

Some photos that Scott McAda had brought to the *careo* were lying on the table as Holbert spoke. McAda was pictured in US Air Force fatigues; in the cockpit of a fighter plane; at a factory in China with a neat row of workers in the background assembling computers. There was, too, a decorative memento from WNC Satcom Group congratulating him on his efforts. "All the photos and trophies are very impressive," said Holbert, "but what have they to do with this case?"

The official record of the second *careo* concluded in the same manner as the first: the participants had not come to an agreement; the authorities had given them time to talk and come to an agreement; the time allotted to the participants ran out before they could reach any such agreement. . . . *This meeting is closed at twelve noon.*

But this second time it was different: Scott McAda had scored a direct hit, and the DA's team knew it. William Dathan Holbert had been outwitted.

In retrospect, McAda said that all Holbert had needed to construct a story about him was learning a few snippets of his past: "Holbert found out that I had lived and worked in China, so he invented a tale about trafficking Chinese nationals. He knew that one of my sons had spent a couple of years at college in Moscow and had learned the language, so that prompted the fantasy that I was trading illegal arms from Russia." Scott McAda's restrictions on movement were eventually lifted by the Panamanian authorities, some eighteen months after Holbert had accused him on national TV of being a Mafia boss. He calculates that his defense cost him around $40,000 in legal fees and other expenses. Daniel Anaya—whom Holbert accused of being a crooked lawyer—says that the experience of being singled out by Wild Bill and included in his gringo criminal cartel fantasy marked him, too. Fingers were pointed at Anaya in Bocas. The general feeling seemed to be that there's no smoke without fire. It hurt his business; it took time for him to recover.

The experience behind them, Scott and Belinda left their comfortable house in Boquete and moved to a sixty-seven-acre farm in a hollow in the mountains of Chiriquí, an hour from David. Belinda cares for her horses; Scott writes his memoir, follows his investments. They swim in their pool. The couple are almost totally self-sufficient. They have cows, sheep, goats, hens, and pigs. They grow vegetables. Lard is a ready substitute for olive oil. Scott McAda appears gregarious, but he says he's suspicious when he meets new people. Belinda McAda says her husband has changed.

Standing in his open-plan farmhouse, a long line of Ayn Rand books on the shelves behind him, with a smaller line of John Grisham thrillers, he says that he was offered the chance to get the whole Holbert mess sorted out faster: "One day my attorney told me that someone at the DA's office [not DA Luis Martínez] told my attorney that he could get the charges dropped more quickly if we paid him $600. Apparently that was more or less this person's salary. My attorney was a bit embarrassed when he told me. But I said, 'No way.'"

William Dathan Holbert submitted, voluntarily, to a series of psychopathic tests on May 3, 2011. (In a brief letter to the authorities in her loopy, girlish handwriting, Laura Michelle Reese declined any such clinical evaluation.) The Panamanian doctors applied the Psychopathy Checklist–Revised (PCL-R), a series of tests developed by Robert D. Hare, a Canadian psychologist, that examine twenty different personality traits and behaviors. To do this, the doctors had to interview Holbert and consult his—at this juncture, rather thin—official case file. Out of a maximum score of 40 points, the threshold for the designation of psychopathy is generally agreed to be 30. Reading the findings, you get the distinct impression that Holbert enjoyed the experience. Certainly, he managed to convey a superficial charm:

> *Mr. Holbert likes talking and is entertaining in conversation. He expresses himself very well and it is easy to establish a rapport with him. His replies are plausible and demonstrate a rich vocabulary and an aptitude for interpersonal relations.*
>
> *Mr. Holbert has a tendency to exaggerate both his sense of self and his capacities. [. . .] Lies and deceit have dominated Mr. Holbert's interactions ever since he fled his home country. The ease with which Mr. Holbert created a dual reality as regards everything around him is surprising and explains why his crimes were not discovered sooner. [. . .]*
>
> *Mr. Holbert made no mention whatsoever of the suffering he caused to his victims and their families. He talked about remorse, but his words clearly showed that he understood that it was important to mention repentance. There is no genuine empathy for his victims. [. . .]*

Mr. Holbert describes a limited range of emotions. He is able to communicate extreme emotional experiences, but—despite his eloquence—is unable to describe [the subtleties of] intermediate emotions. The doctors found out that Holbert had fought hard for shared custody of his three children when he got divorced, but during the interview he could not remember their birthdays.

The Panamanian doctors noted Holbert's grandiose, exaggerated sense of his own worth and what he felt the world owed him: *Throughout his life, it is clear that Mr. Holbert never considered working for someone else and was only interested in plans—legal or otherwise—to get rich "overnight."* They concluded that William Dathan Holbert had an antisocial personality disorder. He scored 31 points on Hare's PCL-R scale and could thus be described as being a psychopath. He was a point above the threshold.

They are three sheets of lined paper ripped out of an exercise book, all signed "William Dathan Holbert" at the foot of the page. In neat, regular handwriting, the first is drafted in Spanish and is headed *To the Good People of the Republic of Panama.* It is dated January 5, 2011, and reads:

> *Allow me to say that I am sorry. My actions were bad and they were selfish. I ask for your forgiveness.*
>
> *My crimes are NOT a reflection on Panama. Panamanians are good people and are always friendly to everyone.*
>
> *I was hired by a criminal enterprise. My crimes are lamentable, and if I could change the past, I would do so. [. . .]*
>
> *My wife knew nothing about my serious crimes and did not participate in them. She is a good person and requires no punishment. She is also one of my victims.*
>
> *Thank you for this opportunity to change. May God bless you.*

The second letter is written in English, also dated January 5, 2011. It begins with Holbert's social security number and a mention of Chiriquí Public Jail, which is where he was when he wrote it:

To the People of the U.S.A.,

Please allow me to apologize for my crude, selfish and felonious actions. I have brought shame to the Country, my family and myself.

The letter repeats much of what Holbert wrote to the people of Panama, and concludes: *I realize now, I must repay the world for what I have taken from it. I pledge myself to the reform of my person. I commit myself to only a good, responsible life, from this moment forward. Recently I have accepted Jesus Christ as my personal savior. I will live in his image of love and compassion.*

The third letter is headed *To the Brown family, Icelar family and Hughes family.* It was written on Christmas Day, 2010. It reads:

> *My name is William Dathan Holbert. I would like to tell you that I am sorry for my horrible crimes and I am repentant. I know that nothing I can do will be of any comfort to you at Christmas without your lost loved one. I want you to know that I recently accepted Jesus Christ as the captain of my soul, heart and mind. I ask him for forgiveness for my great sins. I also ask you for forgiveness. I know that this is an impossible thing to forgive, but it is possible that this letter will help you in the process of grieving.*
>
> *For many years I lived a selfish life. I caused you pain. I promise and I guarantee to you that, from this day onwards, I will do good and will repair all the wrong I have caused.*
>
> *I am sorry. Please forgive me. Please know that I suffer, too, for my crimes.*

But the letter to the three American families was written in Spanish, not English. In submitting to psychiatric evaluation, in taking part so enthusiastically in a later reconstruction of the murders in Bocas del Toro—and in writing to his victims' families—William Dathan Holbert was showing that he was willing to cooperate fully with the Panamanian authorities. But the letter in Spanish to the Brown family, the Icelar family, and the Hughes family was not really written with any of these declared recipients in mind. The choice of language proved it.

It was, rather, a letter intended for DA Luis Martínez.

9. Life Behind Bars

Stormy weather in Bocas del Toro in the fall of 2014 kept some expats indoors, afraid of getting an unwelcome soaking on the way to their favorite bar. That is, if their favorite bar was still there. Angry waves broke the floating dock that led to the Riptide, the popular watering hole housed on the former shrimper transplanted from Florida. The dock was repaired, after a fashion—you had to be careful where you trod, and walking the length of it drunk was asking for trouble—and the Riptide continued to serve its fish and chips and its happy hour specials. In November 2014 the old hulk of a vessel finally sank. According to a comment posted anonymously on an Internet message board, *The RIP Tide was a great floating restaurant/bar that attracted a lot of expats so there was always a bunch of crusty Gringos hanging around swapping lies.*

With the shrimper on the seabed, the owners of the plot where the boat had been moored put their piece of land up for sale. Quite a few other For Sale signs had been pinned to properties hugging the shore on the outskirts of town, but the Riptide was considered special. Along with the Buena Vista—the town's original gringo hangout—it was a piece of

Bocas history. Many expats have nursed a cocktail propped up on one of its gently rocking bar stools. Wild Bill was a regular patron; he drank there all the more frequently after he moved into Bo Icelar's house in Big Creek in late 2009, as the Riptide was on his driving route into the town center. At the Riptide, as in most places, Wild Bill had a reputation for being loud, aggressive, and quarrelsome—not exactly on the lookout for a fight but never one to back down when provoked.

It was at the Riptide in May 2010 that Mark Johnson, the American real estate agent, had cornered Holbert and asked him where his friend Cher was. Holbert had exploded. Johnson needed to make a fast exit down the floating dock before Holbert had the chance to throw him overboard. But the expat realtor had found Wild Bill out and, figuratively, scored a direct hit. Holbert and Reese's days in Bocas were numbered. Whatever his behavior, Holbert had earned the right to have a signature cocktail on the drinks list at the Riptide (*BILL CORTEZ SPECIAL, Corona+Seco Shot, No Lime, $3.00*).

Things were to get worse, weather-wise, in the new year. It was the morning of January 4, 2015, and a gale was brewing. Maggie, the long-serving housekeeper at Cocomo-on-the-Sea, Douglas Ruscher's guest-house at the north end of Bocas Town, could hardly take her eyes off the waves as they rolled into shore. "The sea wants something from us," she said, shaking her head. She sensed her job and her livelihood were at stake. The Caribbean Sea, so often glassy and blue, was showing another face. Bocas was confronted with a fierce storm coupled with a particularly high tide.

Suddenly, the sundeck of Cocomo-on-the-Sea, which measures about eighteen by thirty feet and stands on stilts above the sea, took a direct hit from a powerful surge of brown water. The dining room, overlooking the deck and covered by panels of corrugated iron, seemed secure, even though it, too, had been built on stilts over the water. The bedrooms at the rear of the property were built on dry land and were, presumably, safe. But it was difficult to know for certain. For the time being, Ruscher's young guests gathered nervously around the dining table and took photos of the scene of the disintegrating sundeck, grave expressions on their faces. "I just can't look at it," said Ruscher, who had had the deck built eleven years before. Ruscher retired to his bedroom in the property next door, which, like his guesthouse, is a single-story wood and corrugated metal construction painted blue and white. When Ruscher remembered he had taken out an insurance policy on his property, his mood lightened a little. Meanwhile, the waves sent spray flying over the roof of his guesthouse. The storm still had a way to go before it was over. Other people had it far worse: one local family living in a shack nearby lost their home to the waves that day.

In the first hit, the brown water had surged under the sundeck and forced the planks at its center upward. The wood folded with a creaking sound. No more than ten other strong waves were what it took to finally destroy Ruscher's deck, which detached itself from the dining room and started to crash against what was left of Cocomo-on-the-Sea, breaking apart as it did so. The rain poured, and frigate birds, their big, wide beaks pointing downward, glided over the waves in search of sustenance. What the birds saw in the foamy water were planks of wood from Ruscher's sundeck and parts of other buildings torn apart by the sea, discarded plastic bottles, shreds of cloth, seaweed, coconut husks, and—closer to shore—dozens of violet-red petals.

When news broke in July 2010 that Cher Hughes's corpse had been buried in a shallow grave behind Holbert and Reese's house in Darklands, with another body in a more advanced state of decomposition close by, the Bocas expats had to try to make sense of it all. The Riptide's drinks board was quickly wiped clean of the Bill Cortez Special, and a group of gringos tore down the Casa Cortez sign on the dock of the renamed Casa del Sapo. That was the easy part. The realization that Cher Hughes, a well-loved and gregarious member of the expat community, had been slaughtered at Wild Bill's place at Darklands—and that there was at least one other victim—made people angry, but it also made them introspective and prompted some difficult questions. Could it have been me? Was I being groomed, too? And why did no one realize what Holbert and Reese were up to until Cher Hughes was dead?

Mike Smith and his wife, Fran Tilbury—regulars at Holbert's Jolly Roger Social Club—found the period especially difficult. But some things started to make sense to them as Holbert and Reese's modus operandi of killing to steal assets became clearer. "He was always trying to get us together so we could take the *Sea Turtle* [Smith's yacht] on a trip to Cartagena or Venezuela," said Mike Smith. "But it never happened. Fran and I were often apart, she was in Loma Partida [Split Hill] and I was building our house in David." Then there were a couple of strange calls that Reese made to Smith and Tilbury in the months between what turned out to be Bo Icelar's murder and the killing of Cher Hughes: "Jane calls, and it's like, 'He's beat me up.' Or, 'I've hurt my ankle,'" recalled Smith. "That could have been a bait to get me to come over the mountain. It could have been another setup.

"I hate that I was lied to," said Smith of the younger man. "He said he used to own a town, right outside Cancún. He said he inherited it from his father. He said his parents were dead." Holbert had told his interrogators that Smith and Tilbury were his "dear friends." Scott McAda told Smith about it; Smith replied to McAda that it bothered him.

"I'd love to confront him," said Smith. "Mike Brown's son, he was a good kid, he was just a boy . . ." Smith's sentence trailed off in disgust. Holbert had executed Michael Brown, his wife, and seventeen-year-old son to grab their home and suck Brown's bank account dry to fund a spending spree on a Jet Ski, gas for speedboats, and liquor. With Holbert apprehended, Smith now had to put his faith in Panamanian justice. But Wild Bill was cunning: "I've never met anyone who could keep his lies so straight, even when drunk," said Smith, referring to Holbert. His drunkenness was sometimes faked, too. Holbert and Reese kept sober at some of their parties by keeping a close watch on their own bottle of vodka, kept separate from the bottles everyone else drank from. "This one's for me and Jane," insisted Bill. No one was supposed to drink from Bill and Jane's bottle of vodka. But the bottle contained only water.

The waves that pummeled the houses on the shore came from the same sea that gave the town's surf schools their income. As the January 2015 tempest raged, Bocas was buzzing with the news that Kelly Slater, the world's most illustrious surfer, was in town. Over dinners of soda and tacos, Thai noodles and Panamanian lager, Slater's name was on the lips of all the expansively tattooed young surfers vacationing in Bocas. He was said by some to be riding the powerful breaks at Wizard Beach on

Bastimentos Island; others placed him at the exposed Bluff Beach or Punch Beach on a wild stretch of coast on Columbus Island, twenty minutes from Bocas Town. But everyone's mood soon changed. It's easy to underestimate the power of the sea, easy to get lulled into a false sense of security. A young Canadian man went out for a swim with two friends at Red Frog Beach—like Wizard, an exposed stretch of sand on Bastimentos. It was the morning of January 6, the third day of the storm, and there were large swells. The friends got into trouble in the water. Two managed to make it back to dry land. A body was recovered the next day, washed up in the tide. It was the young Canadian man. He was twenty-five years old.

The storm of early January 2015 also temporarily interrupted the expat bush telegraph that since mid-December had been passing on the latest piece of news of William Dathan Holbert. Remarkably, the man they had known as Wild Bill had just set up his own church, accepting members of all denominations. An e-mail link to a rudimentary Web site from an outfit calling itself the Panama Prison Ministries operating out of the male wing of David prison had been posted on a couple of Internet message boards. Holbert clearly wanted his former friends and neighbors to know what he was up to.

The chair of the group was a man calling himself Brother Bill. Its statement of purpose read: *We few workers of the harvest strive to fulfil the will of our King the Lord Jesus Christ in the form of caring for those forgotten by family, friends and society. Caring for the spiritual and physical health of the 1,187 men incarcerated for all sorts of violent and horrific crimes in the region's most antiquated prison system, and said system's most antiquated prison, we fulfil the commandments our King laid out clearly for us in his holy Word.*

The Web page opened with a large photo of a smiling William Holbert standing behind what appeared to be a brand-new wooden pulpit. In the photo, Holbert was wearing gray trousers and a yellow T-shirt, his face smiling, beatific. In the background was a cinder-block wall, a high wire fence, weeds. The snarl of his Bocas days was gone. He wore his hair short; it was darker, too, and he had a neatly defined goatee beard. Holbert's shoulders were broad—this had not changed—but he was carrying little excess weight. He looked pretty slim, in fact, and paler. Another picture showed Holbert in a black shirt buttoned up to the collar, dark necktie, grinning; his right hand was making a thumbs-up sign. When Douglas Ruscher saw the picture he said, "I just can't believe that's Wild Bill. He looks so different." That was the predominant reaction among the expats: how could Holbert have changed his appearance so much?

Scrolling down the page there was another photo, this one of what appeared to be Holbert's congregation: brown-skinned youths in T-shirts and shorts, some wearing baseball caps. All were sitting—or were slumped—in neat rows of white plastic chairs. There followed a truncated version of Matthew 25:34–40: *Then the King will say to those on his right . . . I was in prison and you came to me. Then the righteous will answer him, saying, "Lord . . . when did we see you sick or in prison and visit you?" And the King will answer them, "Truly, I say to you, as you did it to one of the least of these my brothers, you did it to me."*

Another picture showed a smaller group of middle-aged men poring over what appeared to be Bibles or prayer books. A couple of the men were white. I knew that there was a convicted American pedophile serving a lengthy term in David prison. Was he one of the group? Like all the other pictures, it had been taken with a mobile phone and was rather grainy, so it was difficult to know for sure. The photo was labeled: *Daily Prayer Service.*

Health care is not provided. Many [prisoners] die due to simple illness. A mild heart attack is a fatal and normal everyday occurrence. We provide care for special needs prisoners as well as for a cell of 8 tuberculosis infected prisoners. The impression given by the Web site was that Brother Bill and his Panama Prison Ministries were the people who ran things in David prison. And not only ran things; these inmates were seemingly working hand in hand with the prison authorities to keep David's criminal justice show on the road: *The state has recognized our accomplishments and allows us some liberty and authority inside the prison . . .* Some of Holbert's former acquaintances in Bocas were aghast, even if they were not surprised. Everyone had stories of how unpredictable the criminal justice system was, and how variable treatment by the Panamanian police could be. One man, it was said, had been sentenced to multiple years of incarceration because a couple of cannabis plants were found on his property; another, wealthier, man arrested with a pouch of cocaine in his pocket spent an uncomfortable night in the cells but was released the next morning with charges dropped. Holbert's Damascene conversion was one thing, but was Holbert, a prisoner like any other, really able to call the shots in jail?

It was in June 2010 that Holbert and Reese had fled Bocas del Toro; only then did their fellow expats finally start putting two and two together and realized the couple had been up to no good. Around seven weeks later, Holbert and Reese attempted to cross the San Juan River, the border between Costa Rica and Nicaragua, to get as far away as possible from their stolen house of horrors in Darklands. Many people had gawped at footage of Holbert and Reese, loaded into the back of a pickup truck, visibly overweight and wearing flip-flops. It was a strangely halfhearted attempt at an escape, particularly for a couple who had had over four years on the run to perfect their technique. The pair looked like they were about to spend an afternoon at the beach; they were clearly unprepared for hiding out in the rough bush of Central America.

Over time, the couple's flight from Bocas only prompted more questions. One American expat, speaking for many, said: "There are two possibilities. Either Wild Bill and Jane were so confident, they thought that nobody would ever be smart enough to catch up with them, or else they wanted to get caught." In any event, when Holbert and Reese were arrested by the Nicaraguan authorities, the law appeared to have them firmly in its clutches. With a minimum of red tape to sort out, Holbert and Reese were flown promptly from the bank of the San Juan River to Panama City. Holbert was cooperative with the police and soon confessed to having killed Michael Brown/Salem, his wife, and his teenage son, Bo Icelar, and Cher Hughes, insisting that Reese took no part in any of the killings. Holbert, of course, gave his confession a significant postscript when he tried to implicate Scott McAda and others in his crimes. For her part,

Reese protested her innocence, kept her head down, and made no further comment.

Lying naked on the floor of a filthy cell in "La Joya," the Republic of Panama's most notorious prison [in Panama City], I decided that I would take my own life. I could find no will to live. This is when Holbert says he turned to a Bible he had been given by his mother, who had flown down to Panama to visit him. He had kept the Bible in his cell for several weeks and had nothing else to read. Still, he avoided it. He recalled himself, in November 2010, *never picking [the Bible] up and not even wanting to look at it. It sometimes still amazes me to what length a man will go to hide from God when he is so stained with sin. But finally I picked it up and began reading. I read for hours. And finally I remember on my knees asking God, "What do you want from me?" He answered. Here I am.* Holbert's conversion was complete: *My life has never been the same! I accepted Jesus Christ as my savior there in cell 3 of pavilion 7 in Panama's most violent prison. Soon God sent me help. Preachers, priests, and men of God came to my aid unasked. It was and still is incredible and most definitely supernatural. God is in control. . . . This evil pirate that was, now tends the sick and dying men no one will touch for fear of infection. This black sheep now teaches hymns to special needs prisoners. . . . And distributes free food to poor prisoners. . . . And quiets the conflicts that break out between rival gangs. This man known as Wild Bill in the underworld for his proficiency with a pistol now has become Brother Bill servant of the most high God.*

A final image on the Web site of Holbert's new church sticks in the mind. Brother Bill is standing in front of the sturdy trunk of an old oak tree in the prison yard, loops of razor wire in the background. On either side of Brother Bill are two young men wearing beach shorts and tank tops. Neither can be more than twenty-one or twenty-two years old. Holbert is making his familiar thumbs-up sign; the young men, meanwhile, are leaning into him. The photo may be posed, but the sense of hero worship feels real.

Got a sick mother? Tell Brother Bill to pray for her in church. . . . A dispute near to violence? Call Brother Bill to calm the seas of anger with the words of Jesus Christ. God is real ladies and gentlemen. If God can change a monster like the Wild Bill I was to the gentle loving Brother Bill I am . . .

Well there just isn't anything he can't do, is there? Thanks for reading. May God Bless you. Help us by praying for these poor men and for me. Help us in any way you feel you can.

My story is very unique and filled with horror and sorrow but with a very happy ending.

Back in Bocas del Toro, happy endings can take many different forms: A woman named Barbara* from a small town in New England works tables in a restaurant in Bocas Town. She always appears cheerful, smiling. Life has not always treated her well. Her childhood wasn't easy. There weren't always the right people around to give her the love and guidance every kid needs. Now in her forties, Barbara has tied her flag to the mast of the sunshine and easy living of Bocas and, most days, feels really good about that.

One night after work Barbara went to "Crazy Dave's" bookstore, a mainstay of the expat community. This is a bookstore that turned into a wildly successful pub when "Crazy Dave," originally from Florida, realized that he could make a better living selling bottles of beer and rum and Cokes than secondhand thrillers. Barbara went on to a couple of other bars; the last stop was a bare-bones dive as the night came to its worn-out end, but at least her bed was a five-minute taxi ride away. But there were no cabs to be found. Barbara started walking in the direction of the rather sketchy neighborhood near the airport where she had rented an apartment. On the way, she heard a voice in the darkness. "Let me walk you home, mommy," it said. Three young men appeared in the shadows. "Let's take this road here," one of the young men said.

Barbara weighed her options. She could ignore the young men and try to get away quickly, or she could walk with them. After all, they could be offering her protection. Barbara decided to walk with the men. She was close to home, but everywhere was dark. Suddenly one of the men grabbed Barbara and took her purse. This was especially bad news; Barbara wasn't a wealthy woman, and there was money inside. Another of the men took Barbara's cell phone. "Don't move," ordered one of the men. The men and Barbara stopped walking, and Barbara began to fear the worst. Time was

---

* Not her real name.

passing as if in slow motion. The men sat down on the sidewalk, which was a surprise. Barbara considered running, but she was told to sit down, too. The men had been drinking that night, or were high, or both. They fell asleep. Barbara got up. Time was speeding up now, her heart beating fast. She grabbed her purse and her phone. She put her hand in the pockets of each of the sleeping men. And then she ran.

How much money did she take from her assailants' pockets? Barbara won't give an exact figure: "Let's say it was enough for me to get my hair done the next day."

Holbert's shiny new pulpit was provided by the Catholic Church. Or, rather, it was the Catholic Church's pulpit, which had been taken to David prison for weekly mass given by Father Rory Gutiérrez, a local priest. Father Rory had recently felt the need to take to the local airwaves to tell a radio reporter that he—and no one else—was the preacher at the jail. A comment made by Claudia Alvarado to a journalist had been misinterpreted and the story had spread that Holbert had become a kind of prison chaplain. The prominent image on the Panama Prison Ministries' Web site of Holbert addressing a congregation of inmates from behind the pulpit was "probably Holbert reading a passage from the Bible," said Father Rory. It wasn't, as it seemed, Wild Bill's own church in the pen.

There is a line of people waiting to see Father Rory, all smiling, relaxed, good-humored. The day is blisteringly hot. Some of the women outside Father Rory's door—there are only a couple of men—have made improvised fans from folded pieces of paper in an effort to keep cool. Father Rory has seen Holbert in jail dozens of times. Behind his neat desk with its flickering computer screen, Father Rory is a valuable witness. I get to the point: "Father, do you believe that Holbert has really turned to Christ?"

"I believe he is sincere," says Father Rory.

"Can you describe for me the behavior of an inmate who isn't sincere?"

"Well, you see other cases where prisoners attend mass and then straightaway ask you for things, favors of some kind. That's not Holbert.

He sets out the chairs before mass, he's attentive." Before the weekly mass starts, Holbert is one of the inmates passing from cell to cell to encourage the other prisoners to file into the yard for the service. "But he's a psychopath," continues Father Rory, "and sometimes his psychopathy will get the better of him." The priest pauses. An air-conditioning device on the wall of his office makes a low hum. "Of course, it might be due to something that happened in his childhood."

"No," I say to Father Rory. "I don't think so. It seems his childhood was perfectly normal."

I take a taxi back to David's ragged downtown from Father Rory's church. Suddenly, there is a screech of brakes and the sound of the impact of metal. There has been a car crash on the road ahead of us. The taxi driver shakes his head as he slows down. "There's always someone wanting to get someplace before the others," he says. We pass a couple of men examining damage to their vehicles. One has his hands on his hips; the other is beginning to open his mouth as if about to remonstrate. They disappear from our field of vision. The taxi driver's radio is tuned to one of several religious stations available on the dial. A man's voice addresses a crowd: "There are two types of people in God's world . . . ," he says. But then static interferes with reception and the taxi driver and I don't get to hear what the two types are.

In setting up his Panama Prison Ministries, Holbert was continuing an attention-seeking strategy that began as soon as he was paraded by the police before a row of cameras soon after he was flown in chains to Panama on July 29, 2010, grinning broadly, despite the accusations of multiple murder directed at him. Over time, Holbert posted on a Facebook page a steady stream of selfies taken in the half-light of his cell; these invariably accompanied news items in the Panamanian media on the country's most infamous overseas inmate. There were grainy videos, too. It was against the rules for inmates to have cell phones and access to the Internet. Then again, it was against the rules for them to consume cocaine, but the jailers and the razor wire hardly prevented them from doing that, either. The rules were bent when money changed hands.

Early in 2013, the then governor of David prison, Ismael Flores, had issued a denial to the Panamanian press that Holbert had access to the Internet. This seemed odd, because by that time there was a veritable explosion of pictures on the Web of Holbert on his own or with other inmates. In some photos, the men were cheerfully consuming jail-brewed alcoholic drinks. Flores sent out a detachment of guards to investigate. They went to Holbert's cell and discovered four tanks of *chicha* and sacks of potato and carrot peel. Usually, *chicha* is made from fermented maize, but Holbert's recipe simply replaced maize with the material that was most readily available. Governor Flores also reported that his guards confiscated cell phones and chargers. Holbert sent out a defiant message in Spanish from his Facebook account: *Who says that you can't be free when you're in jail? Hahaha $$$$$ Thank you Heavenly Father. I'm a prisoner but I'm not powerless . . .*

In the middle of the same year, 2013, Holbert started to acquire a national presence in Panama that transcended his crimes. This was no longer Wild Bill, the arrested fugitive, being carted off in handcuffs from one jail to the next. He seemed to be in the driver's seat. He appeared on national television and radio as the self-declared president of a group calling itself the Panamanian Prisoners' Association. Journalists in Panama asked few questions about the credibility of this "association." But in a country with a volatile prison population that from time to time mounts hunger strikes and other forms of protest, often with violence, someone like Holbert could be a useful weather vane to help gauge the mood of prisoners. Demetrio Ábrego, David correspondent for the national TVN television network, took a camera team into David prison to interview Holbert. The former Wild Bill used his time in the spotlight to launch a campaign from his cell for Manuel Noriega's release from jail in Panama City on humanitarian grounds. Noriega was over seventy years old, argued Holbert, and was thus due parole. If that was the principle that applied in Panama, why was it only Noriega, approaching his eightieth birthday, who was denied this right? Speaking into the reporters' microphones, his words were clear, measured. The loud, belligerent Wild Bill of the Jolly Roger Social Club even appeared somewhat reasonable. By this point Holbert had been locked up for close to three years in an almost totally Spanish-speaking environment, and he now spoke fluent Spanish. It was not always grammatically correct, but it had a folksy aspect, a type of Spanish you might hear spoken by men in a neighborhood bar in any hardscrabble section of David.

The expats back in Bocas who watched local Panamanian television news gasped. But in time the story filtered out to just about everyone: chat rooms used by expat residents in Panama were naturally outraged that a self-described killer was being given airtime. To Ábrego's disgust, a couple of members of the TV crew helping set up the report from David prison that day asked Wild Bill for his autograph and wanted their own selfies taken with him. Holbert was only too happy to oblige. Several months earlier, Ábrego's TVN channel had reported a claim from Governor Flores that Holbert had threatened to kill him if the governor managed to get Holbert—the ultimate unpleasant hot potato for a prison boss—moved to another jail. Holbert allegedly had told Flores that he had "a lot of money" and knew "a lot of people." In the end, Holbert stayed in jail in David. Wild Bill had achieved—however improbably—a kind of jail-bound notoriety, even a warped celebrity. Why?

Holbert's Internet sideshow ran and ran. No declarations from prison officials changed anything. In July 2014, Don Winner, the retired US intelligence officer who had helped Diana Motlik and Mary Wittmeyer in Panama City, posted the following on his blog: *Why is it so hard to put Holbert in a tiny little box, with practically no creature comforts whatsoever? He should be provided with whatever is required by law—according to international standards for Human Rights—and nothing else. By that I mean food, bedding, drinking water, and a toilet, enclosed by four solid walls. There's no way in hell this murderous monster should have a cell phone. So he can't talk to his mother in North Carolina. So what? [. . .] This piece of shit will rot in prison until he eventually dies, dreaming about the freedoms he will never again experience . . .*

Holbert's assertions raised still more questions: Where was the money that Holbert was boasting about, and which was apparently used, in part, to bribe the prison guards? Did it really exist? Holbert had killed principally to steal real estate, but Jeffrey Kline had been murdered solely for money, and many expats in Bocas—including his victims—were the sort of people to keep at least part of their savings under the proverbial mat-tress. Given that Holbert and Reese had fled Bocas in a hurry, nobody there doubted that he had left stolen money hidden in the archipelago. Some people openly worried that Holbert could find a way of escaping or simply bribing his way out of prison. And if Laura Michelle Reese was found not guilty of murder, or found guilty of a lesser charge and released because of time served on remand awaiting trial, she would likely know where the money was hidden and pass it on to Holbert so as to keep the bribes flowing to the jailers at David prison. Theoretically, the couple had the time to discuss all of this during their marital visits—two hours together, once a month, in a hut equipped with a rudimentary bed on the grounds of the jail.

There was just one problem. Reese had found herself a new man.

The story came from the prison itself and it was difficult to be certain of all the facts. A gardening detail from the men's wing of David prison was picked to do some weed clearing in the women's wing of the prison. The prison authorities selected Reese to deliver food and drink to the men. One of the men on the detail was a prisoner in his mid-twenties; it was rumored that the prison authorities had selected him especially and encouraged him to make a move on Reese, as a revenge for Holbert's per-sistent taunting. Claudia Alvarado, attorney to both Holbert and Reese, denied this. She said that it was a decision made by the prison's "technical committee." But it does seem strange that the prison authorities should choose the non-Spanish-speaking Reese to deliver meals to the men on the gardening detail when almost everyone else in the women's wing spoke the local language. One rumor had it that the young prisoner was especially handsome; according to another one, he wasn't particularly good-looking. But he was certainly kind and respectful to Reese. The prison gardener was serving a relatively short sentence and was released some months afterward. He continued to visit Reese in jail, along with—on occasions—other members of his family who, according to some sources, approved of the relationship. For her part, the former Jane Cortez, onetime tongue-tied bartender at the Jolly Roger Social Club, needed little encouragement. After Holbert had wondered out loud sev-eral times how it was that when he called her on her cell phone late at night the line was frequently busy, she told him what was up. By this time the rumors in jail had already started anyway. Laura Michelle Reese announced to Holbert that she was with someone else. The amorous young gardener was still in prison at this point. Holbert could have attacked him. But this would have been tantamount to an admission that he had been duped. Wild Bill, therefore, did nothing.

Love is in the eye of the beholder, of course, but a new and wholly objective possibility opened itself here. Holbert and Reese had never married. They presented themselves as man and wife, and Holbert claimed that the couple had tied the knot in Costa Rica, although he said he didn't remember exactly where. As a result, they enjoyed the prison visiting privileges of a married couple, and these privileges remained in place even when it became clear that they were not married at all. But Holbert and Reese were also the only suspects in the murder of Jeffrey Kline in Costa Rica. The case prepared by the Costa Rican authorities presented the pair as suspects on an equal footing. Given the gravity of the crime, Costa Rica would surely apply to extradite Reese even if she walked free in Panama. But if Reese married and sought the Panamanian citizenship that would therefore be her right, she would place herself out of the reach of the Costa Rican prosecutor. The reason was simple: Panamanian law did not provide for the extradition of its own nationals, period.

Meanwhile, Claudia Alvarado confirmed that young women came to visit Holbert, too. The rumors that had reached the city of David and elsewhere in the country were that Holbert had a large bag of cash from his crimes buried somewhere in the islands of Bocas del Toro. It was widely assumed that the women visiting Holbert in prison had more than half an eye on the possibility of getting their hands on the spoils of his crimes. In 2014, something like five young women in as many months had come to the general visiting room to talk with Holbert. They were mostly from western Panama, but one had traveled to David from a satellite town outside of Panama City. Holbert had befriended the women on the Internet. However, Holbert appeared to have a cash-flow problem. He was usually only able to give them $40 or $50 to cover their transportation costs. The women surely expected more evidence that Holbert was solvent. It appeared that they all lost interest.

Other prisoners might have been in a position to be more generous. The possibilities of smuggling scarce resources—cell phones, drugs, and weapons—into jail created a number of moneymaking activities in prison. But Holbert was not involved in any of them. Cash reached him, somehow, but the amounts were meager. His lawyer was his only face-to-face contact with the outside world, so it was widely assumed that she passed money on to him. If, like many inmates, Holbert had a cocaine habit in jail—and he didn't—his money would run out in no time. As it was, Holbert could hand over much of the little he had to the young women. But the $40 or $50 he gave the ladies was not a sufficient incentive for them to return. Whatever sentence was handed down to Holbert, he would still face a trial in Costa Rica over the killing of Jeffrey Kline—unless he married a Panamanian.

The testimony of Raymond Stuart Davies on the subject of Holbert and Reese's activities in Costa Rica seems compelling; for the Costa Rican authorities now to accept Holbert's story that he had sailed out of Puerto Viejo, Costa Rica, with Kline, killed him in Panamanian waters—a hundred yards from the Riptide, to boot—and then returned to Puerto Viejo to bury the American would be supremely counterintuitive. Under the Costa Rican criminal code, the couple would face a sentence of twenty to thirty-five years for the murder of Jeffrey Kline. Holbert and Reese were not going to escape a trial in Costa Rica so easily, unless figurative wedding bells rang out in the prison yard.

If Holbert didn't marry a local girl—and if Reese did end up the wife of her Panamanian gardening ex-con—might Holbert take it out on Reese at the trial? After years of insisting that Reese had known nothing about his crimes, might Wild Bill decide to implicate his former lover in the murders to which he had already confessed, just to get his own back?

As the storm of January 2015 gradually abated, progress toward a conclusion in the charge of multiple murder against William Dathan Holbert and Laura Michelle Reese had ground to a halt, and delays had added salt to the wounds of the victims' families. On March 3, 2011, Mark Fry, the then consul general of the US embassy in Panama, contacted the Panamanian authorities asking about progress on the case and requesting to know approximately how long it would be before it would come to trial, given that Holbert and Reese had been arrested on July 26, 2010. Four and a half years after Fry's note, the date would still not be known. Also in March 2011, the US embassy wrote to Panama's Foreign Ministry wishing "to bring to the Ministry's attention on-going delays in document-ing the death and releasing the mortal remains and property of the U.S. Citizen Bo Icelar. . . ." Icelar's corpse was still at the morgue in Bocas Town, where it had lain since being exhumed from the bush behind the former Brown family home at Darklands. "Despite the Embassy's repeated enqui-ries and the intervening year since Mr. Icelar's death, the Panamanian death certificate remains incomplete as to the date of death and thus, cannot be issued."

When Holbert, shackled and handcuffed, arrived in Bocas in late November 2011 for a reconstruction of his crimes, Walter Kawano, Bo Ice-lar's good friend, saw him surrounded by policemen walking along Main Street. Holbert and the investigators were making their way to the Bar-racuda Bar, from where Holbert said he and Bo Icelar set off in Holbert's boat one day in November 2009, the ride from which Icelar would never return. Unsurprisingly, some locals heckled Wild Bill as he made his ungainly way through town. He would have gotten more abuse, had the streets not been emptier than usual because of heavy rain. "That's when I thought, now maybe we are a bit closer to justice," said Kawano.

Three separate trials had, in fact, been scheduled for May 2012. The investigation led by DA Luis Martínez was complete and the accusations leveled by Holbert at Scott McAda and others had finally been discounted and discarded. Holbert and Reese were due to go to court charged with the murder of, and robbery from, three members of the Brown family in the first planned trial, set for May 7, 2012. A second trial would deal with the killing of Cher Hughes on the twenty-first of May. Finally, Hol-bert and Reese would be tried for the murder of, and robbery from, Bo Icelar on May 29, 2012.

These trials would have gone ahead in May 2012 had it not been for a formal request lodged by Claudia Alvarado to join the three separate charges against Holbert and Reese into one indictment—all of which would ordinarily have led to individual sentencing or acquittal. Panama, and other jurisdictions, too, allows such "joinders" when a string of offenses are similar in character or are clearly part of a series. Typically, joinders are permitted in instances of shoplifting or burglary where the techniques used might be very similar. The idea is to prevent a series of expensive trials dealing with substantially the same facts. This argument of economy was the one put forward by Alvarado to the regional court in David to support her request. Sometimes a joinder is an advantage for the prosecution, as it demonstrates to the judges, or to the jury, that there is a pattern. But—particularly when there is a guilty plea—it can be a boon for the defense, as it can ensure that the sentencing will be concurrent and not consecutive.

The regional court in David rejected Alvarado's call for a joinder in a ruling handed down on April 27, 2012; serial killers are not the most obvious recipients of this mechanism, and a firm of Panamanian lawyers hired by Cher Hughes's family in the States insisted that the murders were carried out in different places for reasons that were not identical, and so a joinder should not be allowed. But Alvarado appealed, and the lower court's finding was overturned by the Supreme Court in Panama City, a decision announced in the Panamanian media in January 2014. The appeal had added a year and a half to Holbert and Reese's wait in the sweltering jail in David. There had to be a good reason for this: if the joinder maneuver wasn't going to help their case, Alvarado would not have taken the matter as far as the Supreme Court. Subsequently, red tape delayed matters further. In December 2015, the case file—now a unified file of three sets of indictments—was still awaiting a couple of signatures at the Supreme Court before it could be sent back to David.

Meanwhile, the lead prosecutor had changed. In July 2013 Betzaida Pitti de Castillo replaced Luis Martínez as district attorney in David. The new DA would be tasked with prosecuting a case for which she had no firsthand knowledge. As soon as the files arrived, her team would have to start work to prepare the trial. Claudia Alvarado, who had represented Holbert and Reese since 2011, had the advantage of familiarity with the case over a much longer period.

"Hypothetically, if we received the file tomorrow," said a woman working in the court clerk's department in David in January 2015, "this case would be tried in September, although we might be able to move it forward a little." This didn't happen, but it gave a good idea of typical waiting times. The problem, apparently, was a backlog of cases, violent crime in particular; the courts in western Panama could barely cope. The woman added that, as it was a complicated case, essentially three files in one, Holbert and Reese's trial "might well take more than one day." After a wait of many years for the cases to come to trial, the speed of the trial itself was another surprise of the Panamanian courts system.

Usually, defendants had the choice between trial by jury or trial by a panel of three judges. But Claudia Alvarado explained that, since Holbert and Reese had been charged with more than one crime in the killings of the Brown family and of Bo Icelar (i.e., murder and robbery, thus aggravated homicide), they would have to be tried by a panel of judges without a jury. In Panama, trial by jury was only an option for Holbert and Reese in the original, separate indictment for the killing of Cher Hughes, since this case had been prepared by the DA on the basis of homicide only. And since the usual practice in Panama is limited to the cross-examination of each side's legal counsel—rather than an exhaustive examination of the defendants and as many witnesses as is needed, as is the case in the United States and elsewhere—the single trial would be a quick affair. Holbert and Reese and the victims' families would get their day in court, but it would likely not be much more than a single day. Next, the judges would retire to deliberate their verdict. A sentence would be delivered two or three months later. For some friends and families of the victims—Diana Motlik, Cher Hughes's sister, and Sharon McConnell, Bo Icelar's close companion—the wait for justice had been long and it had been painful. But with a trial that in North American terms was likely to be inexplicably brief, precisely what kind of justice would be served in the David courthouse?

10. The Lights That Don't Go Out

It is a moist, windless night in March 2015. I had been on the trail of Holbert and Reese for just over a year. Sitting at the kitchen table of her home in Como, Mississippi, Sharon McConnell, Bo Icelar's friend, has a question for me: "Can you tell me something? I want to know how Bo died."

After he was arrested and charged with five counts of murder, William Dathan Holbert told Panamanian investigators that he killed Bo Icelar with a .38-caliber revolver on his cigar boat in the middle of Bocas Lagoon, far away from land and from any other craft. After initially saying that he wouldn't do so, Holbert agreed to participate in a reconstruction of the crime, a routine procedure in Panama. The purpose of the reconstruction was to show investigators if the acts as described by Holbert were materially feasible. There was also the chance that in carrying out the reconstruction Holbert might, unwittingly, give away some other information or clues as to what happened.

The reconstruction of the Icelar killing started at the police station in

Bocas Town on November 23, 2011, at 8:20 in the morning.* Rain was pouring hard. DA Luis Martínez, Holbert's attorney Claudia Alvarado, two police surveyors, two ballistics experts, two forensic photographers, an interpreter, and several police officers were in attendance. Holbert, for his part, was handcuffed and manacled. This was the day that Icelar's realtor friend Walter Kawano spied Holbert being led by a pair of law enforcement officers along Main Street. Kawano had wondered if this unwelcome sighting of Wild Bill on his old stomping ground might have meant that closure in the case was not too far off.

Holbert told the investigators that on the day in November 2009 when he killed Icelar, he had piloted his cigar boat from Darklands to Bocas Town and left it at a dock next to the Barracuda Bar, a drinking spot on the main drag. He then walked to one of the cars he owned, a 2001 Chevrolet S-10 pickup he had left there, drove it to Icelar's house in Big Creek, and sounded the horn when he arrived. Icelar came out and walked across the yard to the gate. In the reconstruction, the DA's team used a Nissan Frontier and drove to Icelar's house from the center of Bocas Town along the coast road. It was, and still is, the only route between the two locations. When they got to Bo Icelar's house, in the interests of similitude, Holbert was asked to sit in the driver's seat with his handcuffs still on and sound the horn as he had done the day of Icelar's killing. Alberto Concepción, a policeman playing the role of Icelar, came out of the mansion precisely as Holbert had indicated. The group then drove in convoy back into the center of Bocas Town to the Barracuda Bar, where Holbert said he had moored his boat. For the rest of the reconstruction, the police provided a slightly larger vessel than Holbert's cigar boat. Alberto Concepción played the role of Bo Icelar throughout. The large group climbed aboard, Holbert still handcuffed and manacled. The volume of the radio was turned up to blaring; the craft was skimming across the water at 30 knots. Back in 2009, Holbert had been at the controls, with Icelar standing forward of him. Icelar thought he was going to Darklands to meet with Holbert's attorney to check something to do with the shell com-

---

* Laura Michelle Reese did not take part in the reconstructions of the murders of the Brown family, Bo Icelar, and Cher Hughes. She wrote to the authorities: *I know nothing about these cases. . . . Thank you for your time.*

pany that, formally speaking, owned the house and land at Big Creek. Holbert showed graphically how he had shot Icelar once in the neck. His victim fell forward, his body crumpled on the bottom of the boat. Holbert said he wrapped Icelar's corpse in a tarp, "like he was a tuna fish," and pressed on across the lagoon, as fast as he could, through the channel separating Darklands from Split Hill, to the Browns' old house.

According to Holbert, it was a Saturday or a Sunday when he got to Darklands with Icelar's corpse. His house was deserted. Holbert's two workers had that day off. Reese was not around, said Holbert. They had had an argument and Reese had stormed out. The DA asked Holbert what had caused the argument. By way of explanation, Holbert said: "I'm a well-known womanizer and have had extramarital relationships with many women, and I said something and it all came out, and it upset my wife." Icelar weighed around two hundred pounds and Holbert said he himself weighed close to three hundred pounds at the time. Nevertheless, Holbert claimed that, acting alone, it was "very easy" to remove Icelar from the boat and drag him up the floating dock. Next, Holbert loaded Icelar's lifeless body into Michael Brown's old four-wheel-drive pickup, the blue Toyota Hilux that Holbert kept permanently on the property. At this point, the DA's team improvised and produced a stuffed black refuse bag to represent Icelar's lifeless body in the tarp. One of the photographers took a picture of Holbert maneuvering the bag as if it contained a corpse. From there the group made the sad trek to the clearing in the bush, three hundred yards from the house, where Holbert buried Icelar in a shallow grave.

But we only have Holbert's word for this chain of events. Time has blurred memories in Bocas as it does everywhere, but a local resident saw Holbert carrying a tarp with something heavy wrapped inside in the last weeks of 2009. For what it is worth, this sighting has Holbert approaching one of the communal jetties that jut out the length of the crescent-shaped bay of Big Creek near Bo Icelar's house. Holbert unloaded the tarp, and whatever heavy object it contained, from his pickup; he then loaded it into his speedboat. Another day, another sighting: just before Christmas 2009, Wild Bill was spotted outside the Barracuda Bar carrying another heavy load wrapped in a tarp. Someone called out, "Hey, Bill, what you got there on your shoulder?" That's when Holbert replied, "Half a cow." For her part, Sandi Hodge, Bo Icelar's former neighbor, is convinced Icelar was killed in his house and his corpse removed sometime later.

In the United States and Great Britain, and in other countries where witnesses are routinely cross-examined in courts of law in murder trials, visual evidence dating back several years is notoriously unreliable. Skilled attorneys know the tricks that make witnesses look unsure about what they think they remember. But even without the stress of a courtroom appearance, people often confuse places, dates, and events. However, if one or another of the sightings in Bocas of Holbert dragging heavy objects obscured by a tarp is accurate, the implication is that Holbert alone, or Holbert and Reese together, killed Bo Icelar at his house. This opens the possibility that Holbert might have tortured his victim. Icelar very likely had to show Holbert the documents in his possession—the bearer shares and the corporation charter—that demonstrated ownership of the assets. But Icelar had no reason to tell Holbert where he had hidden cash (a relatively modest amount, $8,000) on his property. Choosing to kill Icelar in the open waters of Bocas lagoon implies that Holbert had the bearer shares in his possession, or knew that Icelar was carrying them, and that he was confident that he could find the cash Icelar kept in or near his mansion in Big Creek. The autopsy of the decomposed remains of Icelar's corpse contained in the shallow grave under the scorching sun recorded that Icelar had been shot in the head, but there is no way of establishing whether or not Holbert tortured Icelar before he killed him. The autopsy also provided no clue whatsoever as to where the killing took place.

In a second reconstruction set up to cast light on the Brown family murders, Holbert insisted to the DA's team that when he murdered Michael Brown just before Christmas 2007 during an inspection of his Darklands property, he did so with a single shot to the back of the head. He had been strolling around the property with Brown and had killed him, execution-style, while Brown was showing him a well. Holbert then called out for Watson, Brown's teenage son, on the pretext that his father wanted him to give him a hand with some task or other. Holbert then shot Watson Brown in the bush near where his father had fallen, again with a single bullet in the back of the head. Finally, Holbert strolled back to the residence and executed Brown's wife, Manchittha, as she was kneeling down gardening in the yard with, once more, a bullet in the back of the head.

Strangely, in Holbert's account neither did Watson Brown hear the gunshot that killed his father, nor did Manchittha Brown hear—and act upon—the shots that killed her husband and, subsequently, her son. Holbert explained this away by telling investigators that many people living in that part of Darklands were setting off fireworks to celebrate the impending arrival of New Year's, as commonly happens in Latin America in the last days of December. Quite simply, in Holbert's version the noise of the fireworks obscured the sound of the gunfire. The DA's file records no challenge to Holbert's account of his murder of the three members of the Brown family. Moreover, there is no indication in the DA's file as to how Holbert might have gotten hold of Brown's PIN to access his victim's HSBC bank account, from which he was able to withdraw cash from local ATMs. It is virtually out of the question that Michael Brown handed the PIN to Holbert along with the bearer shares and the corporation charter Brown had used to set up his Panamanian shell company, named Latitude 9.10, Inc. It is only a little less improbable that Holbert might have caught a glimpse of the PIN written down somewhere during the course of the negotiation to sell the shell company and the assets it sheltered. Brown wanted to sell a piece of real estate; he didn't want to give a stranger his nest egg. Also, Holbert admitted to stealing around $80,000 in cash from Brown when he killed him. Brown kept his cash in a safe. How could Holbert have gotten the cash and the PIN without torturing Brown? If Holbert's account of his killing of Bo Icelar seems a little suspicious, his version of the murder of the Browns strains all credibility.

To a loved one, of course, such details matter.

The plan was for Bo Icelar to sell his house and land at Big Creek, Bocas del Toro, and then stay at Sharon McConnell's house in Como, Mississippi, while he looked for a new place for himself. McConnell and her husband, David, were expecting to give Icelar a temporary roof over his head at the end of 2009 or, at the latest, at the beginning of the following year. "Bo realized he made a mistake a couple of years after moving to Bocas," said McConnell. "The party scene just wasn't for him." McConnell's home in Como, a graceful Queen Anne house dating from the turn of the nineteenth century, has a history. In the early twentieth century, when Como, now a town of around fifteen hundred inhabitants, was a comparatively wealthy place—indeed, home to some grand families of the South—actress Tallulah Bankhead had set tongues wagging by attending soirees at the residence in her undergarments. Casting her few inhibitions aside, Bankhead would dance with wild abandon across the creaking floorboards of Sharon McConnell's Queen Anne.

Things are quieter today. In her first-floor atelier, there are dozens of McConnell's resin face masks of notable blues musicians. The white resin looks much like plaster of Paris. The masks lie in rows on a large table, preserving their subjects' features for posterity. A couple of disrobed, life-size male statues occupy corners of the workspace, white like the masks. For McConnell, who is blind, making a statue is an intensely tactile experience. And on a wall of McConnell's atelier, there is an oil painting with the faintest of reliefs, enough—just—to trace with a fingertip the dark blue silhouettes of two women. One is standing, painting another woman, who is seated. Both subjects suggest an easy, confident elegance. McConnell says she is the painter in her own picture. She has placed herself in the scene. Hands on hips, facing the painting, she asks me: "Does my ass look big in that picture? I'm not sure, but I think it does."

Some months after the police found the second shallow grave at the Browns' former house in Darklands, and the remains were positively identified as belonging to Bo Icelar, Sharon McConnell was doing some yard work. She felt a butterfly flutter around her neck and land on her shoulder. Something made her stop in her tracks. "It was Bo. I'm sure of it," said McConnell. She asked the butterfly if it was okay and what heaven was like. A second later, she felt the insect fly away.

Como lies two miles off Interstate 55 south of Memphis, between the Mississippi hill country and the Mississippi delta. From here, dead-straight country roads fringed with rampant kudzu plants—blue-gray before the arrival of the warm days of spring—descend gradually, barely perceptibly, to the delta proper. Morris Cummings was born in Clarksdale, a town in the heart of the delta, in 1955. The town was the best and the worst of the American South: the best, because the skill of delta blues musicians would give America its first homegrown, grassroots sound track; the worst, because this was a place of stark inequalities, barely disguised hostility, and, for many, grinding poverty. Cummings grew up in a one-bedroom shack he shared with six other family members. Down the road was a little hamburger joint that was segregated, but everyone there ate food prepared by the same black cook.

Cummings went blind when he was four years old. Some six months later he was given 50 cents by a stranger who took pity on him, and he used the money to buy a "harp"—delta language for a harmonica. Music was everywhere in the delta in those days. Cummings concentrated on playing the trumpet while he and his siblings were watched over by Miss Gertrude, their babysitter: "She always had a Bible to hand, and a big voice, but no big stick," says Cummings. At the age of five, Cummings was sent to a school for the blind in Jackson, Mississippi. "I was all alone, it felt like my parents had let me down and there was no one to care for me. But you make friends. You overcome it." Cummings would sit at the foot of his bed, wondering what his brothers and sisters were doing back in Clarksdale. He got letters, but infrequently. Talking on the telephone with his parents was out of the question on account of the cost. As he grew, his shoes broke and his pants got too small. One day, he picked up the harmonica he had acquired for 50 cents, and worked hard at playing it. The school had a music program, and Cummings joined and began to travel around the state. He went home just twice a year. One time, he went back to Clarksdale to find that his family wasn't living there any longer. It turned out that they had sent him a letter announcing that they were moving to a new home in Greenville, another delta town, seventy miles south of Clarksdale. But Cummings never received the letter. "They came back to get me," said Cummings, referring to his family. "I was one scared child."

Cummings finished school in 1970 and has worked as a musician ever since. "I spent my whole life on Beale [Street], worked all over Memphis. Gradually, the music changed. It got slicker, maybe, but something was lost." There had been a fierce sense of community in the days when you would get together and make up a song on a porch after nightfall against the drone of ten thousand crickets. People moved out of the delta and got work in factories in cities to the north. That broke the link with the cotton fields. Factories offered minimum-wage jobs and, as hard as the work might be, at least the former plantation workers were not trapped like before. "The owners had the stores. That's where we spent our money. Our schoolbooks were from the 1920s, and it was the 1950s. They kept you dumb, a mule, a tool to be used."

Bo Icelar had briefly had the idea of starting up a music club in Bocas and wanted Cummings to play there, but nothing came of it. Meanwhile, Cummings played in blues festivals in North America and Europe, shared stages with Muddy Waters, B. B. King, and Bill Wyman of the Rolling Stones. Money was always tight, however, and playing the harmonica was Cummings's only source of income.

Cummings ran into a minor spot of trouble with the police in Clarksdale one day, back in the mid-1990s, Cummings isn't sure of the exact date. Icelar was in Mississippi at the time. Icelar bailed out Cummings right away. He didn't ask Cummings for the money back. Icelar could be cantankerous; that was clear to the people who knew him well, and also to quite a few people who knew him much less well. "But he loved me, he loved Sharon, he loved all his friends. Bo hated to see another person in despair. He loved the blues and he was a good listener." Cummings can stand in a person's presence, he says, and pick up on things. That's how he reads you, understands your character. No need to say too much.

Cummings is in a park on the banks of the Mississippi, below the low bluff where the careworn buildings of downtown Memphis rise. He is wearing a black coat and pants and smart, shiny shoes. Cummings's large frame takes up much of the bench I am sharing with him. By now, the sun has burned through the morning mist. In 2009, the blind musician was waiting for his friend Bo Icelar to return to the delta, this time for good, but Icelar never came. The following year, after a Sunday-night gig in downtown Memphis, Cummings was returning to his house in the suburbs with his wife, Melody. They gave his drummer a ride home and then stopped by a Cracker Barrel for something to eat. The restaurant parking lot was full, so Cummings and his wife left their vehicle on the street. When they returned a short time later, they discovered that someone had broken into their car. The thief had stolen around fifty of Cummings's precious delta harps. He felt empty; it took time to get over the shock. Cummings's son pawned his own guitar to help pay for a new harmonica. All over Memphis, folks rallied around him. There was a veritable avalanche of new harps for Morris Cummings. It made the musician happy that so many people cared.

In the park by the big river, Melody hands Cummings a delta harp and the big man starts playing, marking a rhythm with his tapping foot; the thrum of the traffic on Riverside Drive and the wail of a far-off siren are blotted out for a minute or two.

Bo Icelar had a song waiting for him, a song Cummings would have played for him on the back porch of Sharon McConnell's home in Como, a song that would have meant "welcome home." But in the meantime Icelar replied to the ad that William Dathan Holbert had placed in the *Bocas Breeze*, the one that promised *HASSLE FREE AND FAST CLOSINGS*, the one that gave a cell phone number with a dollar sign before and after it, but no name.

Thirty minutes south of St. Louis, Missouri, vehicles taking the ramp to exit the freeway make wide arcs around a piece of roadkill, most likely a fox. The GPS plans a route to the settlement of Fletcher along tight roads with no center markings. Half the homes in this part of Missouri are simple wooden cabins, unpainted. An old school bus parked on a dusty plot is "for sale or trade." A taxidermist's workshop appears—a Web address advertising its services is an incongruous flash of the contemporary—close to the hulk of an old barn. A handwritten sign offers four acres of land for $19,500. Price-wise, there seems to be a race to the bottom going on as, a minute or two farther along the same road, someone else is selling three acres for $12,500. After crossing a bridge and taking a road along the side of a gulley, a notice says *Jefferson County Maintenance Ends* and the road turns to hard, rutted dirt, birch trees all around. A lady in a purple pullover walking a dog waves a greeting and

I make a U-turn as I figure I have gone too far. And then I see it: another sign, this one with a horse on it.

Cher Hughes, Judy Barber, and Diana Motlik were born with the last name Hodecker. The five Hodecker siblings—there was a brother and another sister, too—lived in Fletcher at their maternal grandmother's stables for around four years. Hughes, the eldest of the five, went to high school in De Soto, the nearest town. "Grandma boarded horses," said Motlik, "and we kids cleaned the stables and scrubbed the saddles. There was a fifth of an acre of vegetables: tomatoes, carrots, green beans, zucchinis, you name it." The vegetables were sometimes bartered for hay for the horses. Fruit in the fall was turned into jam, slowly, over the heat of a stove. There was little money with which to make ends meet. The Hodecker children slept together in an attic, a few mattresses on the floor to sleep on. The washroom was in an outbuilding. Because of the sloping ceiling, if you stood up anywhere other than in the center of the attic, you would bump your head. The kids learned to ride bareback, and even rode the horses to a nearby church, which was a Baptist congregation, although the family was nominally Catholic. In the summer, when they were done with tidying the stables and polishing the saddles, they would take the horses to a nearby creek and use them as diving boards, shrieking as they crashed into the water. The horses scared off the snakes, too, which was no bad thing. Prior to moving to Fletcher, the Hodeckers had lived for ten years in the city of Sunset Hills in the suburbs of St. Louis. Mom and Dad Hodecker were still together at this point; their split prompted the move to Fletcher. In Sunset Hills, where Cher Hodecker attended middle school and started high school, the family lived in a neat brick house. Money was not as short as it would later be at the stables. On Saturdays the Hodecker children would walk for an age from their house in Sunset Hills, Motlik thinks it might have been as much as four or five miles, to see the Saturday morning matinee feature at the nearest movie theater. But in Fletcher the kids were so deep in the country, and the household budget was so much tighter than in Sunset Hills, that the kids had to make their own amusements. Close by, the screech of trains traveling along a railroad was a reminder of the wider world, a call to wanderlust. More than anywhere else, Cher Hughes's lessons in life came from her grandmother's stables in this corner of eastern Missouri: you worked hard, and then you played hard.

In high school in De Soto, Cher Hodecker, blond and vivacious, turned heads. "Everyone wanted to be her friend," says Motlik. Diana and Judy were in awe of Cher. "She was beautiful and popular," said Motlik. "She saw the good in people, she was able to home in on people's intrinsic value." Motlik was the Hodecker girl who stayed in Missouri and had children, made a home there for the long haul. Cher never had any children, but she doted on Motlik's daughter and son, goofing around in the swimming pool with them, running up and down the aisles of the toy section at Kmart, always the fun aunt. In Florida, Cher Hughes worked long hours at her sign business and—from the far-off perspective of her family and friends back in Missouri—when success came to her, it seemed to happen fast. In what spare time she had, Cher Hughes went boating off the blinding white beaches of the Gulf coast. Motlik saw it all for herself with her husband and children on vacation: the green-blue water, the excitement of sailing up to an island in your own boat and getting sand between your toes. You could pretend, for just a minute, that the place was all your own. Did places like Sanibel Island, off Fort Myers Beach, spark the dream of the house that Cher and Keith built next to the ocean in Darklands? Diana Motlik thinks so. Meanwhile, Hughes bought a home for herself in St. Petersburg and another to rent out. This Florida rental property was the forerunner of what would, one day, be Cher Hughes's Casa del Sapo on Carenero Island in Bocas del Toro.

"By her mid-thirties, Cher had basically made it," says Motlik. We are sitting in a sports bar off a freeway chosen because it is approximately midway between her home in a small town northwest of St. Louis and a hotel I'm staying at in the city. In these first days of spring, temperatures have reached the upper sixties but clumps of compressed snow line the streets, the thaw revealing pieces of garbage that were last exposed to the sunlight in the depths of winter. Lake St. Clair is still frozen over; grass hereabouts is mainly the color of peanut butter. At the sports bar, big screens are showing a hockey game. Behind Diana Motlik's shoulder I see, momentarily, a player with his stick raised to strike the puck; then I notice tears welling up in Motlik's eyes. "I thought this would make me feel better, but somehow it doesn't," she says, her gaze direct, frank. "I miss her. It hurts so much that she'll never come back." After a few seconds, Motlik takes a photo out of an envelope and smiles. It was taken somewhere in Panama. Hughes is standing between two young policemen, an arm around each of them. She is wearing jeans and has one hip raised coquettishly in a way that underlines that the photo is set up, posed. Cher Hughes is smiling broadly; the young policemen look a bit shy. The photo says, in effect: Cher could charm anyone. "Cher had nothing left to prove," said Motlik.

In 2002, in her mid-forties and with money safe in the bank, Cher Hughes sold her sign business in St. Petersburg after sixteen years of toil. With Keith Werle, the man who would become Hughes's second husband, the businesswoman from St. Louis moved to Bocas del Toro, trading Florida's warm seas for Panama's even warmer ones. "She knew what she wanted and she went for it. Cher always wanted a house on an island," said Motlik. "And she really loved it in Bocas. She wasn't afraid living there, and for the most part she was happy."

When Cher Hughes traveled from Bocas to Panama City in mid-March 2010 to see an apartment she had her eye on, and to talk to an attorney about her impending divorce, there was another part to the plan she had for her future. Hughes wasn't going to live in Panama full-time any longer. A change was on the horizon: "She wanted to come back to Missouri and look after Dad," said Motlik. And that's why, when Hughes's father received no call from his eldest daughter on June 10, 2010, her whole family became deeply worried. That date was her dad's birthday, and Hughes had never missed a single one. On June 10, Motlik and Barber came to realize something had to be very, very wrong. That's when they knew.

On August 1, 2010, a Sunday, around a hundred of Hughes's and Icelar's Bocas friends crowded the Toro Loco bar off Main Street for a memorial service. Inside the bar it was dark, and one of the tables was covered with candles. The expats took turns recounting their favorite memories of Icelar and—especially—the supremely sociable Cher Hughes. The choice of venue was apt under the circumstances: the Toro Loco was the last place in Bocas Town where Hughes had been seen before her disap-

pearance. Don Winner, the blogger and former air force intelligence officer, flew in from Panama City. Winner had helped Diana Motlik and
Mary Wittmeyer press the Panamanian authorities to take the case of the
missing middle-aged *gringa* seriously, and for many of the expats present, his blog was their main source of news as the disturbing story
unfolded. They had only just learned from him that Holbert and Reese
had been arrested in Nicaragua. Many thanked Winner, shook his hand,
and patted him on the back. But Winner found it difficult to walk through
the door of the Toro Loco that day. He wrote in his blog: *It was too tough.
I kept thinking, "Why am I here?" I had never met either Cher or Bo while
they were alive, as far as I can recall. I don't live in the Bocas del Toro area
and I felt like some kind of an outsider or an intruder for some reason.* The
expats asked themselves why they had lost two of their own, how it could
have happened. As Winner put it, at the Toro Loco they collectively wondered *what winds of fate had blown this pain and suffering into their lives.*
Three weeks later, in St. Petersburg, Cher Hughes's US-based friends and
family converged on the Don CeSar Hotel. The portion of deck used for
the "Celebration of Life" had pink and white balloons tied among the
flower arrangements. Don Winner made the trip, once again, as did Keith
Werle. Somebody wrote out Cher's name on the sand, and then everyone
watched the sun go down over the Gulf of Mexico.

As the strange, exotic story of American expats murdered on a faraway Caribbean archipelago came to the attention of the media, Judy
Barber gave interviews to Tampa Bay–area newspapermen and a couple
of local TV channels. *I was glad to tell everyone how wonderful my sister
is*, wrote Barber. *Even the reporter said it is sad how this person could have
caused so much hurt to so many people and not even have a regret. He said
he hopes he rots in prison . . .*

On August 10, 2010, Mary Wittmeyer e-mailed her niece, Judy Barber,
from Panama to tell her that she and Keith Werle had recorded an interview for the NBC show *Dateline*. The producers of *Dateline* were putting
together a show on Cher Hughes called "Stealing Paradise." This was now
a national story. For Barber, if not for all of Cher Hughes's family, there
was a pressing need to let the world know whom Holbert had killed. She
also accepted the request from the *Dateline* producers for an interview.

The question of the advisability of publicity split Cher's family pretty much down the middle. Diana Motlik turned down the offer to appear on the show. Judy Barber flew with her husband to New York City on September 16 and was picked up by an NBC driver at JFK Airport. Barber, wearing an elegant blue blouse, was interviewed by NBC's Kate Snow the next day. At Barber's feet, out of shot, were loops of cables and bits and pieces of TV paraphernalia. *For now*, wrote Barber, *I am just taking life one day at a time*. It was Judy Barber's first visit to New York City. She was overwhelmed that her sister's story had spread so far.

In the first week of October 2010, Barber wrote in her diary: *I cannot stop thinking about going to Panama. How can I get there?* And then it occurred to her that she still had the unused ticket from May, for the trip that had been canceled due to Cher's disappearance. Barber e-mailed Expedia, the online travel agency: *To whom it may concern, my name is Judy Barber. . . . I am wanting to go to Panama to see the place that made my sister so happy. Her birthday would have been November 15th. It was suggested to me that since I did not use my ticket in May that I could use the ticket in November. I am asking if this could be considered due to the circumstances.* The travel company swiftly credited Barber with the money she had spent earlier in the year, and soon she was on her way to the far side of the Caribbean.

Visiting Sandi Hodge's house in Big Creek, Barber established an immediate rapport with Jack, Hughes's faithful Doberman pinscher. "Jack came right up to me and laid his head in my lap," said Barber. And when Judy Barber went to see Cher's house at Darklands on the little island offshore, she was amazed at how far Jack had swum to the Browns' old house, the place Holbert had called Hacienda Cortez, where he had killed and buried Jack's mistress. On Carenero Island, where Hughes built her rental property, the Casa del Sapo, some of the children who Hughes had doted on, grown a little older now, came up to Barber and hugged her. Barber tried to teach the kids words in English; the kids tried to teach her words in Spanish. And lying on the path that weaves its way behind the houses on Carenero Island, Barber saw a half-dozen butterflies. Later, on her last day in Panama City, before flying back to Florida, she saw a butterfly painted in primary colors on a slab of rock in a park. Barber wrote: *Ever since Cher passed I have been seeing butterflies.*

November 15, 2010, was the day that would have marked Hughes's fifty-third birthday. Under a blazing sun, Keith Werle and Judy Barber and a solemn group of friends from Bocas dug a deep hole in the black earth on the little island where the house with the deck and the swinging bench made for two overlooked the turquoise water. An urn was placed in the hole. Everyone took turns kneeling down to pat the dirt back into place, the thatched, dusty party room of the property looming behind them. "Keith got Cher's ashes and we buried them on her birthday on the island she loved," said Barber.

Judy Barber had kept her promise and buried her big sister's ashes on the little island in Darklands. Despite the gloomy reasons for being in Bocas, she had enjoyed meeting her sister's friends. But Barber had made another promise to herself. With her second marriage floundering, in November 2009 she had taken up Hughes's offer of running the Casa del Sapo, her sister's rental property on Carenero Island. It was a rational decision, but it was guided by emotion, too. Barber had written that she was listening to her *heart and head* and would *hopefully find the life I had been wanting.* In December 2011, she checked in for a second time on a flight to Panama. The most recent manager of the Casa del Sapo, the American Renay Hallman, had left. "My plan was to see if I liked living there. This had been what Cher and I had been talking about," said Barber. "My view was, Wild Bill took my sister. Are we going to let him take the whole dream away, too?"

Barber discovered the Casa del Sapo full of cobwebs and spiders. There was rat poop on the floor. Some of the door handles didn't work. A huge pile of garbage in the narrow yard made Barber feel physically sick. "That trash was six feet high. I cleared it up. I felt that it disrespected [Cher]. I was scared and I left." There was also a mattress dumped outside that someone had tried to set on fire, which seemed strange. Barber stayed away for a few days to collect her thoughts and then went back to the Casa del Sapo, determined to make a go of it. One day, two surfer guys were walking by and saw Barber in the yard. "One of them asked me, 'Is this

Wild Bill's museum?' That just broke my heart. I told them who I was. They apologized."

Despite knowing little Spanish, Barber got the Casa del Sapo back on its feet, bit by bit. It was a handsome house, after all, with its red-stained clapboards and deck over the lapping waves. One good early sign was that quite a few of the North American expats on Carenero Island reached out to her. But Barber worried about what she called the "sinister side" of Bocas. The beaches were beautiful, on Carenero and on the other islands, but Barber didn't like to go into the water for a swim. She thought there were people waiting in the jungle for the chance to jump out and rob her stuff. Every month there were mysterious burglaries at the rental house. By the first weeks of 2012, Bocas Town's boisterous New Year's celebrations over, Barber's conclusion was that she didn't know whom to trust.

In the late sixteenth century, the nautical practice of careening—leaning a ship on its side to repair its hull or to caulk cracks with fibers and tar—gave the island its name. On the same sheltered, white-sand beaches on the leeward side of Carenero Island that Barber grew afraid of, pirates would get their ships ready to raid Spanish galleons loaded with treasure looted from their colonies on the Pacific coast of South America. As Bocas del Toro was thought to have little mineral deposits or gold to plunder, the Spanish committed few resources to the region. Carenero Island offered the pirates abundant freshwater, fish, seafood, turtle flesh, sarsaparilla, fruit, and timber. Everything could be bartered from the locals for a few trinkets. It was the perfect hideout.

In February, three months into Barber's stay at the Casa del Sapo, a TV crew from a prime-time American crime show arrived at the rental house. "It was surreal," said Barber. "It was all happening again."

The visitors to Carenero Island were a TV crew from the CBS show *48 Hours* accompanying James and Lillian Faust, a couple from upstate New York, and several family members. James Faust's daughter, Lillian's stepdaughter, Yvonne Baldelli, had disappeared from her rental accom-

modation on Carenero Island the previous November. Don Winner, the
investigative blogger, had been hired by CBS as a consultant. He was
back in Bocas del Toro for another missing persons case that made everyone fear the worst. Baldelli's rental accommodation had been one of the
units at the Casa del Sapo.

In 2011, Baldelli, forty-one, a divorcee, had been living in Southern
California working as a manager for Procter & Gamble. She was laid off
and found herself at a figurative fork in the road. With her boyfriend of
two years, a former marine named Brian Brimager, five years her junior,
she decided to start a new life in Panama. Baldelli planned to design and
produce bikinis and beach wraps to sell to tourists, and shipped over a
couple of sewing machines for that purpose. Brimager packed a guitar
and hoped to make a living playing in the bars of Bocas Town. They
arrived in Bocas del Toro in September 2011 and moved into Cher
Hughes's former rental property.

In a matter of days, the couple found their niche in the partying expat
crowd in Bocas, and Baldelli, with her sunny, optimistic personality,
made friends easily. A Facebook page named "Justice for Yvonne Baldelli"
has a compilation of photos of her, always with a wide smile, chestnut-
color hair falling to her shoulders. Powerfully built, with close-cropped
hair, Brimager, known as "Brim," was as much a fixture in the bars of
Bocas Town as Baldelli was. But Brimager's relentless, heavy drinking—
in a place where everyday alcohol consumption is nonetheless the norm—
alienated some of the expats. Worse was to come: some of the expats said
they started noticing unmistakable signs of violence; for a time, Baldelli
sported a black eye, which she did her best to hide by wearing large sunglasses. She had bruises on her arms. Neighbors on Carenero Island heard
yelling and loud noises coming from the couple's rental unit. Renay Hallman, the then manager of the Casa del Sapo, remembers seeing Baldelli
crying and upset one day. Baldelli told Hallman that she and Brimager
had gotten into a fight at a bar and, subsequently, Brimager had tried to
choke her in the street. Another time, Hallman heard a lot of banging and
thought that Brimager was slamming Baldelli against a wall. A young
woman walking on the coastal path on Carenero Island, just yards from

the couple's room, saw Brimager choking Baldelli and dragging her into the rental property. The young woman said she heard Brimager tell Baldelli, "I am going to kill you." In an uncomfortable near echo of William Dathan Holbert, Brimager commented to several expats that he was one of a small number of people in the world capable of killing someone.

Yvonne Baldelli stopped answering calls from her family and friends in late November 2011, but e-mails from her account mentioned that she had split up with Brim, had moved to Costa Rica with a new man, and was "having a great time." She said that she expected to make it to Southern California for a family get-together in January. That gave the family a small degree of reassurance. But the date of the get-together came and went, and Baldelli didn't show. Worryingly, the e-mails sent from Baldelli's account rang false to her family in the United States. They just didn't seem to have been written by her. It was another echo of Holbert and the strange, rambling text messages he sent out in the middle of 2010, purporting to be from Cher Hughes. In the meantime, Brimager had returned to Southern California and married an old flame with whom he had had a young daughter. The e-mails from Baldelli's account related that she had previously known nothing of Brimager's love child, and—angry at the deceit—split when she found out. Baldelli adored kids but couldn't have any of her own, and news of the love child, which had been kept secret by Brimager, would have surely upset her. The *48 Hours* team, meanwhile, tracked down a machete that Brimager had put up for sale online, with the comment that it had *only [been] used to chop up one stripper*. With the CBS cameras filming, the local police, the family, and dozens of volunteers searched the dense bush behind the ragged wooden shacks on the fringe of the settlement hugging the sheltered side of Carenero Island. The bush stretched all the way to the exposed, uninhabited Atlantic shore of Carenero. The FBI sent a team of divers to investigate the waters offshore—the second time in eighteen months that the FBI had sent a crew to Bocas del Toro to investigate the suspicious disappearance of a US citizen. In fact, the agents the FBI sent to search for Baldelli were "pretty much the same guys" who came to Bocas del Toro when Cher Hughes was murdered, according to George Ingenthron, owner of the Pickled Parrot, a beachside bar on Carenero Island.

"I'm sitting on my sister's porch and another girl has been murdered. How do I feel? I can't even tell you how I feel," said Judy Barber. Baldelli's stepmother approached Barber and told her, "I'm sorry we are disturbing you." The two women hugged each other and cried. Forensic tests revealed traces of blood in the two-room unit where Baldelli and Brimager had been staying. The charred mattress Barber had found, dumped in the yard of the Casa del Sapo, was also splattered with blood. For the time being, there was no corpse: Yvonne Baldelli's parents returned to the United States not knowing for sure that their daughter was dead, but understanding that this must surely be the most likely outcome. Speaking to James and Lilian Faust on camera, *48 Hours* presenter Peter Van Sant said, "You can't make this stuff up, can you?" Before he left Carenero Island, Don Winner came over to Barber and whispered in her ear, "Your sister is proud of you."

At the end of June 2013, a Panamanian man was working in the bush close to the windward side of Carenero Island, on the wooded, swampy ground near where the search parties had begun looking for Yvonne Baldelli eighteen months earlier. The man was not, in fact, far from the rocks that, it is said, gave Bocas del Toro its name. Hearing the seawater rush over a rocky outcrop in the sea, Spanish explorers thought that it made a sound like so many bulls roaring, and the islands of the lagoon received their name: literally, the Mouths of the Bull. The man discovered three military-type duffel bags and a couple of garbage bags. These contained dismembered body parts, shown by DNA tests to belong to Yvonne Baldelli. Initially Brimager had been charged in California with covering up Baldelli's presumed death, and not given bail. Now it was found that the duffel bags in the bush were the same ones that featured in some pictures on both Brimager's and Baldelli's laptop computers. The circumstances of Baldelli's fate were becoming clearer, and in February 2014, Brian Brimager was charged with the murder of Yvonne Baldelli.

Barber's mind still spins with questions. Above all: "Why was [Yvonne Baldelli] murdered at Cher's hotel?" The parallels between Wild Bill and Cher Hughes, and Brimager and Baldelli—another beautiful, vivacious American woman full of dreams for her future, slaughtered brutally, almost casually—are difficult to grasp, difficult to digest. For example, Holbert drained the bank accounts of some of his victims, and Brimager reportedly also used ATMs to withdraw money belonging to Yvonne Baldelli. Brimager could not have been unaware of the Wild Bill case— conjecture and rumor about Holbert and Reese were staples in every drinking house on the islands in the short period the couple lived in Bocas del Toro. So Brimager would have known about the heroics of Jack the Doberman pinscher, who on several occasions swam a mile and a half from Cher's island to the former property of the Brown family, where Holbert had buried Jack's mistress. Yvonne Baldelli also had a dog, Georgia Mae, a King Charles spaniel she had brought over from the States. After Baldelli disappeared, there was no sign of Georgia Mae. Had Brian Brimager taken note of the Jack episode and eliminated Baldelli's beloved pet? After all, everyone had remarked that Cher Hughes would never voluntarily have left Jack behind.*

In July 2012, seven months after she arrived, Judy Barber locked the front door at the Casa del Sapo for the last time. She returned to St. Petersburg. "I got a taste of it," she said of her stay in Bocas del Toro. "That was what I needed." Does Barber think, somehow, that the expats in Bocas—and in Volcán and maybe elsewhere—could have done more to alert the authorities to Holbert? Could they have acted to save a life? After all, Holbert repeatedly boasted that he had killed people. In the Riptide Bar, Holbert once announced that he had found an Indian on his dock, asked him, "What the fuck are you doing," didn't like the reply the Indian gave him, and "so I shot him." Holbert said he got a permit for a firearm and sent a text message to a group of friends and acquaintances saying he had a *license to kill all you gringo motherfuckers*. On another occasion Holbert said, "I'm evil and I like it that way." Yet it is almost certain that no one approached the police or the US embassy to register any concerns about him. And in the few months he lived in Bocas del Toro, Brimager, too, boasted of a violent past. He even loudly threatened to kill Yvonne Baldelli within earshot of people going about their business on Carenero Island. But, once again, nothing suggests any action was taken by Bocas residents, expat or Panamanian.

---

*Having been charged by a federal grand jury in California with the murder of Yvonne Baldelli, Brian Brimager is due to stand trial in the first half of 2016.

So, could the expats have done more? Barber pauses before replying. She says, slowly: "No, I don't really think so. I don't blame the expats [for not acting sooner]. People there are always coming and going, you know?"

"Cher was an angel," said Barber. Holbert killed Cher and "that put a stop to it." It was like Hughes's husband, Keith Werle, said so many times: Holbert killed the wrong girl. He killed someone who was bound to be missed. He got too confident, and he slipped up.

For Barber, the years have passed and there remain so many unanswered questions. For instance, when Holbert and Reese were apprehended, Reese was wearing some jewelry: a necklace, a diamond ring, and a bracelet, all of which Barber says her sister designed. "I would want my daughter, Jennifer, to have that jewelry," said Barber. When Reese was interviewed in Panama City after being flown back from Nicaragua, she complained to the public prosecutor that some of her jewelry went missing when she was arrested on the San Juan River, implying that it had been stolen from her. The DA's file makes no further reference to these items in Cher's jewelry collection.

It is the end of April 2015. The fifth anniversary of Cher Hughes's murder has come and gone. There is still no news of Holbert and Reese's trial date. More than five years after their sister was murdered, the lack of a conclusion weighs heavily on Diana Motlik and Judy Barber. No one can quite understand why it is taking so long to set a date and haul Holbert and Reese into the dock. For Barber, the ill-fated stay on Carenero Island will not be her final visit to Panama. She will make one more trip across the Caribbean Sea. Nothing will keep her away from the trial, however brief it is under Panama's legal system.

"I want to be sitting there in the courthouse and I want to see that bastard," said Barber. "I'll be holding up a picture of Cher so that he knows she wasn't just another victim."

Epilogue
"I Am Your Worst Nightmare"

In March 2014, I had made my first visit to the city of David. Holbert and Reese had passed through here in 2007 and hadn't lingered. But since their Panamanian crimes took place in the west of the country, and David has its only big courthouse, the pair had to await trial in jails in the city. A newspaper reporter covering the crime beat in David introduced me to Demetrio Ábrego, a Panamanian TV reporter working out of an office of the TVN channel covering western Panama. Ábrego had interviewed Holbert in his cell six months previously. It was a weekday, mid-afternoon, and Ábrego had just filed that day's story with the channel's HQ in Panama City.

A dark-eyed man in his forties who describes himself on Twitter as a *Journalist, Lawyer, Teacher and Farmer*, Ábrego was relaxed and expansive. A half-dozen watercolor caricatures, widemouthed, bug-eyed—one for each member of the TVN team working in David—stood on a shelf in his office against a wall whose paint was peeling like a bad skin disease. I mentioned to Ábrego that I planned to ask Holbert for a meeting. Ábrego's tone changed. He recalled going into David prison with his camera team, feeling the stares of the prisoners in the exercise yard, and entering Holbert's dark, stinking cell. The interview done, a couple of younger members of the television crew sent to the jail took selfies in the yard with Holbert, much to Ábrego's displeasure. It simply wasn't professional. Selfies with the American prisoner would only serve to shore up his notoriety among the other inmates—surely the reason why Holbert was happy to be in the frame when the TV men asked him if he could be in their pictures. With his smiles and back-slapping, Holbert had—on some emotional level—won over those junior crew members. But he certainly hadn't won over their boss.

"Don't trust anything Holbert ever tells you," warned Ábrego. "He is the ultimate manipulator."

At Panama's 2009 general election, Claudia Alvarado ran for deputy in the Panamanian parliament. Alvarado had worked for some twenty years running various prisons in Panama, including David's men's prison. Now a youthful-looking fifty-something, who wears her black hair long, Alvarado was at a crossroads in her life. Her political party lost the election and—in a country where the posts of civil service functionaries are sometimes reassigned to pay back political favors—Alvarado found herself surplus to requirements in the prison system. So she switched sides, becoming an advocate for some of western Panama's most problematic inmates, young members of urban gangs, often still in their teens, identified by gang tattoos. In 2011 the newspaper *Panamá América* reported that there were at least fifteen rival gangs battling for control of the men's prison in David, including Los Kilimanjaros, Carne Frita (Fried Meat), Los Frogs, and Los Kill the Frogs. The same year, *Panamá América* opined that the violence among prisoners and, above all, the severe overcrowding made the jail "a ticking time bomb." Alvarado told me that the prison was built seventy years ago and designed to accommodate 450 prisoners. They had added ten extra cells, but this made little difference. "That added space for another 250 prisoners, 300 at most," said Alvarado, who had become Holbert's attorney when Holbert found out about her from a fellow prisoner and wrote her a note on a scrap of paper, asking for a meeting. Alvarado showed up at the jail and Holbert became her client on the spot.

Previously, the American had not had the best of times with his legal representatives. Soon after his arrest, when he was incarcerated in the capital, Holbert had turned down a state-appointed attorney in favor of his own choice of a prominent Panama City law practice. He was disappointed that his case wasn't taken up by one of the more experienced partners; instead he was allotted a relatively junior associate. That didn't stop one of the lawyers in the firm from making a reputation for himself by attempting to extract cash from US journalists hoping to interview the self-confessed killer. But with Alvarado, something clicked. In one of their conjugal visits, Holbert told Reese about his new attorney. Reese asked Alvarado for a meeting and she, too, asked the polite, well-dressed grandmother to represent her. The impression I got was that Claudia Alvarado wasn't in it for the money. This was not the kind of attorney who would try to make a fast buck for herself by selling access to a client. But she did give the impression of being a woman who knew how to get things done. When I approached Alvarado to see if Holbert would agree to see me, once her client had assented—and Alvarado herself had agreed, which took several meetings—she turned out to be an agreeable but firm gatekeeper. In the end, Alvarado arranged the permit to enter the jail within two days of approving my request.* In David and in Bocas, people wondered out loud how anyone could take on Holbert and Reese as clients. The implication was that common decency meant that somewhere an attorney should draw the line at these two. Over a buffet lunch in the dining room of a boxy, modern hotel a few blocks from the center of David, Alvarado attempted to answer the question. She laid both palms flat against the starched white tablecloth and gave the stock lawyerly response to the effect that everyone deserves legal representation, even people who have committed terrible crimes. Her job was "not to excuse, but to explain and defend." Still, the way she referred to Holbert and Reese

---

* Laura Michelle Reese did not respond to my appeal for an interview.

by their given names, never their surnames, suggested that a degree of cordiality was present in her relationship with them.

David prison was a fundamentally insecure place. In May 2014, Holbert managed to grab a fellow inmate, jailed on suspicion of the murder of a prominent local print journalist, and hold him hostage in his cell. Holbert was attempting to force a concession from the prison authorities. He wanted them to allow him more time in the prison yard to, as Alvarado later put it, "carry out a number of activities." Meanwhile, with the hostage crisis unresolved, another prisoner used a cell phone to call paramedics outside the pen to report that a jailer had been injured. Farcically, when the paramedics arrived at the jail, the authorities did not let them in, saying that no one had been hurt.

Later, Alvarado told local media that Holbert had not, in fact, taken anyone hostage. David Dell, the Welshman who had met Holbert in Volcán in 2007 when the American opened his Harley-Davidson shop, sat down at his desk in the highlands and wrote: *From seeing his smiling face on the television news, it seems clear he is enjoying every minute of it. He is getting his "fifteen minutes" of fame, and more.* But the television items that disturbed Dell and others were a warning, of sorts—for me and anyone else chronicling Holbert and Reese's crimes. Was there any way of recounting events without giving Holbert the oxygen of publicity? In Bocas, one of Cher Hughes's friends told me that "this is a story that should not be told for a long time." When I asked how long, she replied, "For about a hundred years." People felt shamed by Reese and Holbert. And yet, others were adamant that Holbert's crimes needed to be recounted. To do that, you had to be clear about the details. To take the hostage incident as an example, some sources said that Holbert had taken a man prisoner in his cell; others said that he had not. Not for the first time in Panama, it was difficult to tell fact from fiction. Still, there was a job to be done. Four months after the alleged hostage-taking, I was patted down and walked into a meeting with William Dathan Holbert in the men's jail in David. The facility had not, as yet, exploded, as *Panamá América* had predicted.

From outside its main gates, the entrance to the prison looked like an abandoned car-repair shop. There was razor wire on the perimeter walls, but this was unexceptional for the area. At the side of the gates, painted on the outside wall in uneven script where prison visitors, mainly women, stood in line, there was a quote from Proverbs 22:6: *Train up a child in the way he should go, and when he is old, he will not depart from it.* Next to this was a dress code for the waiting women specifying length of skirt or shorts, the kind of tops that were acceptable. "No high heels," it also said.

On one side of the empty entrance yard, several men were sitting at tables in a wire cage, seemingly on metalwork detail. Opposite the metalworkers was a low, whitewashed single-story building. A young man in hand and leg cuffs—the latter fixed fairly loosely—came out a door of the building and walked slowly toward the gates with a prison guard. They left the facility together in a van.

In the other direction went food packages dropped off at the gates by the women waiting in line. Several of them used umbrellas as sunshades. A couple of female guards sitting at an ancient wooden desk made notes in a ledger as the food packages were taken away, only occasionally glancing at the women at the gates. And there were more regulations on a paper pinned to a board behind the desk: "No citrus fruit. No fatty soups." This was a scene that was played out just about every day. There wasn't enough food in the prison to go around and inmates relied on supplies from family, as they do in every prison in Panama.

I was, as it turned out, the first non-Panamanian to visit Holbert in David. No family or friends had come from the United States to see him here; nor, for that matter, had any family or friends come from America to visit Laura Michelle Reese. Two male prison guards at the gate signed me in. There was mild interest from the guards that Holbert, nearly four years after being transferred here from custody in Panama City, should finally have a gringo visitor. Alvarado chatted with the guards; after all, she had been the boss here back in the day and still knew most of the staff. We waited a few minutes for the permission slip, signed by the governor, to arrive. There was a last-minute hiccup when I emptied my pockets and the guards saw I had $26. That was about five times the permitted amount. But Alvarado smiled at them and I got to keep my cash. Behind the guards, a television with its sound turned down was showing a cooking program.

A prison guard strolled across the empty yard and escorted Alvarado and me to the administrative wing of the jail; the rule forbidding high heels apparently didn't apply to Alvarado. Someone had brought out three chairs and placed them in the narrow space in front of a counter, behind which four or five young women were processing stacks of paper files. Behind them you could see the figure 1,124 written on a board on the wall—the number of men locked up in David prison that day. Guards shuffled in and out. We were in an exposed place, but we were entirely ignored. This was clearly a world away from those prison interviews conducted through a telephone line across a thick plate of glass.

Holbert arrived with a smile and a brisk "Hey, I'm Bill," and offered his hand. He sat next to Alvarado on an identical, straight-backed chair. He wore no handcuffs and was not, as far as I could see, restrained in any way. I faced Holbert, sitting lower down, in an armchair. He was wearing baggy shorts that extended past his knees, a yellow T-shirt, and a large crucifix made from two pieces of wood tied at the center with a rubber band. He looked physically fit, though pale, and had a goatee beard like the one in the Panama Prison Ministries photos. I tried to put to the back of my mind the thought that the finger that pulled the trigger to take the lives of at least six people had squeezed my palm.

Holbert started by getting some complaints off his chest: "We're only allowed an hour a week of exercise. That violates every law on earth. And you get just one phone call a week. That's another gross violation!" But he confirmed that he had a cell phone and access to the Internet. "If you don't have money here, you can't live. Prison here is a joke. For a man who's intelligent, being locked up in a box is terrible." Inmates took drugs to get through the day, even though no drugs were supposed to enter the facility. Holbert said that 90 percent of the prisoners took them, although he said that he didn't. "I never did do cocaine. . . . But if you took the drugs out of here, there would be a bloodbath."

I inquired about Laura Michelle Reese, but Holbert had nothing to say. I remembered the business about how Reese was chosen to serve food and drink to the gardening detail from the men's pen who were sent to the women's jail, and about how she fell for one of them.

Holbert preferred to talk about his brushes with Ismael Flores, the previous prison governor: "We had no sports program, and being a sort of a politician I started a fight with the governor." Holbert got some of the other prisoners to protest. "We striked and we rioted. Nobody could enter. Anyone who wanted to come in, you'd beat them with a stick. I used the news media to fight the system."

That seemed a good moment to bring up the fact that he had used journalists to press for the release of Manuel Noriega from his own jail cell in Panama City. Holbert shook his head sadly. "It makes no sense. He's over seventy years old. He's a really nice guy. He can serve the rest of his sentence at home. . . . In Noriega's time there was no delinquency. There was corruption, but no murders, no madness. . . . I spoke to him six, seven times."

Holbert was not forthcoming about how he came to get Noriega's phone number in prison in Panama City. The last time Holbert had called Noriega was in 2013. In his telling, Noriega asked him for help, and Holbert accepted. Holbert shrugged, as if to say that calling the former dictator was the most normal thing in the world. "I don't have nothing else to do. They [the Panamanian authorities] look fuckin' stupid. I'm famous. Things I do affect people." Holbert picked up a pretend phone. "I said to him, Uncle Tony, what's up?"

"Do you think much of your life back in the States?"

No, Holbert preferred not to think of the life he had led before prison. In high school, he said, he had played everything except basketball. He had played defensive end on his high school football team. On top of that, he had done wrestling, boxing, and the discus and shot put. He said that he had been class president, which I knew was untrue—he had been almost perfectly anonymous at North Henderson High. I could have confronted him about this, but I chose not to do so. The world is full of liars and fantasists. But it's not full of multiple killers. Better to move on. We talked about his life after graduating from North Henderson. Holbert leaned forward, resting his chin on his thumb and forefinger. He looked me in the eye all the time, but now his stare was deep, borderline aggressive. A narrow shaft of sunlight picked out particles of dust, rising and falling.

"I made a gain every month. I sold heavy equipment. I was working eighteen hours a day. But I fell apart after my divorce. I said fuck it and left.

"When they took my children away from me, I became a different man. I appealed, and lost. They put the same judge there. I played the game by their rules and lost. I was really pissed off about the States."

"It was a kind of tipping point?"

Holbert looked at me, quizzical. I said, you know, like in chemistry class, when a piece of litmus paper turns from pink to blue, it happens in just a moment.

"Yes!" said Holbert. "I didn't want my house of cards to fall down. I had six houses. It was an empire!" But things started to unravel for him. "I robbed Peter to pay Paul." Holbert had been looking past me, but then concentrated his gaze. "We are brought up thinking that money is every-thing!"

I wanted to talk about the period when Holbert and Reese set up a white supremacy bookshop in Forest City, North Carolina. About how Holbert took to the street with a megaphone to get people to attend his meetings.

"That was nothing to do with racism," said Holbert curtly. "It was anti-immigration." He wanted to move on from that line of questioning: "I don't think about my life outside anymore. If I did, I'd go insane."

But Holbert was still thinking about western North Carolina. This whole time, Claudia Alvarado had been sitting next to Holbert, upright like a pole, not saying a single word. Then I realized: she doesn't under-stand English. Holbert started talking to Alvarado in Spanish, apropos of nothing, about the 250-room Biltmore House, just outside Asheville, erected by George Vanderbilt, grandson of railroad tycoon Cornelius Vanderbilt. Holbert told Alvarado, with perceptible pride, that it was the biggest private home in America, and that he was from nearby.

Holbert moved closer and slapped me on the knee jovially. A tiny ball of spit landed on my cheek.

I needed to establish a timeline. I had a list of dates, states, countries, the wheres and the whens. I asked him about the car chase in Wyoming in the winter of 2006, after his real estate fraud on the North Carolina shore. "What happened next? How did you get to Central America?" A smile came across Holbert's lips. He winked at me. I thought about Scott McAda and the way that Holbert had winked at him in the *careos*, after he had told the most preposterous stories, just when the DA's team wasn't looking.

"No, I can't talk about it."

I pressed him.

"Okay. It took four days. It was planes, trains, and automobiles. We went through the Bahamas and Grand Cayman." Holbert said he spent two years in Costa Rica and saw the whole country: "I was a man on the run, looking for tomorrow." It was the obvious place to go. "I had been to Costa Rica on vacation, maybe in 2002."

Arriving in Central America was a culture shock. "Personal space doesn't exist. You think people are fucking with you, and they're not. It took me two years to get comfortable.

"You have to know how to circumvent the rules. My biggest fear was getting caught. I had seven passports. Easy as hell to get 'em. I ran arms from Nica [Nicaragua] to Colombia. It's much better than drugs. You get back ten, fifteen times your investment."

I was pretty sure that Holbert was laying the groundwork for the same type of story he tried to sell to DA Martínez and his team when he attempted to implicate a number of his fellow expats in a fictitious organized crime ring. I scribbled all this down in a notepad (recording devices were not allowed in the prison).

I asked him about his time in Boquete. "I didn't like it. I want to live with Panamanians. Americans, they bitch about everything. I set up a fraudulent psychiatry office. Dr. William Reese! I was right on the main square. In no time I had twenty clients. All of them were old women who just wanted to talk. Out of every hundred expats, ninety-seven are damaged." Holbert wondered out loud why so many of his compatriots came to live in Central America, concluding that there was no big savings to be made on housing prices these days. So it must be because here you could get servants on the cheap.

Holbert looked at me, inviting more questions. I had many, but he jumped in and started talking about the reconstruction of the murders of Bo Icelar and the Brown family in Bocas del Toro. Once again, Holbert appeared aggrieved:

"They paraded me through Bocas in chains. They said I worshipped Satan. They said the house [in Darklands] was haunted. That's madness!

"The reconstruction was hard. I went back and everything was the same except for the house. They had robbed everything. They stole the damn toilet. I lost my temper. 'You motherfuckers destroyed it!' "

Holbert said that he told the police officers that if they tried to force him to do things, "someone else is going to die." That someone won't be Holbert, though: "Suicide won't ever happen. I don't know if it's because I like to live or if I'm afraid to die. I look on the bright side. I have nothing, no responsibility. It's liberating."

What about the families of his victims?

"I feel horribly. I killed innocent people. I killed my friends."

From where I was sitting, Holbert's contrition felt not at all convincing.

"It was a bad decision from a moral standpoint. Ridiculously bad. I don't know why I did it." So why did he kill Cher, for instance? "I wanted to show myself I'm a coldhearted bastard. I went against my instincts. I don't know why I did it. Everything was screaming, Don't do it! But I did it anyway. I killed my friend.

"It's all my fault, all of it. I am your worst nightmare.

"But I'm pragmatic. I want to heal the past. I'm interested in the future. I work with the Catholic Church. It's a karma thing. I lived a shitty, selfish life and I want to make up for it."

I asked Holbert: "What would you say to people who think you deserve to die for your crimes?"

As quick as a flash: "What people?"

"Some people in Bocas, for instance. It can't be a surprise to hear that there are folks who think you deserve to be put to death for those murders."

Holbert shook his head like I was missing something really obvious.

"Back home the best you can expect—the best—is not to get out of prison again. In America we have to punish, take a sledgehammer. But here it's a more forgiving society. They're not judgmental. Life is laid-back.

I'm not an American anymore. I feel half Panamanian. They [Americans] make me want to vomit! The US mentality makes me sick. But Panamanians are more intrigued than shocked. They want photos and autographs." Holbert brightened. "I love it here! Here, chicks call me!" More spit fell, this time on my lower arm. The man facing me was animated.

"In America they think of me as Hannibal Lecter or Charles Manson. I'm infamous. But here I'm loveable. I speak ghetto Spanish. I'm Bill, nobody special." Holbert said that in North Carolina nobody could believe he had turned out this way, that this was the man they had known. "There's a stigma," he said.

"I've done some cool shit and some bad shit. No one wants to be a mass murderer."

Holbert turned to Alvarado and said: *"El panameño está más interesado que asustado."* In English this means: "Panamanians are more curious than afraid." Alvarado nods her head.

An hour had passed, and the prison guards were bustling all around us. The typists behind the counter were filling out forms. It seemed we could stay here on these rickety chairs as long as we pleased.

"Now I read a lot. They sent books [to the prison] from a library that closed in the Canal Zone. They're mainly textbooks. It's not a curriculum. I like the ones on anthropology." It turned out that Holbert was writing some books of his own. He counted them on his fingers. There was an autobiography ("I think it's pretty good") and also what Holbert described as a "parable."

"You've read *The Alchemist* by Paulo Coelho? Well, it's a bit like that." A third book was going to remain a secret for the moment: "There's another one, but I don't want to talk about it."

I had started to feel nauseous. But there was still one big question I wanted to raise. It was in my notepad, circled. I was thinking now of a photo in the DA's file of a family scene. Ever since I saw it for the first time, I could not get this photo out of my mind. The image was of Michael Brown and his wife, Nan, and Brown's sons Marco and Watson. Watson was sixteen or seventeen when the picture was taken. He was seventeen years and two months old when Holbert put a gun to his head and pulled the trigger. The photo was taken by Brown's daughter in the muddy yard of the Brown residence in Darklands. I have a black-and-white copy, although the original was almost certainly in color. I can imagine the blue of the sky at the corners of the picture, the green of the banana leaves in the background. With the colors drained, the life has gone, too. Marco, on the left, long-limbed, exudes a boyish confidence. In the middle stand Michael and Nan Brown. Watson is on the right of the photo, next to his mom, shy, squinting slightly, locks of hair falling over his eyes. He is, I imagine, small for his age. Probably when folks looked at him and imagined how old he was, they guessed a year too few.

"How do you kill a seventeen-year-old boy?"

Holbert looked like this wasn't a question he was expecting.

"How do you kill a seventeen-year-old boy like Watson Brown? Tell me, how exactly do you do that?"

Holbert said he was following orders. It was that old Mafia story again: "They said, 'Take care of this.' It's what happened. The kid, he was there. I ran out of money. I'm not justifying what I did. . . . And they were people trafficking, the Browns. They were doing some real bad shit. The boy, too. . . ." I thought I heard Holbert say that the Browns were killing and raping. But I felt sick and suddenly I realized I wasn't hearing right. I put my pen down. I thought of a disinfectant gel I had back at my hotel that I wanted to rub into my hands and arms. I needed to get out of this place.

One more time, now a bit louder, and in a different tone, despite myself: "How do you kill a seventeen-year-old boy? How is this possible?"

Claudia Alvarado, Holbert's attorney, fired an inquisitive glance in my direction. For me, the conversation had ground to a halt right there. I now felt like I was about to vomit. But Holbert had moved on to talk about other things.

"It's going to be an interesting ride. I'm not beaten. I'm not going to lay down and die.

"Before I'm forty I'll be out. There are just too many loopholes."

Cyndy Hughes, a professor in the Department of Criminology and Criminal Justice at the Western Carolina University at Cullowhee, North Carolina, teaches a course titled "The History of Serial Killers." Although

Hughes teaches it only during the summer recess, it's her most popular course. "There are students who stay on campus just to take it," said Hughes, a young academic who has researched the way that the criminal justice system deals with murderers across the United States, and particularly in her home state of Florida. In her academic work, Hughes concentrates on here-and-now cases. The general public's interest in crime stories played out in real time dates back, says Hughes, to the low-speed car chase in 1994 when police and a half-dozen news helicopters tailed a white Ford Bronco that had O. J. Simpson as its fugitive passenger: "People saw Simpson riding down the freeway and they wanted to know what had happened, they wanted to understand the backstory, they quickly felt intensely involved in events."*

Why do her college students sign up so readily for Hughes's serial killers course? "It's a facet of the world and a type of life that we will never properly understand. Serial killers are, quite simply, different from us." That's not the case with some kinds of robberies, for example. Even if we don't steal, we can generally grasp why people get greedy and do steal things. "We can make that mental leap," said Hughes.

In the case of Holbert—and Reese, also—the distinction between sociopaths and psychopaths is relevant. Sociopaths live on the fringes of society and are aware of their differentness. We soon become aware of it, too, if we come across them. If they commit murder, it is usually haphazard, poorly planned. These are people who can never fit into normal society, unlike psychopaths, who can even thrive in the communities they choose to live in. Despite a profound narcissism, they are sometimes superficially charming and even gregarious. But they have an utter lack of emotional attachment. They care not a jot how their actions affect others; in the extreme example of murder, they show no remorse. Hughes insisted that psychopaths are "broadly intelligent, either street-smart like the Son of Sam [David Richard Berkowitz, the American serial killer convicted of a series of shootings that began in New York City in the summer of 1976] or more conventionally bright like Ted Bundy [who confessed

---

* Simpson was subsequently found not guilty of the murders of Nicole Brown Simpson and her friend Ron Goldman.

to around thirty murders]." These are people with a strong intuition and the ability to "read" people. If sociopaths are, figuratively, small children holding a loaded gun with the safety catch off, psychopaths are the equivalent of snipers.

Hughes's main caveat when discussing serial killers is that there is—thankfully—still an insufficient critical mass of subjects for this ever to become a mainstream area of academic study. In the United States, at least, serial killers are predominantly white males who begin killing at some point between their mid-twenties and their mid-thirties. There are four recognizable types of serial killers, said Hughes, defined as individuals who have murdered at least three people with a minimum thirty-day "cooling-off" period between the crimes. In all cases, there is a compulsion to kill.

At the beginning, there is a "testing of the waters." The individual, not yet a killer, seeks to experiment to see where the boundaries are. Typically, this phase will allow him to adapt if needed and, figuratively, regroup. Holbert tested the waters with the real estate fraud in Oak Island, North Carolina, where he used fake property deeds to dupe an investor out of $200,000. Whatever the truth of Laura Michelle Reese's involvement in the subsequent killing spree in Panama, the Costa Rican prosecutor considers the murder of Jeffrey Arlan Kline to be the equal work of Holbert and Reese. Holbert didn't know how to kill someone until he tried. Did he need Reese to be there for the first murder and then go it alone, with her backing and knowledge, in the case of the killings in Bocas del Toro?

The first three types do not seem to fit the bill in the case of Holbert's self-confessed murders: There is the "visionary," a killer who perceives—and in his hallucinatory state, likely really believes—that he is answering a call to murder. Next, the "mission-oriented serial killer" concentrates on one type of victim, such as prostitutes or gays—crimes that come from hate. Then there is the "hedonistic" killer. This is probably the best-known type of serial murderer. He commits his crimes because they excite him sexually. The crimes are messy and, sometimes but not always, triggered by sexual inadequacy. The killings of Ted Bundy and the unsolved murders committed by Jack the Ripper in London in the nineteenth century fall into this category.

A fourth type is the "power and control–oriented" serial killer, whose goal is absolute control over another human being. This personality seems much closer to what witnesses in Bocas del Toro have described when they talk about Holbert, who was determined to be recognized as a successful real estate operator transplanted to the Caribbean. Hughes points out that this type of serial killer invariably targets members of their own race: "A white man driving through a black neighborhood is immediately noticeable, so serial killers will avoid this type of situation. They don't want to get detected and they tend to enjoy and take their time planning their crimes," says Hughes. The victims are sometimes easy to control, almost always trusting. Many serial killers use a ruse to attract their victims. Ted Bundy's arm in a fake sling found its echo in Holbert and Reese's bottle of vodka filled with water—the bottle of "liquor" that only they would drink from at the parties they hosted.

Yet the theory does not necessarily apply neatly to reality: serial killers are different from "normal" criminals (such as bank robbers brandishing firearms) in that the motivation of the latter to kill is external to the crime. But this seems to clash with what we know about Holbert, since the killings he's been charged with—Jeffrey Arlan Kline, the Brown/Salem family, Bo Icelar, and Cher Hughes—had the external motivation that he wanted to steal his victims' homes and assets. On the other hand, Holbert and Reese never made a penny from the real estate they stole. The Brown house gave them a roof over their heads for two and a half years, but—aside from a couple of parties—Holbert and Reese made no use of the house Cher Hughes and Keith Werle planned and built in Darklands. (Hughes's Casa del Sapo rental property could hardly have been a cash cow for Holbert, as he operated it for too short a period.) Most pertinent of all, Holbert and Reese were incapable of flipping, and so converting into cash, the prime piece of real estate in Big Creek that Holbert stole from Bo Icelar after firing a bullet into the back of Icelar's head.

So might Holbert and Reese's motivation be external to the crimes after all? Was it all about a warped desire for notoriety? Laura Michelle Reese told her expat neighbors, "Folks aren't going to believe what we've been doing here when we're gone."

Serial killers become more disorganized over time. They are not usually caught because the cops catch up with them; rather, they develop an exaggerated sense of their own power and intelligence. They think they are several steps ahead of everyone else, become sloppy, and make mistakes. Keith Werle said that in killing Cher Hughes, his estranged wife, Holbert had "picked the wrong girl." But the sloppiness was there early on, too. Holbert and Reese's crude, fake Dutch passports were remarked on but went unreported; they were even considered par for the course for the sleazier type of expat in laissez-faire Panama. Holbert carried a Dutch Antilles driver's license that was such a poor fake as to be laughable. It is counterintuitive to believe that during his relatively frequent forays into the Panamanian heartlands—to Boquete, Volcán, and so on—he was never stopped by the traffic cops. So how come when he showed the fake driver's license he was not hauled off to the nearest police station for questioning? Had that happened, the police could have found out that Holbert and Reese were in Panama illegally. They had slipped into the country from Costa Rica in early 2007, unnoticed. The same Panamanian immigration data that in 2010 had shown police that Bo Icelar and Cher Hughes never left the country, could earlier have demonstrated that Holbert and Reese had never lawfully entered it. The most likely conclusion is inescapable: as far as the traffic cops were concerned, Holbert was able to buy his way quickly out of trouble with a couple of twenty-dollar bills. Meanwhile, the attorneys who processed the changes to the directorships of the shell companies that Holbert stole needed to ask to see his ID. These attorneys did not pause for very long over the oddity that a young American man might introduce himself as a Dutch national. There was a fundamental lack of curiosity, even though they did everything the law required them to do. Most important of all, Holbert's repeated boast among the hard-partying gringo crowd that he had killed people in the lagoon, usually Native Americans who had gotten in his way, was never reported to the authorities.

In jail, Holbert said that in North Carolina nobody could believe that the William Dathan Holbert they knew had turned out this way. He thought Americans put him in the same group as (the fictional) Hannibal Lecter or Charles Manson. As he said to me in jail, in North Carolina there was a "stigma."

In fact, in his old stomping ground of Beechwood Lakes, in Hendersonville, North Carolina, people now barely recognized his name, said Dianne Prohn, who knew Holbert when he was a boy living on Mallard Trail and later, as an adult, when Holbert was handed a contract for the landscaping in the subdivision. Dianne and Ken Prohn, both retired teachers, have lived in Beechwood Lakes for over thirty years. Like Holbert's parents, William and Karen Holbert, they had been among the first buyers there. "But there aren't many people who have lived here for anything like as long," said Dianne Prohn. "People come and go. A lot of new folk arrived in the last few years." The near-constant movement in Beechwood Lakes was one reason why the name William Dathan Holbert meant nothing, or little, to most people there.

John Boyle, the reporter for Asheville's *Citizen-Times* who had covered the breaking Holbert and Reese case in the summer of 2010, went further: "It slipped a lot faster from people's consciousness because he [Holbert] was in another country and the victims had no local ties." In retrospect, people moved on from the story "surprisingly quickly." In contrast, in the mid-1990s, soon after her graduation, a young local woman had been sexually assaulted and murdered in Asheville. It was a "horrible case," said Boyle, but it was one that "still resonates" because in the mountains of western North Carolina communities are tight and extended families tend to stick together. Of course, people's interest in news stories of all kinds can be dulled by practical, everyday worries. Just as a travel Web site was crowning Asheville, in early 2015, "The Coolest City in America," a man wrote to Boyle's newspaper to complain that the city "is most certainly a playground for the rich. No affordable housing and by affordable I mean homes that are priced to where a person earns the median income of $8 to $10 an hour." But then, seemingly out of nowhere, a community—any community—can be shaken by a tremor of evil.

Hendersonville Road, south of downtown Asheville, is a ribbon of usually slow-moving traffic. Here are fast-food places, pawnshops, dollar stores, office blocks where people earn their non-hipster livings. Here, too, was the Body Shop gym where William Dathan Holbert met Laura Michelle Reese. Guys with beards aren't skinny in these parts; it's real lumberjacks who put on lumberjack shirts. On the hillsides are nice, unpretentious homes with big yards, tall trees all around, fresh air: the sort of place you might consider if you were going to raise a family. It's also countryside familiar to anyone who has seen *The Andy Griffith Show*.*

In the spring of 2015, the name William Dathan Holbert elicited quizzical looks in Saluda, the town of the runaway trains. Hardly anyone remembered who he was. At a fund-raiser organized by the Saluda Downtown Foundation, no one appeared to know anything at all about the Holbert and Reese case. Mr. Leon at the M. A. Pace General Store, which—with its black-and-white photos of sports teams, old Coke bottles, and dusty lace dresses—doubles as an informal museum of Saluda life, didn't recognize the name. You want a famous resident of Saluda? He pointed to a picture of Perry Como, who had spent the latter part of his life in Saluda and would treat Mr. Leon's customers to an occasional impromptu song. In any case, with the town's annual Coon Dog Day Festival approaching, Saluda was packed to the gills. Retirees from out of state were taking gentle strolls and young thrill seekers were signing up for white-water rafting trips. For businesses, the warm weather brought visitors and there was work to be done, incomes to be earned.

It was the late summer of 2015, and Holbert and Reese's trial date had still not been announced. Every call to the Supreme Court in Panama City got the reply "The file still needs a couple of signatures." Only then would the file be sent to the David courthouse for the clerk there to pencil in a date for the trial. The situation had been precisely the same at the start of 2015: then, too, the only thing left was for a couple of top functionaries at the Supreme Court to sign on a couple of dotted lines. The media relations officer at the Supreme Court couldn't explain the delay. The impression

---

* The series ran in the 1960s and featured the mishaps of widower sheriff Andy Taylor and his bumbling deputy, Barney Fife, in the fictional North Carolina town of Mayberry. Even in the sixties, the show was something of a nostalgia trip.

was that there was no desire to proceed, that it mattered little if Holbert and Reese were tried at all. Or was someone on the Supreme Court deliberately stalling things? It was difficult to know for sure. What was clear was that Panama had locked up the former Wild Bill and Jane and, figuratively, thrown away the key. Sharon McConnell, Bo Icelar's close friend, and Cher Hughes's sisters Judy Barber and Diana Motlik, and her aunt, Mary Wittmeyer, were frustrated by the wait. For these four women, the situation was beyond comprehension. They needed closure, but there was no sign they would get it.

Then, in November 2015, out of the blue, came news from David: Laura Michelle Reese had gotten married. The groom was the young male inmate who had charmed Reese when he was on gardening detail at the women's prison. Reese's attorney Claudia Alvarado told reporters that her client had wanted to wed "away from the eyes of the media," revealing that the ceremony had taken place at the women's prison the previous month and that Reese's new husband was named José Edgar. No one traveled from the United States to attend the ceremony, said Alvarado, but an American woman living in Boquete who had spent time in jail on drug charges in the same facility as Reese, and had made friends with her there, did return to prison to see Reese and José Edgar make their vows. Marriage to José Edgar, a Panamanian, entitled Reese to Panamanian citizenship and ensured that she would never be forced to stand trial in Costa Rica for the murder of Jeffrey Arlan Kline, or in any other country on any other charge.

Shortly after Alvarado spoke to reporters about Reese's nuptials, a photo surfaced on the Web of a grinning William Dathan Holbert, his arm around the waist of a young biracial woman. In another image, Holbert's puckered mouth was kissing the woman on the cheek. The pictures had been taken in the prison yard. In both of them, the woman is staring squarely, even defiantly, at the camera lens. Alvarado's cell phone started ringing incessantly. Who was this woman with Holbert? It turned out that she was named Daphne—only her first name was given—she was twenty-one, and she was Panamanian. Holbert had met Daphne over the Internet. Alvarado said that Holbert would shortly be getting married, too, just as soon as his new American passport was delivered (formal identification of the couple contracting marriage was required by the judge officiating at the ceremony). On a local Web forum, someone commented under the pictures: *"STUPID WOMAN!!"* Like Reese, Holbert would not be subject to extradition to any foreign country on any charge if he married a Panamanian and, in so doing, acquired her citizenship.

Over the mountain in Bocas, the ebb and flow of life and lives brings new folks in and takes others away, just as it always has. Near the bookshop in Bocas Town that "Crazy Dave" turned into a raucous bar, an elderly man looks out from the porch of a neat, single-story detached house. It's the man who, back in the day, was known to just about everyone in Bocas as Manuel Antonio Noriega's close friend and bagman. Dense plants placed carefully on the porch let him see out but make it difficult for passersby to see in. Not that most of them would have any reason to: this block of Bocas Town is one of the busiest, crammed with college kids on vacation looking for good deals on boat trips out to the best beaches and tanned surfers grabbing tacos and beers. The elderly man has had a fall; his health is failing. He hasn't been out of his home in nearly a month. "When you get old," he says in a faint voice from behind the row of plants, his face mostly hidden, "it's best to die."

In Bocas, with every sun that rises and sets on the archipelago, the memory of Holbert and Reese's passage through the community fades a little more. Long-term expats tell newcomers their macabre story, of course. It's a neat fit with the pirate theme underpinning the gringo perception of Bocas generally, the one that had led to a veritable explosion of skulls and crossbones on flyers and signs for dive boat operators and hostels. At the same time, the fear that Holbert might break out of jail and kill again has dissipated, which can't be a bad thing, notwithstanding the occasional news of escapes from Panamanian jails.

At Cocomo-on-the-Sea, the guesthouse in Bocas Town, Douglas Ruscher looks out from the vantage point of a worn armchair on his deck toward the green tip of Carenero Island across the bay of Big Creek. Some months after Holbert's arrest, Ruscher got a phone call. "It was Wild Bill. He was calling me from jail. 'You've got a big mouth, Doug,' he said. I hung up straight away." Douglas Ruscher put the memory of the phone call in the back of his mind, which is where, by and large, it stays. Meanwhile,

Casie Dean prospers at her newspaper, the *Bocas Breeze*. Walter Kawano sits at the desk at the real estate agency where he used to greet his buddy Bo Icelar when he passed by. Sandi Hodge, Cher Hughes's friend, tends her garden with its profusion of bird-of-paradise flowers. Mike Smith and Fran Tilbury spend more time in David than they used to do, now that their new house is built, rather than in Bocas. Keith Werle remarried and returned to the States. Don Winner still blogs in Panama City. Scott McAda recently became a grandfather. People wanting—needing—a hideout from the law or the tax office or an angry ex-spouse can still easily find one in Bocas del Toro.

Through it all, in the archipelago of Bocas del Toro, indigenous beliefs persist, passed from mother to daughter, father to son. They survived the arrival of Christian missionaries, the Catholic Church, and, later, the encroachment of technology and the modern world. Some you could dismiss as superstitions, but in this corner of the world the fear of spirits and curses is real, and they are told in earnest. One example: Peel an orange without a break and hang it to one side of the main window in your house. Peel another orange without a break and hang it to the other side of the window. No evil spirit will pass between the two peels.

Here's another: If you set out on a journey and find you have left something behind, never go back for it. That way, your journey will be safe. You leap, confident, fearless, into the next chapter of your life. You don't look back.

Selected Bibliography

On the history of the Panama Canal and the early years of the Republic of Panama, I found the following books particularly useful:

David McCullough, *The Path Between the Seas: The Creation of the Panama Canal, 1870–1914* (Simon and Schuster, 1977).

Matthew Parker, *Panama Fever: The Epic Story of the Building of the Panama Canal* (Hutchinson, 2007), also available as *Hell's Gorge: The Battle to Build the Panama Canal.*

Ovidio Díaz Espino, *How Wall Street Created a Nation: J. P. Morgan, Teddy Roosevelt, and the Panama Canal* (Four Walls Eight Windows, 2001).

Earl Harding, *The Untold Story of Panama* (Athene Press, 1959).

On the Torrijos and Noriega years, there is no more compelling account than *In the Time of the Tyrants: Panama, 1968–1989* by R. M. Koster and Guillermo Sánchez (W. W. Norton, 1990). I found the chapter on the last journey of Hugo Spadafora particularly useful. Other books that informed my research on this period are:

Frederick Kempe, *Divorcing the Dictator: America's Bungled Affair with Noriega* (G. P. Putnam's Sons, 1990).

Graham Greene, *Getting to Know the General: The Story of an Involvement* (Simon and Schuster, 1984).

Luis Murillo, *The Noriega Mess: The Drugs, the Canal and Why America Invaded* (Video-Books, 1995).

Kevin Buckley, *Panama: The Whole Story* (Simon and Schuster, 1991).

Manuel Noriega and Peter Eisner, *America's Prisoner: The Memoirs of Manuel Noriega* (Random House, 1997).

Daniel González, *Los Reyes del Lavado de Dinero* (first edition published privately, 1991).

William Shawcross, *The Shah's Last Ride: The Fate of an Ally* (Simon and Schuster, 1988).

Amir Valle's biography of Hugo Spadafora, *Bajo la piel del hombre* (Aguilar, 2013), is a wonderful and moving book and deserves an English-language translation. I also learned a lot from *Bribes, Bullets, and Intimidation: Drug Trafficking and the Law in Central America* by Julie Marie Bunck and Michael Ross Fowler (Pennsylvania State University Press, 2012).

Malcolm Henderson has written a delightful account of setting up home in Darklands called *Don't Kill the Cow Too Quick* (iUniverse, Inc., 2004), which I found very helpful, as I did his *Superstition, Pirates, Ghosts and Folklore of Bocas del Toro, Panama* (published privately, 2012). Both books are easy to find in shops in Bocas Town. I also gleaned useful historical pointers from Clyde S. Stephens's *Outline of the History of the Province of Bocas del Toro, Panama* (SPS Publications, 2008), and *Bocas del Toro y el Caribe Occidental: Periferia y marginalidad, siglos XVI–XIX* by Celestino Andrés Araúz Monfante (Editorial Mariano Arosemena, 2007).

Scott McAda showed me an early draft of his memoir, provisionally titled *The Road to Reason*, which provided some useful context on the accusations made by William Dathan Holbert in this regard. I'm also indebted to Judy Barber for giving me access to e-mail correspondence included in her tribute to Cher Hughes, *A Sister's Promise* (Outskirts Press, 2015). Don Winner's Web site Panama-Guide.com was invaluable in tracing the early contours of the Holbert and Reese story from pieces he posted online.

Acknowledgments

Writing this book would not have been possible without the generosity, kindness, and encouragement of a large number of people in Panama, the United States, and Europe. First, I'd like to thank Malcolm Henderson for his hospitality at Finca Tranquila in Bocas del Toro and in the city of David, and for facilitating numerous introductions. In the—thankfully rare—moments when the outlook for this project seemed bleak, Malcolm reminded me that this was a story that needed telling. Scott McAda gave me full access to a large collection of file papers and recounted his life story over a half-dozen meetings with consummate good humor; I am very grateful to him, too. In Volcán, David and Lydia Dell told me about the expats in their corner of Panama, welcomed me to their home, and were full of ideas and leads. In Como, Mississippi, I made a friend in Sharon McConnell and am hugely thankful that she found the strength to tell me her story. And my visits to Panama City were brightened up to no end by the laugh-out-loud anecdotes and wise words of Dick Koster—his influence is everywhere in this book, not only in the passages on Torrijos, Noriega, and the Canal Zone.

I would also like to thank Douglas Ruscher and his team at Cocomo-on-the-Sea in Bocas Town; Amir Valle, biographer of Hugo Spadafora (particularly for telling me about Spadafora's time in Costa Rica); Okke Ornstein; Cyndy Hughes; Morris Cummings; Demetrio Ábrego; Elmer Quintero; Diana Motlik; Judy Barber; Mary Wittmeyer; John Freivalds; Steve Salem; Marie Hoover; George Ingenthron; Mark Johnson; Sandi Hodge; Casie Dean; John Lang; Mike Smith; and Fran Tilbury. Dianne and Ken Prohn helped with the history of Hendersonville, North Carolina, and John Boyle and Dan Ward did the same for Asheville, North Carolina. For explaining his version of the history of the Republic of Panama, and his sense of fun, I'm indebted to Ovidio Díaz Espino. For reading through some of the early drafts of this book and giving valuable feedback, I'd like to thank David Ellard, Mark Cowan, Gerry Noonan, Frank Ledwidge, John McGartoll, and Chris Goldberg.

My gratitude to Penguin Random House and David Higham Associates for granting permission to quote from *America's Prisoner: The Memoirs of Manuel Noriega* by Manuel Noriega and Peter Eisner, and from *Getting to Know the General: The Story of an Involvement* by Graham Greene, respectively.

The Jolly Roger Social Club might never have seen the light of day without the dedication and counsel of Alex Christofi, my first agent at Conville & Walsh; thanks, too, to Sophie Lambert, at C&W, who picked up where Alex left off. Serena Jones, my editor at Henry Holt, dragged my mid-Atlantic English to within sight of the North American shore, and did so with much flair and a keen eye for pace.

Finally, my heartfelt thanks to my wife, Katiana, for her precious support: you never stopped believing, not for a single second, and that made all the difference.

Nick Foster was born in Liverpool in 1966 and read Spanish and French at University College London. He worked as a European Union diplomat in Venezuela and Brazil and has contributed news stories on Latin America to the *Daily Telegraph*, *The Times* and many other outlets. Foster spent three seasons working as a football reporter for UEFA.com and now writes features for the *Financial Times* and the *International New York Times*. He is currently producing a documentary about one of France's highest-profile cold cases. Foster lives in Belgium with his wife and two sons.